The Law of Things

The Law of Things examines how law operates not only through words but through things, systematically conferring upon the world, the State, the people, sex, race, nature, and culture a thingly materiality treated as outside language, representation, and perception. It argues that law, in thingifying what it encounters, makes use of a precritical and authoritarian epistemology that forecloses contestation across legal and political life.

Drawing on intellectual history, critical theory, poststructuralism, linguistics, and Science & Technology Studies, the book offers a wholly original framework for understanding how thingness functions as a mode of governance. It reveals the discursive mechanics by which law renders its objects aconstructed and self-evident, producing zones of uncriticability that silence the speaking observer and narrow the space of critique. Chapter by chapter, it defines thingification as a distinct epistemic operation, traces its lineage through the history of thought, diagnoses its contemporary resurgence, maps seven domains in which law endows what it encounters with thingness, exposes the fascist grammar that shadows such epistemologies, and develops a counter-posture (countermateriality) that upholds a minimal materiality necessary for law to remain a tool of interruption and resistance. The book thus does not merely lament the return of precritical thinking. It also defends the constructivist conditions under which critique itself can survive.

This book speaks to legal scholars, legal philosophers, intellectual historians, and critical theorists, as well as anyone engaged with contemporary debates in epistemology, discourse studies, and political thought.

Jean d'Aspremont is Professor of Legal Philosophy and International Legal Theory at *Sciences Po Law School*. He also teaches at *the University of Manchester* and at the *Graduate Institute of International and Development Studies* (IHEID) in Geneva. His work spans multiple disciplines within legal theory and philosophy. He has authored more than two dozen books and published over

200 articles addressing questions of legal theory, international legal theory, philosophy of law, hermeneutics, and poststructuralism. His scholarship also encompasses the history of international legal thought, contributing to a deeper understanding of how legal ideas have evolved. His intellectual influence extends globally, with his work translated into numerous languages, including Spanish, Portuguese, Russian, Mandarin Chinese, Hindi, Japanese, Persian, and Turkish.

The Law of Things

On the Return of the Precritical

Jean d'Aspremont

Routledge
Taylor & Francis Group
LONDON AND NEW YORK

First published 2027
by Routledge
4 Park Square, Milton Park, Abingdon, Oxon OX14 4RN

and by Routledge
605 Third Avenue, New York, NY 10158

Routledge is an imprint of the Taylor & Francis Group, an informa business

A GlassHouse Book

© 2027 Jean d'Aspremont

The right of Jean d'Aspremont to be identified as author of this work has been asserted in accordance with sections 77 and 78 of the Copyright, Designs and Patents Act 1988.

All rights reserved. No part of this book may be reprinted or reproduced or utilised in any form or by any electronic, mechanical, or other means, now known or hereafter invented, including photocopying and recording, or in any information storage or retrieval system, without permission in writing from the publishers.

For Product Safety Concerns and Information please contact our EU representative GPSR@taylorandfrancis.com. Taylor & Francis Verlag GmbH, Kaufingerstraße 24, 80331 München, Germany.

Trademark notice: Product or corporate names may be trademarks or registered trademarks, and are used only for identification and explanation without intent to infringe.

British Library Cataloguing-in-Publication Data
A catalogue record for this book is available from the British Library

ISBN: 978-1-041-27350-9 (hbk)
ISBN: 978-1-041-27351-6 (pbk)
ISBN: 978-1-003-75394-0 (ebk)

DOI: 10.4324/9781003753940

Typeset in Sabon
by Deanta Global Publishing Services, Chennai, India

"The extravagances of an age are never anything more than variations on what that age makes thinkable"[1]

Note

1 Jacques Rancière, *La Leçon d'Althusser* (La Fabrique, 2011) (orig. 1974), at 14 (« Les extravagances d'un temps ne sont jamais que des variations sur ce que ce temps rend pensable »)

Contents

Preface

This book presents itself as discussing how law thingifies the world we inhabit. Because legal thought is not a type of self-standing and autonomous thought but rather serves as the receptacle of how contemporary thought articulates itself more generally, this book tells us a story about how people think today. It particularly sheds light on how people, especially decision-makers, have come to increasingly resort to the creation of universalizable necessities by the simple invocation that "This is how things are!", as if the world were a warehouse of self-evident objects awaiting inventory rather than a contested terrain of representations, exclusions, and struggles. Such mode of creating necessities has always been at work in legal thought and practice. But, especially in the Global North, it is now becoming a more general way of thinking about the world mobilized well beyond legal circles. It is because lawyers have long practiced this mode of thinking that they ought to alert everyone to the dangers thereof, namely its resuscitation of a precritical epistemology, one that bears the trappings of fascist thought.

The foregoing should suffice to demonstrate that this book aims to contribute to a number of questions and controversies that have become urgent as a result of our present political conjuncture. This conjuncture is marked by a decline of constructivism and intellectualism as well as the multiplication of zones of "uncriticability" around certain actors, certain situations, certain systematic injustices, certain societal controversies – zones where the stamp of thingness has rendered contestation unthinkable and dissent illegible. In that sense, and in contrast to some of my previous inquiries into modes of thinking, this book carries with it a great urgency and could not be more topical. It is written against the clock of a world that is forgetting how to think otherwise.

This book, as will quickly become obvious to the reader, mobilizes a great deal of philosophical works (in the broad sense). Yet, despite venturing well beyond legal thought and practice to offer considerations about contemporary thought more generally, it does not claim to be a book of philosophy.

Not only because its author, albeit a passionate reader of philosophical works, has no academic training in philosophy and does not seek to secure any credentials in that specific field. But also because the author of this book has always remained rather sceptical of the disciplinary ordering of thought, especially in the West, for it is an ordering that too often mistakes boundary-policing for rigour and confuses the administration of concepts for the life of ideas. This book's borrowing from many intellectual traditions is simultaneously a way to blur the disciplinary boundaries between them, demonstrating that it remains possible to develop fresh thoughts in the humanities precisely by refusing to corner oneself within one discipline or one tradition. This may come at the price of taking liberties with the semantics specific to the disciplines concerned. One can easily anticipate how self-labelled philosophers will frown at the use of certain philosophical notions in these pages. So be it. Taking a fresh and hard look at contemporary thought requires doing away with orthodox hermeneutics, essentialized conceptual thinking, and the modern disciplinary ordering that has too often made intellectual orthodoxy a professional virtue. Philosophy, after all, was never meant to be a guild.

As is commonly practiced in our disciplines, prefaces are regularly taken as the place where the genealogy of the (making of the) story that is told in the ensuing chapters is explicated. On earlier occasions, I have myself indulged in such – often navel-gazing – expository exercise. I will refrain from doing so here. The matters discussed in the following pages are too important and too pressing for the genealogy of the making of the thoughts that populate the following chapters to be of any relevance. There is no time for such stories. It suffices to say that this book was simply born out of the stupefaction of witnessing how political discourse, especially in the Global North, has been backtracking at breakneck speed on all that critical thought has taught us over these last decades, while enabling (if not supporting) mass murders at an industrial rate as well as nurturing the resurgence of that old folly, i.e. the figure of the interior enemy who is allegedly threatening the thingly pureness of our daily lives. The thing has returned, not as a philosophical curiosity but as a promoter of the essence as well as a weapon of cancellation. It should not be a surprise to the reader if the following pages occasionally read as a call for all the constructivists in the humanities to rally and take to the streets to remind everyone that the world never is as it is!

A stylistic practice I will not escape in this preface is that of thanking those who helped me make this book possible. My gratitude goes first to my friend and colleague Laurent de Sutter, whose encouragement proved invaluable from the very start. I am extremely grateful to Colin Perrin at Routledge for his vision, experience, and guidance and without whom this book would have never come to life. I am thankful to all those colleagues who have provided me with the opportunity to present the book before academic audiences that offered me useful insights and allowed me to streamline the argument herein. I am also indebted to my colleague Mostafa Taherkhani, who kindly commented on an earlier version of the manuscript and who decisively contributed to making the following better, sharper, and richer. My greatest gratitude goes to Rebecca Mignot-Mahdavi without whom this book, and the space for writing it, would have remained in the realm of the impossible.

March 2026

Introduction

It is commonplace to say that much of what law does to the world and to people it does with words. Yet, as argued here, law does not only do what it does through words but also through things. This book examines how law thingifies the world we inhabit and operates as a thing maker, whereby the world, law, the State, the people, sex, race, nature, and culture are conferred a thingly materiality treated as hors langue, outside representation and perception. This book is thus about the modes of thinking that govern how law is thought, mobilized, represented, practised, and contested, and especially those modes of thinking that come to thingify what law encounters.

It is important to note that, in contemporary societies, especially in the Global North, law – just like the sciences – occupies a central place within the discursive and institutional pyramids that authorize perception, representation, and action. This is why a book that reflects on the modes of thinking informing legal thought and practice is also a book about contemporary thought as a whole. Just as those who, like Canguilhem, Foucault, Latour, and Jasanoff, dissected the modes of thinking at work in the sciences and thereby taught us how a form of thought that centres the sciences functions, this book holds that legal discourse is a modest receptacle of patterns of thought that extend well beyond it. In that sense, this book is thus much more than a book about law. It is a book about contemporary thought.

One of the main claims developed in this book is that thingification – which is defined as the discursive action that attributes thingness to the world one inhabits – constitutes a highly efficacious mode of governance, one that legal thought and practice have enabled for years. By rendering the world a-constructed and *hors langue*, law's resort to thingification can be read as epitomizing an epistemology that predates the Kantian critical revolution and bears the mark of a fascist grammar: It forecloses representation, suspends the speaking observer, and narrows the scene of contestation. Claims about the thingness of law, the State, the people, sex, race, nature, and culture are routinely accompanied by an uncriticability that excludes

DOI: 10.4324/9781003753940-1

representation and blocks contestation. It is further submitted here that the return of a precritical epistemology with fascist overtones is not merely an ailment of legal thought and practice. It is a mode of thinking enjoying a major comeback across contemporary discourses worldwide. Thus, the critique of law's enabling of thingification is simultaneously a critique of authoritarian epistemologies that have reinstalled themselves across domains, where legal relays now fix the world, divide and classify people, exploit bodies and nature, securitize borders and populations, essentialize identities and cultures, naturalize property and extractive entitlements, codify gender and sexuality as immutable categories, reify public order and the "national", instrumentalize health and biopolitical registers, sanctify heritage, tradition, and the family as self-signifying, territorialize land and water as pure resources, and objectify platforms, protocols, and infrastructures as givens. As will be demonstrated in this book, such resurgence of authoritarian epistemologies is certainly not the end of law. On the contrary, the resort to thingness has long supplied law with a formidable toolbox. The task, then, is to reopen the space of critique, that is reinstating the speaking observer, representation, and contestation against the production of necessities that thingification processes install.

It should be clear from the outset that while law's thingification of law itself, the State, the people, sex, race, nature, and culture bears the marks of a fascist grammar and signals a precritical epistemology, thingification is not the sole mode through which contemporary authoritarian forces operate. These forces optimize their discourse by continuously recalibrating their epistemologies: They thingify race, the State, the people, culture, and sex, while simultaneously de-thingifying other domains – adopting an ultra-constructivist posture toward, for example, climate science[1] – in order to unseat evidence, suspend witness, and disarm representation. In practice, precritical epistemologies that award thingness are nested within broader, multilayered sequences of discursive moves. The same holds for legal thought and practice, which routinely accommodate multiple, at times contradictory, discursive operations. In that regard, the precritical epistemology by which law confers thingness is but one modality among others within law's shifting discursive apparatus that alternates between producing necessity and loosening it to strategic effect.

Some readers may find it paradoxical that I write a book warning against the return – within law and beyond – of a precritical and authoritarian epistemology articulated around thingness, after more than a decade spent diagnosing what goes wrong in modern thought, especially in its constitution of (and by) law. Indeed, to some extent, this book can be read as a defence of a limited modernity, one indebted to Kant's constructivist epistemology insofar as it re-centres critique, the speaking observer, and representation. The alleged contradiction with my earlier charges against modern thought does not bother me, for coherence has never been the organizing principle of my work. If there is a tension, it lies only in a narrow corridor: The constructivist posture endorsed here does not rehabilitate modernity wholesale but secures the minimal materiality and discursive conditions under which critique can operate against the production of necessity through thingification processes. In this sense, the present argument does not retract past critiques of modern thought but redirects them toward resisting the self-effacing epistemology of thingness by reinstating the scene where the speaking observer and representation can return. Whilst being very critical of modern coherence,[2] modern epistemology,[3] modern textuality,[4] modern historicism,[5] modern comparativism,[6] modern consensualism,[7] modern institutionalism,[8] modern temporality,[9] modern institutionalism,[10] modern scienticism,[11] modern subjecthood,[12] modern secretism,[13] I do not believe there is any escape from modern constructivism that does not relapse into precritical thinking and its authoritarian grammar. Abandoning constructivist epistemology simply restores the regime in which thingness appears as necessity without witness. In that regard, it is not surprising that the most compelling charges against modernity in recent decades – those we owe to poststructuralist, feminist, postcolonial, decolonial thought – have all remained anchored in a constructivist epistemology of sorts. This is because the latter preserves the very conditions of critique, i.e. the capacity to name, to reframe, and to interrupt the discursive actions that produce thingness.[14]

It must be acknowledged at the outset that engaging with the theory of the thing is not new, least of all in relation to law.[15] Classical philosophy has long treated the idea of thing extensively, as Chapter 2 recalls, and contemporary literature and art studies have renewed such focus. In that respect, Bill Brown's *Thing Theory* is a prominent point of reference.[16] Brown distinguishes "objects" as familiar, utilitarian entities from "things" that interrupt use and assert material presence, drawing attention to the moments when mediation fails and materiality becomes insistently legible. He tracks how cultural forms (frames, narratives, and genres) activate or arrest this insistence. It is important to emphasize that the following chapters do not transpose in any way *Thing Theory* into legal scholarship. Rather, they pursue their own discursive and epistemological account of thingness and thingification. As Chapter 1 establishes, thingness names the attribution of necessary material existence that imposes itself on the speaking observer, seemingly outside perception, language, and representation while thingification names the specific discursive action through which such thingness is produced. While Chapter 6 will show that certain insights from Brown can support the preservation of a minimal materiality – so that critique can remain possible without effacing the scene of the speaking observer – what follows builds an independent framework for what being-a-thing entails and the necessities that accompany it: The exclusion of perception, witness, representation, and agency, the self-signifying and self-effacing registers of materiality, and the legal relays through which thingly actuality is conferred.

This book, as it engages with legal thought and practice as well as contemporary thought, is yet another venture into discourse studies.[17] It is ordinary in most critical works about discourse, like the present book, to begin by saying a word on the role of agency.[18] In fact, any inquiry into discourse, knowledge, or epistemology is quickly met with the objection that discourses do not act by themselves, as if one had first to locate a conscious subject whose intentions animate every operation of a concept or a system of thought. I feel the need to say a word about this question too. I do not deny that discourses and epistemologies require uptake, practice, and use. Nor do I deny that people act.[19] Yet, I claim that one can analyse what discourses and epistemologies do (their effects, regularities, and affordances) without first centring questions of agency or intention. This is particularly true for the discourse of "thingness" examined here, which crystallizes as a set of classifications, perceptual habits, and practical schemas that become effective through repetition, circulation, and institutionalization, not through any master plan designed by a set of rational and conscious agents.[20]

There is yet another standard formula one finds in the introduction of most works of discourse studies like the present book to which I cannot turn a blind eye. The manner in which thingness and processes of thingification are defined, theorized, and discussed will at times itself denote a treatment that confers thingly actuality upon them. What is more, in the ensuing discussion, law, legal thought, legal discourse, lawyers, and the legal discipline will at times be approached in ways that imply they are provisionally awarded some degree of thingness. Not to mention the terminology used in the following chapters, which regularly employ idioms that imply forms of thingness (e.g. object, fact, constitutive dimension, worldmaking effect, artefact, device, inscription, etc.). One could thus claim that this book does exactly what it laments. Such performative contradiction is not to be feared, but a necessary move, for critique is always entangled with its object. What is more, as Chapter 3 will discuss, thingness and thingification often operate not merely as epistemic postures but as modes of communication, scripting how claims travel, stick, and acquire the appearance of necessity. More fundamentally – and this will be a decisive argument made in this book – not all of law's material supports should be rescinded. A minimal materiality must remain in place if law is to function as a tool of interruption, repair, and resistance when necessary.

A word on the tense in which this book speaks of philosophers and their work. Throughout the following pages, the reader will encounter descriptions of philosophical thought in the present tense rather than the past tense that historical fidelity might seem to demand. This choice is deliberate and rests on several considerations. First, this book does not purport to offer any kind of exegesis of the philosophical works it mobilizes. It cherry-picks from various traditions, borrowing concepts and insights to construct its own story about thingness and thingification. What matters for the following discussion is not what a philosopher meant in their historical context but what their words can be made to do in the present argument. Second, the use of these works is primarily synchronic rather than genealogical. Aside from presenting thingness as the expression of a precritical epistemology that does away with Kantian constructivism and correlationism – which is the object of Chapter 2, this book does not seek to trace causal or developmental links between the thinkers it summons. They are treated as interlocutors convened around a shared problem. Third, the present tense honours a convention long established in philosophical writing, namely, that arguments, once articulated, acquire a life independent of their authors and continue to speak across time. Fourth, and perhaps most importantly, the present tense enacts a central claim of this book: That thought is never simply past. The thingification of the world proceeds as if certain ideas were settled, inert, and no longer contestable. To speak of philosophers in the present is to refuse that very foreclosure and to insist that the critical resources assembled here remain available for deployment against the precritical complacencies of our time.

This book is organized as follows. Chapter 1 defines thingness and thingification, and identifies the precritical epistemology of which they are the manifestations. Chapter 2 situates this epistemology historically within the history of thought, tracing its intellectual lineage and recurrent returns. Chapter 3 explains why we are witnessing a new golden age of precritical epistemologies grounded in thingness today. Chapter 4 examines seven legal situations in which law endows what it encounters with thingness, including law itself, the State, the people, sex, race, nature, and culture. Chapter 5 shows that epistemologies based on thingness bear the mark of a fascist grammar and recall sinister precedents. Chapter 6 develops an attitude of resistance called countermateriality, arguing that critique requires upholding a minimal materiality that nevertheless keeps the speaking observer and representation on the scene. The book closes with an epilogue staging a fictitious debate among seven protagonists whose work has always been deeply invested in the questions of thingness and thingification.

Notes

1 Bruno Latour, *Face à Gaïa* (La Découverte 2015) 39–40.
2 See Jean d'Aspremont, 'The Chivalric Pursuit of Coherence in International Law' (2024) 37 *Leiden Journal of International Law* 191–98.
3 Jean d'Aspremont, 'A Worldly Law in a Legal World' in Andrea Bianchi and Moshe Hirsch (eds), *International Law's Invisible Frames: Social Cognition and Knowledge Production in International Legal Processes* (OUP 2021) 110–23.
4 Jean d'Aspremont, 'Two Attitudes towards Textuality in International Law: The Battle for Dualism' (2022) 42 *Oxford Journal of Legal Studies* 963–84.
5 Jean d'Aspremont, *The Critical Attitude and the History of International Law* (Brill 2019); Jean d'Aspremont, 'Critical Histories of International Law and the Repression of Disciplinary Imagination' (2019) 7 *London Review of International Law* 89–115.

6 Jean d'Aspremont, 'Comparativism and Colonizing Thinking in International Law' (2020) 57 *Canadian Yearbook of International Law* 89–112.

7 Jean d'Aspremont, 'Consenting to International Law in Five Moves' in Samantha Besson (ed), *Consent in International Law* (CUP 2023) 117–34; see also Jean d'Aspremont, 'Current Theorizations About the Treaty' in Duncan B Hollis (ed), *The Oxford Guide to Treaties* (2nd edn, OUP 2020) 46–58.

8 Jean d'Aspremont, 'The Love for International Organizations' (2023) 20 *International Organizations Law Review* 111–59; see also Jean d'Aspremont, *The Experiences of International Organizations: A Phenomenological Approach to International Institutional Law* (Edward Elgar 2023).

9 Jean d'Aspremont, 'Time Travel in the Law of International Responsibility' in Samantha Besson (ed), *Theories of International Responsibility Law* (CUP 2022) 252–76.

10 Jean d'Aspremont, 'The Love for International Organizations' (2023) 20 *International Organizations Law Review* 111–59; Jean d'Aspremont, *The Experiences of International Organizations: A Phenomenological Approach to International Institutional Law* (Edward Elgar 2023).

11 Jean d'Aspremont, 'International Law and the Rage against Scienticism' (2022) 33 *European Journal of International Law* 679–94.

12 Jean d'Aspremont, 'The Law of Statehood as a Constellation of Hybrids' in Jure Vidmar, Sarah McGibbon and Lea Raible (eds), *Research Handbook on Secession* (Edward Elgar 2022) 29–41. Cf Jean d'Aspremont, 'The International Law of Statehood and Recognition: A Post-Colonial Invention' in Thierry Garcia (ed), *La reconnaissance du statut d'Etat à des entités contestées: approches de droit international, régional et interne* (Pedone 2018).

13 Jean d'Aspremont, *The Epistemology of the Secret: International Law as Revelation* (CUP 2025).

14 On the idea that breaking away from modernity cannot come from modern epistemological frameworks themselves, see Walter Mignolo, 'Delinking: The Rhetoric of Modernity, the Logic of Coloniality, and the Grammar of Decoloniality' (2007) 21 *Cultural Studies* 449–514; Michel Foucault, *Dits et écrits*, vol I (1954–1975) (Gallimard 2001) 1284.

15 See Margaret Davies, *Law Unlimited: Materialism, Pluralism, and Legal Theory* (Routledge 2017).

16 Bill Brown, 'Thing Theory' (2001) 28 *Critical Inquiry* 1; Bill Brown, *Other Things* (University of Chicago Press 2015).

17 A discourse is understood here in a rather generic way as to refer to any system of meaning and set of connected utterances through which one speaks about and comes to experience the world and human phenomena. On the notion of discourse, see generally Hayden White, *Tropics of Discourse: Essays in Cultural Criticism* (Johns Hopkins University Press 1978) 4–5; Michel Foucault, *Dits et écrits*, vol I (1954–1975) (Gallimard 2001) 623; Stuart Hall, *Race, ethnicité, nation: Le triangle fatal* (Editions Amsterdam 2019) 27–28. On the idea that a discourse does violence to things, see Michel Foucault, *L'ordre du discours* (Gallimard 1971) 55.

18 For a classical work on agency, see E P Thompson, *The Making of the English Working Class* (Penguin Classics 2013).

19 On the central role of the judge in the performance of thingification and the hiding of it, see Peter Gabel, 'Reification in Legal Reasoning' (1980) 3 *Research in Law and Sociology* 25–51, 32 and 39.

20 See eg Foucault's idea that technologies of exclusion or normalization on questions of health and sexuality were not the result of a decision of the bourgeoisie

but only of their interest for very efficacious and economically convenient modes of governance: Michel Foucault, *Dits et écrits*, vol II (Gallimard 2001) 183 and 379; Michel Foucault, *«Il faut défendre la société»: Cours au Collège de France, 1976* (Gallimard 1997) 29–30. Cf the idea that ideological devices were not created out of the blue by a decision of the bourgeoisie but are the product of a long-lasting struggle: Louis Althusser, *Initiation à la philosophie pour les non-philosophes* (Presses Universitaires de France 2014) 232. See also Louis Althusser, *Pour Marx* (La Découverte 1996) 241–42 (first published 1965).

Chapter 1

Becoming a thing

For the sake of this book, *thingness* refers to the quality of being a thing, i.e. of having a necessary material existence irrespective of how the latter is perceived, experienced, named, or thought. To put it differently, thingness refers to a type of materiality that imposes itself on the speaking observer and which always is independent of the latter's perception, observation, language, discourse, and representation. Thingness thus is the attribute of what is necessarily in-the-world and owes such necessary existence to its being as a thing and not to what a speaking observer may think or say about that thing.

One of the main arguments made in this book is that thingness, so understood, is not an intrinsic quality but, on the contrary, always is an attribute that is produced by the discourse, including the legal discourse.[1] That thingness is always produced explains why the quality of being a thing is inseparable from the process that generates it. In fact, thingness, although it presents itself as being independent of perception, observation, language, discourse, and representation, remains the upshot of a specific discursive action. This specific discursive action that produces thingness is called, for the sake of this book, *thingification*. There never is thingness that is not the result of a process of thingification.

Thingness and thingification, as they are understood here, enjoy some fundamental kinship: One is the product of the other. Yet, it is of the utmost importance to highlight, at this preliminary stage, that thingness and thingification are simultaneously exclusive of one another. Indeed, thingness being the product of a process of thingification, there cannot be thingness as long as the process of thingification has not been completed. And once the process of thingification succeeds in producing thingness, it ceases and is discontinued.

It is the aim of this chapter to unpack the inseparable notions of thingness, i.e. the quality of being a thing, and thingification, i.e. the production of thingness. This chapter starts by defining what thingness, once it has been produced by a process of thingification, stands for (1). It then expounds on the main discursive effects of thingness (2). Finally, a few insights are

DOI: 10.4324/9781003753940-2

provided as to how thingification compares with other contemporary modes of creation of necessities (3).

Before substantiating the notions of thingness and thingification, two observations are in order. First, it must be stressed at this preliminary stage that the notion of thing, despite its mundane usage in everyday language, constitutes a highly sophisticated philosophical concept whose discursive effects, as will be demonstrated here, are multiple, intricate, and subtle. This is why the following sections, in order to fully apprehend how thingness and thingification function, draw on a wide and rich body of philosophical and theoretical materials that may appear to be at odds with the apparent simplicity of the idea of thing. In fact, it is one of the main aims of this chapter to demonstrate that our seemingly straightforward experience of thingness is invariably produced by a complex discursive machinery, the comprehension thereof demanding substantial theoretical resources to be dissected.

Second, a terminological observation is warranted. For ontological inquiries commonly focus on determining which types of entities one can credibly claim to exist,[2] the following discussion of thingness and thingification may be read as a critique of a dominant type of ontology, one that elevates the structure of things as the structure of existence.[3] Yet, it is important to stress that the following remarks are not phrased in terms of ontology but are rather presented through a discursive lens (*what can be thought, said, and experienced?*) as well as an epistemological one (*what can be known?*). In other words, thingness is understood here as a specific way to speak about the world and to make sense of it, rather than a system of thought that determines the categories of beings that can validly be said to exist. Such a preference for a presentation in discursive and epistemological terms can be explained as follows. Even though thingness is an ontology that is self-effaced and that makes itself invisible,[4] unpacking its status as an ontology is, according to the author of these lines, less pertinent than examining its discursive and epistemological consequences, especially given this book's ambition to articulate a critique thereof. Indeed, the critique of thingness that is provided in this book does not seek to supplement a specific ontology with another but, more modestly, to describe what thingness does from a discursive and epistemological perspective and how it can be resisted. Since this book ultimately aims at offering tools to resist what thingness does in discursive and epistemological terms, it is unnecessary, subject to a handful of exceptions,[5] to venture into the treacherous and slippery terrain of ontological debates. Incidentally, framing thingness in ontological terms would risk misplacing the argument made here by situating it between incommensurable registers, thereby rendering the central claim conceptually unintelligible. Indeed, as will be shown in this book,[6] thingness is defined by reference (and in opposition) to Kantian constructivism, which itself replaced the ontological claims of premodern philosophy with claims concerning the conditions of representation, perception, and judgement.[7] To capture and evaluate thingness by reference to constructivism while simultaneously deploying an ontological register would be to contradict the very epistemological framework that renders the concept intelligible.

1. Thingness defined

What possesses thingness is a necessary being-in-the-world.[8] Indeed, thingness, as is understood here, is the quality of what has a necessary material existence in the world by virtue of being a thing and not by virtue of what a speaking observer may perceive, observe, name, represent, etc.[9] In other words, thingness is the yardstick through which necessary existence is ascertained: Being is to be a thingly being.[10] This section further substantiates the notion of thingness and sheds light on the six main discursive and epistemological traits of how the quality of being a thing is understood here. It particularly defines thingness as being composed of six specific modes of being, namely the being-in-itself (1.1), the being-without-a-witness (1.2), the self-signifying being (1.3), the self-caused being (1.4), the ancestral being (1.5), and the self-effacing being (1.6).

1.1 The being-in-itself and the exclusion of perception

The main epistemological characteristic of thingness is the possibility that it is meant to refer to material existence outside the perception of any speaking observer.[11] In that sense, it can be said that thingness is an a-perception:[12] there is nothing to be perceived, for the thing has already and always been there irrespective of how it is perceived. Such exclusion of perception that defines thingness could similarly be described as a *presence without presence*.[13] What is considered a thing is thus a presence that continues after the speaking observer has left the scene. This means that thingness entails the permanence and total independence of the materiality of the thing that possesses the quality of thingness. In epistemological terms, thingness corresponds to a mind-independent existence.[14] In philosophical terms, thingness can be deemed a type of naïve realism,[15] i.e. the belief in the possibility that the real exists outside its perception by any speaking observer.

1.2 The being-without-a-witness and the exclusion of the speaking observer

The suspension of perception that is entailed by thingness and which has just been sketched out bears a specific epistemological consequence: *The scene of the thing that possesses thingness always is a scene without any speaking observer*. The thing always is a thing-without-the-speaking-observer.[16] Thingness, in this sense, refers to an "absence of human witness".[17] In a universe of things, the world accordingly lives, happens, unfolds without any speaking observer.[18] It is a world where one does not need to have any kind of awareness of the thing for the latter to have thingly existence.[19]

The independence from any speaking observer that is characteristic of thingness, so understood, means that thingness lies outside experience. The thing comes to precede the speaking observer whose agency has become irrelevant in the determination of the meaning of the thing.[20] The thing is awaiting no speaking observer to perceive it.[21] If anything, the speaking observer is neither speaking nor observing, let alone a subject invited to the scene of thingness. This cancellation of the speaking observer by the quality of being a thing can similarly be translated, in philosophical terms, in the following way: The common correlation in Western philosophy between the being (object) and the thinking (the speaking observer) is made irrelevant.[22] The constitutive subject of modern thought vanishes: Only the thing remains, receiving its necessary existence from its thingness and not from its relationship with any speaking observer.[23]

1.3 The self-signifying being and the exclusion of representation

As shown in the previous section, thingness is incommensurable with both the act of perception and the presence of a speaking observer. Thingness needs neither of them for thingly materiality to exist. There is yet another epistemological restriction that is entailed by the thingness possessed by a thing: The annihilation of representation.[24] The thing presents itself and it is in no need of being represented.[25] Thingness is thus a state of a non-representation.[26] Said differently, what enjoys the status of thing by virtue of the thingness attributed to it is supposedly outside representation: The thing does not need to be represented or named to signify.[27] Indeed, the thing that possesses thingness is self-signifying, for it signifies by virtue of itself and not through linguistic representation or naming.[28] In short, thingness is a form of *representationlessness* all representational practices – and thus controversies[29] – concerning the thing enjoying such thingness being systematically annihilated.[30]

Being outside representation also means being outside language. Thus, thingness is also the quality of being *hors langue*[31] or outside symbolization.[32] In fact, such cancellation of representation dramatically encroaches language's signifying empire in that it removes substantial areas of signification to language which, in those very areas in which things signify by themselves, has lost all its signifying credentials. By virtue of thingness, language can no longer provide any mirror in which the thing concerned could be reflected.[33] To put it in structuralist terms,[34] as a consequence of thingness, the sign – that comprises both the signifier and the signified – has vanished and only the fixed and self-signifying thing remains. In that sense, the representationlessness of thingness simultaneously presupposes the possibility of being above language and not dependent on its definitional categories.[35]

1.4 The self-caused being and the exclusion of agency

Thingness can simultaneously be read as a specific regime of causality whereby the thing is the very cause of its own existence: The thing is because it is a thing. In this specific regime of causality, the thing does not owe its existence to being the consequence of an earlier action, perception, or representation but owes it only to itself.[36] As a type of *self-causation*, thingness represents a radical departure from conventional epistemological frameworks that rely on chains of external causation. When one attributes thingness to an entity, one is not merely describing its properties or locating it within a network of relations, but rather acknowledging a form of autonomy whereby the thing generates and sustains its own being. This regime of causality collapses the temporal sequence typically assumed in causal explanations where causes precede consequences. The thing becomes a closed circuit of being, perpetually causing itself through the very fact of its thingness. This regime of causality challenges our epistemological habits, which typically seek to explain phenomena by tracing them back to prior conditions or external forces. In the regime of thingness, explanation becomes tautological in a philosophically productive sense: The thing is because it is a thing, and it is a thing because it is. This is not a failure of explanation but rather a recognition that certain modes of existence resist reduction to external determinants. The thing's opacity to traditional causal analysis is not a deficiency but constitutive of its very quality as a thing. Thingness, from such a perspective, can be seen as working as a creationist narrative.[37]

1.5 The ancestral being and the exclusion of the present

The representationless representational practice as well as the regime of self-causality that accompany thingness, and which have just been mentioned, entail a specific type of temporality. In fact, thingness creates a necessary material existence and simultaneously claims that such existence pre-exists its finding.[38] This means that thingness operates around a very specific temporality whereby the self-signified thing appears as having stood prior to any subsequent encounter. In that sense, what possesses thingness is thus always *ancestral*, as it always belongs to a time that precedes that of the encounter with it.[39] Such ancestrality of the thing and its existence being prior to any encounter make the thing outside knowledge.[40] It is a form of existence, like the existence of God, that does not need to be known, let alone be confirmed through knowledge, for it has always been there, even before human knowledge. From such perspective, it is possible to appreciate the extent to which the ancestrality that accompanies thingness provides the latter with a theological dimension.[41] Such ancestrality of the being as a thing can similarly be deemed the expression of an *absolute*:[42] Whatever enjoys such attribute comes to lie like an immovable stone[43] whose location and existence ought not to be discussed and does not call for any extra verification, for it has always been there. As enjoying an absolute existence, the thing simply is, the use of the verb "to be" in this case sufficing to recall that the thing's absolute existence does not hinge on any signification processes.[44] Thingness is a quality that suspends all types of doubts about the existence of the being concerned.[45]

1.6 The self-effaced being and the clandestinity of thingly ontology

Although this chapter seeks to dissect thingness primarily in its discursive and epistemological dimensions, one cannot turn a blind eye to the ontological aspect of thingness. Indeed, thingness can simultaneously be construed as a specific type of ontology, one that limits valid existence to thingly existence. In that sense, thingness can be said to be a type of thingly ontology. Yet, what is most striking is that, while thingness affirms the necessary being-in-the-world of whatever enjoys such quality, thingness simultaneously hides the type of specific ontology it puts in place. Said differently, thingness makes the existence of its beneficiary – i.e. the thing – beyond doubt and in need of no extra verification but hides that it achieves such enviable status by excluding perception, the speaking observer, representation, and the present time as well as its self-concealing character. In that sense, thingness can be construed as a very *clandestine ontology*. A few illustrations can be provided here. For instance, the thing, albeit deemed outside perception by a speaking observer, remains the product of an experience, namely the experience of a thing-at-hand that has always been there. Likewise, notwithstanding the abovementioned disappearance of the speaking observer, thingness remains the product of a representational practice, i.e. the act of thingification, by a given speaking observer,[46] being always ultimately human-made.[47] This also means that the representationlessness that comes with thingness, and thus the self-signifying character of the being as a thing, is only a specific type of representational relationship[48] whereby representation is concealed and made absent. In other words, what has been thingified and, as a result, possesses thingness, remains the product of a very specific representational practice but the latter is nowhere to be seen.[49] The same goes with the exclusion of the present time and the location of the being as a thing outside knowledge, which is hidden all the way. The foregoing means that thingness is always a materiality-effect produced by virtue of a specific perception, a speaking observer, a particular regime of representation, and a certain type of temporality,[50] all such constitutive elements of thingness being made invisible. Such self-effacement is itself a characteristic of the quality of being a thing.

2. The main discursive and epistemological effects of thingness

This section reviews some of the salient consequences of the creation, through a thingification process, of thingness as it has been theorized in the previous section. As was said already, the focus is here on the discursive (*what can be thought, said, and experienced?*) and the epistemological (*what can be known?*) consequences of thingness and accordingly relates to what thingness allows one to think, say, experience, and know.

Before introducing these main consequences of thingness, a caveat is necessary. It could have been decided to present these discursive and epistemological effects as yet other defining and constitutive features of what it is to be a thing and thus added to those sketched out in the previous section. The consequences of thingness are nonetheless introduced here as discursive and epistemological effects rather than definitional components of thingness, for they do not pertain to a certain type of being that is put in place by the attribution of thingness as envisaged in the previous section but relate to the effects of the encounter, by the ostracized speaking observer, with those beings produced by thingness.

With a view to exposing the various discursive and epistemological effect of thingness, this section examines in turn the extent to which thingness generates contemplation (2.1), differentiation (2.2), dehistoricization and de-originization (2.3), depoliticization (2.4), dehumanization (2.5), interpellation (2.6), interpretation (2.7), prescription (2.8), and abstraction (2.9).

2.1 Contemplation

The first of the discursive and epistemological consequences of thingness pertains to the condition of the (former) speaking observer that arrives at the scene of thingness. As was highlighted in the previous section, thingness generates a being that is outside perception, independent of any speaking observer, self-signifying, ancestral and self-concealing. It is submitted here that, in doing so, thingness facilitates a specific epistemological attitude: Contemplation. Indeed, being totally sidelined, the speaking observer no longer needs to engage with the part of the world that has been thingified. One can afford to be a passive contemplator of the thingly world. In that sense, thingness is instrumental in the rise of a specific epistemology, one which could be called the *epistemology of contemplation*[51] whereby the outside of the subject could be reduced to things whose existence is not up for discussion, let alone conceptual thinking.[52] By virtue of such epistemology of contemplation, the speaking observer can be content with simply receiving the self-signifying things that surround her. Thingness, by virtue of the epistemology of contemplation it puts in place, thus is a dry discursive posture whereby one is relieved from the permanent struggle to ascertain and define the outside world.[53]

2.2 Differentiation

Thingness does not only lay the ground for an epistemology of contemplation. It also facilitates a type of thinking called differential thinking. In other words, thingness allows one to approach the world as a composite world made of distinct and well-delineated things[54] that can in turn be the object of strict taxonomies.[55] In fact, one of the main characteristics of thingness is its enabling of a thinking in terms of difference and distinctiveness.[56] The thing is always a "this" or a "that".[57] Thingness is thus part of an ordering way of thinking, one that allows the organization of the world into distinct practices, states, actors, people, environments, histories, cultures, traditions, races, genders, identities, foreignness, otherness, economic development, discriminations, dominations, oppressions, liberations, injustices, inequalities, aggressions, violences, etc.

2.3 Dehistoricization and de-originization

As was indicated above,[58] the ancestrality of the thing that possesses thingness makes the being as a thing be outside the present. But being outside the present also entails being outside the past of that present. Once produced by the act of thingification, thingness makes the thing appear as if it has always been, without the question of its origin – other than that of its material and mechanical conditions of production – having any relevance. In other words, it does not matter whether there was an origin of the thing in the past. For thingness, the origin does not require to be traced back diachronically. In that sense, thingness entails a rejection of the originist thinking[59] that is commonly constitutive of modern historical epistemology.[60] This means that what enjoys the quality of thingness is not produced historically[61] and accordingly escapes any ascertainment and validation through the tracing of its historical past and of its origins. Thingification thus always entails a move of dehistoricization of what is being thingified and, accordingly, the inscription of the latter in a purely synchronic temporality.[62] To put it differently, thingness always tells *a story of something that is there but that has not happened*, let alone happened somewhere.[63]

2.4 Depoliticization

The consequence of thingness mentioned here follows directly from the previous one. If what enjoys thingness is not historically produced and does not owe its existence to its origin, the act of thingification also entails an act of depoliticization of the existence of what has been thingified. For the sake of the consequence of thingness described here, depoliticization is given a meaning similar to that embraced by Hannah Arendt in her reflection on thingification. Arendt, although she welcomes the thingification of action, speech and thought for the sake of making them tangible and remembered, bemoans the extent to which the thingification of the world, especially that which comes with mathematization, not only is incommensurable with speech but also entails a form of artificiality that *forecloses the sphere of politics and jeopardizes human beings' capacity to remain political.*[64] For her, when political life becomes thingified, genuine human interaction is replaced by bureaucratic systems, statistics, and procedures, which undermine authentic political action. From such a perspective, which is also espoused here, the world composed of thingified entities can be considered a-political, for it is simply there, and no longer needs to be discussed and engaged with.

Jacques Rancière similarly diagnoses a form of depoliticization in any ordering that puts emphasis on thingness. He does so through a famous and much-discussed dichotomy, namely that which distinguishes rigorously between "police" and "politics". By police, Rancière does not primarily mean coercive law enforcement; rather, he names the comprehensive order that distributes the sensible – allocating places, roles, capacities, and the parameters of what counts as visible, sayable, and thinkable – thereby naturalizing the given as the only reality. Politics, by contrast, is not governance or policy but the rare event of dissensus whereby those without a recognized part interrupt this distribution, reconfiguring the field of appearance and contesting what is taken as self-evident.[65] Hence his claim that the permanent exhibition of the real functions as the ordinary form of police in contemporary societies: The injunction to reality and concreteness saturates perception with facts, procedures, and measurements that render the order indisputable and convert disagreement into technical management. In this sense, police is precisely the exclusion of politics: It forecloses the emergence of dissensus by enclosing experience within what already is, just as Arendt worries that the mathematized thingification of the world displaces speech and action.[66] Both diagnoses converge on the insight that when the world is presented as incontrovertibly "there", political life is cancelled, because the very capacity to reconfigure the sensible horizon, and the parameters of what counts as visible, sayable, and thinkable, is denied.[67]

2.5 Dehumanization

With the cancellation of the speaking observer, thingness dehumanizes the process of cognizing and knowing the thing. Indeed, the thing, ceasing to be the object of human perception and representation, becomes an a-constructed given and is no longer the product of human experience,[68] owing its existence only to itself and not to the human gaze possibly thrown at it. In that sense, thingness, presenting itself as being outside human perception and representation, demotes the human being and the human gaze to irrelevant information. This is what makes thingification an act of dehumanization of any encounter with the thing enjoying thingness.

But there is more to the dehumanization that is provoked by the production of thingness as is construed here. In fact, the latter does not leave all possible speaking observers unaffected, even if they are necessarily excluded from the scene of the thing. Indeed, any speaking observer is not only declared absent but can, in turn, become a possible object of thingification on which some thingness can be projected. If practices, states, actors, people, environments, histories, cultures, traditions, races, genders, identities, foreignness, otherness, economic development, discriminations, dominations, oppressions, liberations, injustices, inequalities, aggressions, violences, etc. can be a thing, so can human beings. Said differently, even human subjects – those who had once been elevated into sovereign modern selves – can end up being turned into things.[69] Surely, when applied to human beings, thingness is a sort of *human death*.[70] And, once thingified and dead, humans can be a mass of things that can be handled, differentiated, and even erased.

2.6 Interpellation

Possibly the most remarkable effect of thingness is its capacity to interpellate the (former) speaking observer, despite their being deprived of their status as a speaking observer and excluded from the scene of the thing. Indeed, the self-signifying thing and its necessary being-in-the-world, once encountered by the (former) speaking observer, assign the latter a specific place and role, that of a *subject* of a specific order. The (former) speaking observer is interpellated by the thing which, through its interpellation, indicates its being as a thing and elevates them into a subject of the order of the thing concerned.[71]

Needless to say that these considerations might appear contradictory, for they seem to indicate that the speaking observer is both deprived of their quality of speaking observer and elevated into a subject. Such claims are, however, not discrepant, for the turning of the (former) speaking observer into a subject is the making of the latter, not into a sovereign Cartesian self, but into *a subject of the thing* to which they are subjected. Being a subject here means being subject to the thing and thus ascribed a specific place and role, not as speaking observer, but as a *subordinate* that enjoys no leeway to determine their place and their role. This is what Althusser's famous notion of interpellation points to: The making of a subject as a subject of the interpellator, and not as a sovereign self.

In the light of such understanding of subjecthood, it is now possible to appreciate the extent to which the interpellation of the (former) speaking observer and the turning of the latter into a subject of the thing – which is thus everything but a modern empowerment of the self – constitutes a dramatic epistemological effect of thingness. By interpellating the (former) speaking observer, the thing establishes its epistemological order and puts everyone who experiences its presence in a predefined position of acceptance of the thingly order concerned.

2.7 *Interpretation*

The interpellation by the thing and the making of a subject of the thing only unfold to a certain extent. Indeed, the thing interpellates the (former) speaking observer, thereby assigning a place and a role to the latter, but only when it comes to the thing's necessary being-in-the-world. More specifically, the interpellation only plays out with respect to the being-in-the-world but not as far as the meaning of such being is concerned. To put it differently, interpellation and the making of a subject of the thing do not predetermine the possibility of interpretation of the thing by the (former) speaking observer. In that sense, *interpellation is not the end of interpretation* but, on the contrary, only one of its beginnings.[72] In that sense, interpellation is only the first phase of the encounter with the thing. Whilst interpretation with respect to the existence and being-in-the-world of the thing had been concealed by thingness, interpellation opens up and inaugurates a new phase where the interpretation of the thing becomes central. That means that thingness, although it claims to be outside perception and representation, does not preclude interpretation. It simply recalibrates interpretation by channelling it away from the existence of the thing, postpones it after the confirmation of the existence of the thing, and puts it in the hands of the constrained subjects of the order of the thing.[73]

An important remark is in order. Although interpretation seems to come into motion after thingness – and especially interpellation – has done its work, it is important to stress that *thingness remains interpretative all the way*. It is true that interpretation only becomes called for once the thing's necessary being-in-the-world is affirmed and the (former) speaking observer is assigned a place as subject of the thing. Yet, interpellation is interpretation. In other words, thingness is never outside interpretation, even before the affirmation of the necessary being-in-the-world of the thing.

The claim made here about interpretation can be usefully clarified and further substantiated by Heidegger's famous distinction between the *ready-to-hand* and the *present-at-hand*. For Heidegger, the ready-to-hand refers to the situation where objects are encountered as things that just exist as detached entities. Said differently, a ready-to-hand is a primitive, practical engagement with tools or equipment when they are functioning properly. In contrast, the present-at-hand refers to the situation where one encounters an object in a meaningful context. It thus describes a mode of encountering entities when they're removed from practical contexts. Heidegger's key claim is that *ready-to-hand* is more fundamental than present-at-hand. For him, one's most basic way of relating to the world is not as detached observers, but as beings engaged in practical activities. Heidegger, criticizing the Kantian tradition, argues that Western philosophy has overemphasized the present-at-hand mode, treating it as primary, when in fact it is derivative of our more fundamental ready-to-hand engagement with the world.[74] For Heidegger, the subject-object relationship only emerges once one has gone beyond the primitive ready-to-hand engagement. In particular, before one ever encounters things as objects for knowledge, one is already involved with them in practical, meaningful activity. For him, this is something Kant's framework cannot fully account for. In other words, *Kant starts with the knowing subject and the object*, but Heidegger wants to show that our being-in-the-world is more basic than this subject-object distinction allows. It would be far-fetched to associate the ready-to-hand to a pre-interpretive stage, that is, a stage where the existence of the thing is not being interpreted but is just encountered. This is why, for Heidegger, interpretation is always already at work. Even the *ready-to-hand* is not a suspension of interpretation, but rather a mode where interpretation is practical, embodied, and non-thematic.[75] Heidegger's point that the ready-to-hand is not a suspension of interpretation, but rather a mode where interpretation is practical, embodied, and non-thematic helps one explain why thingness, despite claiming to be outside perception and representation and notwithstanding the act of interpellation, can be construed as entailing no annihilation of any interpretive space. Thingness's interpellation is interpretation.

2.8 Prescription

The foregoing already indicates that thingness cannot be reduced to a mere act of description of a state of fact but must always be apprehended in its prescriptive dimension. Indeed, thingness does not only define what is but carries with it a series of instructions as to how one must relate to what has the attribute of a thing: The thing necessarily is and anyone who encounters it must live with it. In other words, the thing prescribes to the whole world that it cannot not exist. In that sense, thingness always orders an absolute obedience to the existence that is so established. The *is* simultaneously is a *must be*.[76]

The prescriptive dimension of thingness manifests most clearly in what is called here the *imperative of acknowledgement*. Once something achieves the status of a thing, it demands recognition from all who encounter it – not as a matter of choice, but as an existential necessity. This compulsory acknowledgement operates on multiple levels simultaneously. Phenomenologically, the thing imposes itself on consciousness, refusing to be ignored or wished away. Practically, it creates obstacles, pathways, and possibilities that shape action whether one wishes to engage with them or not. Socially, it establishes shared reference points that structure collective life.

The prescriptive dimension of thingness becomes particularly significant when one considers its deployment in legal and political contexts, which will be examined in detail in the following chapters. In fact, as will be shown, the legal discourse fundamentally depends on the ability to transform complex social relations into things – objects, property, rights, corporations, jurisdictions – that then acquire prescriptive force over human behaviour. Similarly, when political actors designate certain entities as things requiring protection, regulation, or elimination, they harness the prescriptive force of thingness to reshape social reality. As will also be discussed later,[77] the contemporary proliferation of thingification processes in domestic and global governance can be explained by the prescriptive dimension of thingness, which political actors and contemporary decision-makers tap into.

2.9 Abstraction

This final effect of thingness that ought to be mentioned pertains to what thingness does to the world of the (ostracized) speaking observer. It is argued here that thingification similarly is a mode of abstraction in that it makes the world entirely notional and ethereal. In other words, the thingification of the world and its being construed as constituted of distinct, ordered, self-signifying beings independent of perception and representation results in a very sophisticated form of abstraction, one that is constitutive of thingness.[78]

Such effect of thingification can possibly look paradoxical. In fact, thingness, being the quality of what has a necessary material existence in the world by virtue of being a thing and not by virtue of what a speaking observer may perceive, observe, name, represent, etc., could be construed as absolute concreteness, one that excludes conceptual thinking and abstraction.[79] From such a perspective, how could a thingified world, that is, a world-in-itself populated by self-signifying beings whose existence is not contingent upon being observed, named, or represented, be deemed abstract? It is submitted here that there is absolutely no paradox in the claim that thingness, as is understood here, simultaneously entails abstraction.

The idea that thingification is a sophisticated mode of abstraction – without this being a paradox – finds an echo in Deleuze and Guattari's account of the State-form. For them, the State objectifies territory, seizing it as an operational substrate for organization and production, and in so doing paradoxically de-territorializes it – the territory ceases to be a *milieu* of practices and relations and becomes a governed object. In their terms, the State's overcoding captures the Earth only to recompose it as an apparatus of calculation. Thus, for them, objectification is inseparable from de-territorialization because the territorial world is evacuated into a schema of predicates, metrics, and programmes. Read alongside the argument developed here, this shows how thingification – "objectification" in Deleuze and Guattari's terminology – operates as abstraction. By installing predicates ahead of presence, it turns territories, bodies, and relations into administrable things, thereby thinning the world into an ethereal plane of notions and necessities, a world whose substance has been replaced by its objectified form.[80]

The claim that thingness entails abstraction will surely also resonate among those familiar with the Marxian concept of commodity fetishism and the more general Marxist concept of reification – to which this chapter will revert below.[81] Indeed, the very idea of commodity boils down to a profound abstraction as individuals and their mutual relations are abstracted from human experience in order to create a form that structures social relations while appearing to be concrete, natural, and objective. In other words, commodities are not things but abstractions that appear as things in a way that shapes not only economic relations but consciousness itself.[82]

Building on all such insights, the argument about the abstraction brought about by thingness can be further elucidated and can be said to bear three specific dimensions. Said differently, thingness is thrice an abstraction. First, it is the abstraction of the thingified world from perception and representation. In that regard, thingness abstracts the world from human experience. It is a bypass of the human[83] and of the historical.[84] Second, thingness is abstraction because it obscures its own abstractive character to present thingness as being the most concrete form of being-in-the-world. In that sense, it is abstract because it obfuscates its very creation of a specific epistemology[85] and of a regime of representation.[86] Third, by projecting a being that is self-signifying, unperceived, and unrepresented, thingness constructs a conceptual entity, i.e. the thing, that is no less abstract than the perceptions and representations it seeks to avoid. So construed, thingness produces yet another abstraction: The thing-in-itself,[87] which has been claimed to be one of the greatest fictions on which modern human thought is built.[88]

3. Thingification compared to other modes of necessitarian thought

As is argued in this book, thingness, although it presents itself as being independent from perception, observation, language, discourse, and representation, is an attribute that is always produced by the discourse. As was said, the specific discursive and epistemological process whereby thingness is produced is called here thingification. This section approaches the process of thingification as a mode of necessitarian thought, that is, as a way to create necessities about the existence of what composes the world. It is submitted here that, in modern thought, the creation of necessities about one's surrounding world can take various forms and paths while using a great variety of methods, ways of thinking, and strategies. In that sense, thingification is only *a* specific mode of necessitarian thought that coexists with other modes of creation of necessities.

With a view to further unpacking the notions of thingness and thingification, this section compares the creation of necessities through thingification, with the necessity-creating processes of objectification (3.1), naturalization (3.2), essentialization (3.3), scientification (3.4), and mathematization (3.5).

A few considerations will also be provided as to how thingification compares with the processes of commodification and reification as they have been theorized in Marxian and Marxist theories (3.6). It will be shown that, whilst thingification bears some similarities with all those other modes of necessitarian thought, it remains a very distinct way of creating necessary existence.

3.1 Thingification, objectification, and consumption

The suspension of perception that accompanies thingness, as is understood here, explains why *thingness* ought to be distinguished from *objecthood*.[89] Indeed, the object is an object for the very reason that it is an object of the perception of a speaking observer. On the contrary, the thing is what is awarded a necessary existence outside perception. The thing, contrary to the object, is not there to be seen by anyone whereas the object can only be an object if it is seen by a speaking observer.[90] To put it differently, the object is what is always produced by the subject's perception whereas being as a thing is always irreducible to being an object form of the speaking observer.[91] In that sense, it could be said that thingness does not name an object but a particular subject-object relation,[92] namely a subject-object relation where both the object and the subject are obliterated and where only the thing remains.

There is a further reason to distinguish what is thingified and what is objectified. Because objects continue to be the object of perception by a speaking observer, they remain caught in a system of meanings where they are no longer valued primarily for their functional utility but for the meanings, signs, and social status they convey. This is the famous argument of Jean Baudrillard that ought to be briefly recalled here. For him, objects form a system of signs within which speaking observers (which he calls consumers) construct their identities and social relationships, turning consumption into a language through which people communicate and distinguish themselves. Baudrillard contends that this shift transforms everyday life, as the symbolic and cultural significance of objects overtakes their practical use, embedding individuals in a network of meanings shaped by consumer culture. As a result, the practice of consumption of objects, for Baudrillard, must be completely rethought. In fact, it cannot simply be construed as the use or purchase of goods to satisfy needs, but as a systematic social and cultural activity centred on the manipulation of signs and symbols. It is a process through which individuals communicate their identities, aspirations, and social positions by selecting and displaying objects that carry particular meanings within a system of signs. In other words, consumption becomes a way of participating in a symbolic order, where the act of choosing, possessing, and showcasing objects is fundamentally about expressing differences, desires, and affiliations in the context of a consumer society.[93] Although thingness, as is construed here, does not escape representation,[94] it constitutes a type of being that posits a radical outside to all systems of meaning, representation, and language, i.e. a self-signifying materiality. For Baudrillard, objects are never simply things but are always already caught up in a system of signs, meanings, and social codes. For him, objects do not signify by virtue of their own materiality or presence, but through their place in a network of differences and relations, i.e. the system of objects. As a result, their thingness is always mediated by cultural codes and consumer practices, for they are meaningful only insofar as they are represented, named, and positioned within cultural and linguistic structures; their value and significance are produced by their representational function within consumer society. Baudrillard's work on objects shows that thingness and objecthood can refer to two very opposite approaches to materiality and justifies a distinct conceptual and terminological treatment.

3.2 Thingification and naturalization

Awarding an uncontested material existence to what composes one's environment in order to escape the need for any extra verification is not unheard of. This is what naturalization does too.[95] One may indeed wonder whether thingness is simply a form of naturalizing thinking,[96] i.e. a way of thinking whereby an entity, the shape of a body, a sexual practice, a colour, a practice, a process, a move, a saying, a geographical ordering, a specific hierarchy, a specific relationship, a certain state of distributive justice, etc. is construed as having a natural necessity[97] and belonging to a fixed and natural state of affairs,[98] thus excluding perception, observation, language, discourse, and representation.[99] In the same way, one may wonder whether thingification can be approached as a type of organismic thinking, that is the thinking – common in social sciences especially to theorize social entities[100] – based on organismic metaphors, which can be construed as a type of naturalizing thinking.[101]

It is argued here that thingification cannot be reduced to a variant or a form of naturalization or organismic thinking but constitutes a broader discursive move which always precedes any such act.[102] This can be explained as follows. Commonly, when an entity, the shape of a body, a sexual practice, a colour, a practice, a process, a move, a saying, a geographical ordering, a specific hierarchy, a specific relationship, a certain state of distributive justice, etc. is held as being natural and corresponding to a natural necessity which is outside language, discourse, representation, observation, construction, it has already been made a thing which is subsequently made a natural thing.[103] In other words, thingification always precedes naturalization and organismic thinking, for the imposition of a natural necessity on an entity, the shape of a body, a sexual practice, a colour, a practice, a process, a move, a saying, a geographical ordering, a specific hierarchy, a specific relationship, a certain state of distributive justice, etc. always presupposes some pre-existing thingly materiality to which a natural necessity can subsequently be ascribed.

That naturalization and thingification ought to be distinguished can be further demonstrated by the idea that not all things are held to be natural things. Thingness comes to attribute the status of things to all sorts of entities in the world that are not natural but held as being solely human. For instance, law, the State, the nation, the national culture, the national cuisine, traditions, social classes, etc. are commonly produced by thingification processes and thus construed as things out there but without them being necessarily naturalized and understood as a product of a fixed state of nature.

Finally, naturalization and thingification seem, in the 21st century, to share very distinct fates. In fact, naturalization, especially when it comes to invoking nature to protect the environment or fight climate change, has lost its formidable discursive bite. As has been convincingly shown by Bruno Latour, the concept of nature now seems discredited, having been demoted to a notion that is moralizing and polemical, especially in conservative circles.[104] In contrast, and as will be discussed throughout this book, thingification is currently in its prime, enjoying a discursive apogee that it had not experienced since the heyday of dogmatic empiricism. The diverging destinies of naturalization and thingification confirm that they ought not to be conflated.

3.3 Thingification and essentialization

In terms of producing a necessary existence and providing it with a neat delineation, thingification could be understood as a type of essentializing thinking, that is, a way of thinking about the world that essentializes the latter and reduces it to some key unitary characteristics, nature, or functions. Such conflation would not be totally far-fetched, at least in the social sciences where most types of realism and mind-independent epistemologies commonly bring about essentialism.[105]

Yet, it is submitted here that thingification and essentializing thinking ought to be strictly distinguished, for at least two reasons. First, not all thingification processes are aimed at capturing the essence of what is being thingified. Surely, thingness fixes the thingly realities which it produces but does not necessarily define their essence, composition, or function. It solely awards them a necessary existence. Indeed, thingness can be deployed strategically and critically without any consideration for the essence of what is being scrutinized. Thingification and essentializing thinking can also be distinguished for another reason. Thingness, as has just been highlighted and will be further discussed below, can be made very alien to any essentializing ambition. Conversely, all essentialization processes always presuppose a prior thingification. In fact, in order to extract an essential characteristic, nature or function, one often needs to have awarded some prior thingly quality to what is being scrutinized for its essential qualities. Essentialization would prove impossible if what is being approached in essentialist terms was simultaneously approached as an ethereal or metaphysical phenomenon.

The abovementioned differences between thingness and essentializing thinking seem to be ultimately corroborated, here too, by the very distinct fates that each of these ways of thinking has undergone in the humanities. Whilst thingness seems to be experiencing a golden age, essentializing thinking seems to have long fallen from grace[106] to be associated with a mythological way of thinking.[107]

3.4 Thingification and the production of scientific facts

It is argued here that thingness is a type of necessary existence produced *outside* scientific laboratories. Indeed, thingification cannot be equated with the production of scientific facts. The thingness produced by thingification is not a type of necessary existence developed in a scientific laboratory or a scientific study.[108] Thingness corresponds to what has been called a "necessity of the real",[109] a status which scientific facts are never considered to be entitled to. In fact, there is nothing more at odds with one another than thingness and modern scientistic thought.[110] Thingness creates an existence that does not hinge on its verification or demonstration by a speaking observer whereas a scientific fact is always up for examination, re-interpretation, contestation, and invalidation. Thingness always is a *definite* quality that is self-produced while the scientific truth is only the *provisional* finding of experience.[111] The former puts in place an epistemology where an existence is necessary by virtue of itself and cannot be proved wrong whereas the latter always modestly considers its findings as tentative and falsifiable.[112] For science, dissent is a tool to promote the advancement of knowledge, while, for thingness, dissent is a denial of the obvious.[113] Such discrepancy may explain why the idea of matter – with which the thing is often conflated – is a metaphysical notion that has long left the scientific discourse.[114]

This fundamental distinction between the necessary existence accompanying thingness and the temporary existence generated by scientific laboratories is further demonstrated by the idea – now very common in Science and Technology Studies – according to which scientific knowledge is embedded in social practices and scientific facts are socially constructed through complex processes involving human and non-human actors.[115] Thingness, because it is meant to be outside perception, independent of a speaking observer, self-signifying and to exist only by virtue of itself and not by virtue of social actors and processes, is the antithesis of what Science and Technology Studies have been articulated around.[116]

The best illustration of the distinction between the necessary existence produced by thingness and the scientific facticity produced by scientific laboratories and scientific studies is provided by the idea of race – to which one of the following chapters will more amply return.[117] In fact, despite sciences having compellingly shown for a very long time that no biological difference between groups of humans can ever be ascertained, race has continued to be the source of a fixed, necessary, and unchallenged being governing the minds of people, and especially of decision-makers and political actors.[118]

The distinction, discussed in the previous paragraphs, between the necessary existence produced by thingness and the scientific facticity produced by scientific laboratories and scientific studies calls for a final remark. That thingness is not produced in scientific laboratories or scientific reviews could make one think that the necessary existence produced by thingness is very vulnerable to refutation and thus always volatile.[119] It is argued here that this is not the case at all and that the being that accompanies any judgement about the thingness of the world is commonly held to be, contrary to scientific findings, unassailable, unfalsifiable, durable, and dramatically compelling. In that sense, thingness is a type of epistemology that – sometimes openly[120] – seeks to eclipse scienticism whose findings, as was indicated above, are accused of remaining weak and temporary.[121]

3.5 Thingification and mathematization

The mathematization of nature has, since Galileo, constituted a central mode of creating knowledge about the world in a way that is independent of the perception of the speaking observer.[122] Such a type of knowledge has proved very convenient and has been deemed most reliable,[123] resulting in many discourses striving to adjust themselves in order to espouse mathematical patterns of thought.[124] This can be explained as follows. With mathematization, the world is made mathematizable in its entirety[125] and comes to be outside and before thought.[126] Mathematization also pulls its findings out of time and de-historicizes knowledge.[127] What is more, as is also illustrated by Cartesian philosophy, whatever can be formulated through mathematical propositions exists by itself and constitutes necessary properties (primary qualities) of the thing as they are independently of one's perception.[128]

In the light of the above, there would accordingly be a strong case to compare the creation of necessary existence through thingification and that based on mathematization. Yet, it is argued here that mathematization radically departs from thingification in that mathematical propositions are only hypotheses that can be either verified or refuted. Although the aim of the mathematization of nature through mathematical propositions is to create knowledge, the outcome, just like the product of science, is always appealable and temporary.[129] What is more, mathematizations of the world never seek to hide the extent to which they constitute a type of representation of the latter[130] and are thus, contrary to the type of necessary being that accompanied thingness, not self-effaced.

3.6 Thingification, commodification, and reification

No doubt that the understanding of thingness and thingification that has been theorized in this chapter will prove reminiscent of one of the core concepts at the heart of Marxian[131] thought, namely *commodity fetishism*[132] as well as the concepts subsequently derived from it.[133] For Marx, one of the main world-making effects of bourgeois capitalism is to transform the subjects and the relations between them into objectified, materialized, extra-social, and tradable things that are fixed and determinative of a class reality which is experienced as being out there and with an irresistible facticity.[134] To put it differently, for Marx, commodity fetishism refers to the creation by bourgeois capitalism of a material and universal reality which hides itself and its transformation of humans into things and accordingly produces an objectified being.[135] It is usually well known that Marx's idea of commodity fetishism was later refined and substantiated by ensuing Marxist thinkers who, on that occasion, generalized a much more self-explanatory idiom – which Marx had hardly used in his work[136] – for the creation of such thingly being by bourgeois capitalism: *Reification*.[137] Since its inception, reification has proved a compelling descriptive tool to capture what capitalism does, how it does it, how it hides what it does, and how it proves inescapable. In particular, it helps explain how subjects and social relations come to be experienced as thing-like objects as soon as they come to be viewed according to their potential usefulness and exchange value in economic transactions.[138]

It is not difficult to fathom here why the idea of reification, and its descriptive potential to apprehend the objectification of the entirety of capitalist society,[139] largely dovetails with the creation of thingness as is understood in this book. After all, reification, as described by Herbert Marcuse, is "the general necessity of things".[140] Given such convergent effects, and especially the fact that reification and thingification both assume the character of creating a mind-independent objectified thing,[141] one may wonder why this book, with a view to capturing the thingification processes under examination here, has not espoused the Marxist terminology of reification. Such a terminological question is even more warranted given the extent to which the concept of reification is etymologically, grammatically, and aesthetically much more apposite.[142] On top of being etymologically, grammatically, and aesthetically very germane, the concept of reification honed by Marxist thought has the advantage of putting the emphasis on the very exploitative dimension of thingness.[143] In fact, thingness is a way to exploit and maximize the value of "the real" with a view to making the most of it. More concretely, besides its epistemological and discursive consequences which have been discussed above, there is a social, symbolic, reputational, professional, and even financial value that can be ascribed to the thingly necessities created by thingness, if only by virtue of the time that is spared by dodging all existential and definitional debates as well as avoiding costly peer conflicts. In that sense, thingness can be deemed part of a larger economy about the creation of (the knowledge of)[144] realities, the thingly character of the latter generating a surplus value of sorts. If the thingly quality of thingified being constitutes a surplus value of sorts which can be the object of all forms of exploitation, there would thus be extra incentives to resort to the Marxist terminology of reification instead of thingification.

Yet another motive for adopting the terminology of reification, rather than thingification, is provided by the autonomy from Marxist thought that the concept of reification has occasionally been able to secure, thereby easing its use and generalization outside Marxist theory. For instance, there have been attempts to describe reification as a human tendency or a feature of social psychology.[145] There have also been broad generalizations of the concept of reification in the legal literature.[146] A similar autonomy of such concept from its Marxist inception has also been witnessed in relation to its use in postcolonial and decolonial studies where it has been relied on to describe the fabrication of an objectified colonial being beyond the bourgeois capitalist society.[147] An even more radical and explicit bypass of the Marxist pedigree of the concept of reification is found in the work of Hannah Arendt where reification is associated with the materialization of the world through work – which she distinguishes from labour, including the transformation of action, speech and thought into worldly things, thereby providing worldliness, permanence and durability without which human life cannot be stabilized and escape futility.[148]

Although in some earlier work I have resorted to the concept of reification,[149] I have chosen, in this book, to refer to thingification rather than reification. The reasons for such terminological choice are multifold. First, it has been decided here since the concept of reification has undergone a serious decline and has been severely discredited – possibly for the wrong reasons – in the humanities over the last decades,[150] this book should not read as an endeavour to rehabilitate such a Marxist critical tool. Second, the pedigree of the concept of reification, namely Marx's work itself, carries with it an ambiguity as it is premised on the idea that the social world actually exists, albeit not transparently and not independently from theory and frameworks of knowledge.[151] Third, although Marxist thinkers have striven to emancipate themselves from Marx's concept of commodity fetishism and the latter's focus on the economic sphere by extending the concept of reification to cover the entirety of capitalist social life,[152] the concept of reification remains too imbued with a Marxist thrust that puts the emphasis on the objectification processes at work in a capitalist society.[153] In order to tell a story that goes much beyond the capitalist economy with which the concept of reification remains most commonly associated, it is felt here that thingification constitutes a vocabulary that most appropriately and most efficaciously captures the idea of a necessary being-in-the-world that is outside perception and representation by virtue of being a thing.

That being said, although preferring the notion of thingification over reification, this book shares an important posture with the abovementioned Marxist thinkers who have theorized and grappled with the concept of reification: Their discontent with the reification at work in capitalist societies and their advocacy of a permanent suspicion towards the human-making and worldmaking consequences of thinking in terms of things. This point is important for it allows us to emphasize once more that the necessary material existence enabled by thingness is always constructed and is never out there.[154] In other words, the self-evidence and self-signification of thingness are precisely what thingness does: Laying thingness outside language, discourse, representation, observation, construction, while hiding such exclusionary move. If thingness always is constructed by thingification processes, as Marxists also tried to demonstrate with their own specific vocabulary, then thingness is the mother of all hallucinations[155] and, thus, should always be approached with the greatest suspicion, the very same suspicion with which Marxists approached reifying processes.[156]

Notes

1 On the idea that any discourse constructs its object while being itself constructed, see Michel Foucault, *Entretiens radiophoniques 1961–1983* (Flammarion/Vrin/INA 2024) 469–70.
2 Manuel DeLanda, *A New Philosophy of Society: Assemblage Theory and Social Complexity* (Bloomsbury 2019) 1.
3 Arnaud Macé, *La matière* (GF Flammarion 1998) 11–13; Martin Heidegger, *Qu'est-ce qu'une chose?* (Jean Reboul and Jacques Taminiaux trs, Gallimard 1971) 45–46.
4 See s 1.6.
5 See s 1.6.
6 See ch 2, s 3.
7 On this point, see Giorgio Agamben, *L'irréalisable* (Seuil 2025) 100–02.
8 Martin Heidegger, *Qu'est-ce qu'une chose?* (Jean Reboul and Jacques Taminiaux trs, Gallimard 1971) 45–46.
9 See the remarks of Peter Berger and Thomas Luckmann, *The Social Construction of Reality: A Treatise in the Sociology of Knowledge* (Penguin Books 1967) 37.
10 Arnaud Macé, *La matière* (GF Flammarion 1998) 12.
11 Maurice Merleau-Ponty, *Phénoménologie de la perception* (Gallimard 1945) 279.
12 Ibid 178.
13 Jacques Derrida, *Parages* (Galilée 1986) 189.
14 The expression is from Manuel DeLanda, *A New Philosophy of Society: Assemblage Theory and Social Complexity* (Bloomsbury 2019) 1.
15 Quentin Meillassoux, *Après la finitude: Essai sur la nécessité de la contingence* (Seuil 2006) 14–15. See also Manuel DeLanda, *A New Philosophy of Society: Assemblage Theory and Social Complexity* (Bloomsbury 2019) 1.
16 Quentin Meillassoux, *Après la finitude: Essai sur la nécessité de la contingence* (Seuil 2006) 14.
17 Bill Brown, *Other Things* (University of Chicago Press 2015) 18.
18 Maurice Merleau-Ponty, *Phénoménologie de la perception* (Gallimard 1945) 384–85.
19 Achille Mbembe, *Critique de la raison nègre* (La Découverte 2013) 61.
20 Michel Serres, *Statues: Le second livre des fondations* (Champs 2014) 208–09. See also Tomonaga Tairako, 'Reification, Thingification, and Alienation in

Marx's Economic Manuscripts' (2025) 55 *Hitotsubashi Journal of Social Studies* 1–39, 5.

21 Jean Baudrillard, *Le crime parfait* (Galilée 1995) 86 and 107.

22 On such correlation being the main feature of Kantian epistemology, see Quentin Meillassoux, *Après la finitude: Essai sur la nécessité de la contingence* (Seuil 2006) 18–19. See also infra ch 2, s 3.

23 This is the reason why what Michel Foucault famously described as "humanism", which he understands as the emergence, at the end of the eighteenth century and the beginning of the nineteenth century, of "man" as an epistemic object and the simultaneous formation of social and human sciences, cannot be construed as putting in place a process of thingification as is understood here. Indeed, in Foucault's critique of the modern episteme, the constitution of the human by psychology, sociology, the study of literature and myth, etc., operates as what Foucault calls a strange empirical-transcendental doublet, thus preserving the human's status as a speaking observer and thus as a condition of possibility for knowledge. For the human emerged simultaneously as both the subject who knows as well as the object to be known and to be constituted; the process is one of objectification and not of thingification as is understood here. See generally Michel Foucault, *Les mots et les choses* (Gallimard 1966) esp chs 9–10; Michel Foucault, *Dits et écrits, I (1954–1975)* (Gallimard 2001) 636, 679; Michel Foucault, *Dits et écrits, II* (Gallimard 2001) 37. On the distinction between objectification and thingification, see infra this ch, s 3.1.

24 It is interesting, if not ironical, that those philosophers who recognize the possibility to make unmediated contact with the world, and thus espouse a certain idea of thingness as is understood here, have sometimes been called the "representationalists" for they take concepts to be representations of reality. See Robert Brandom, *Making It Explicit: Reasoning, Representing, and Discursive Commitment* (Harvard University Press 1994) 8.

25 Jacques Derrida, *Parages* (Galilée 1986) 189.

26 Ibid.

27 In the same vein, see Timothy Bewes, *Reification or The Anxiety of Late Capitalism* (Verso 2002) xii.

28 Roland Barthes, *Mythologies* (Éditions du Seuil 1957) 254 (speaking of the thingifying effect of myths).

29 Cf Herbert Marcuse, *One-Dimensional Man: Studies in the Ideology of Advanced Industrial Society* (Beacon Press 1964) ch 4 (who argues that concreteness, why dominates modern societies, makes all tensions between appearance and reality vanish).

30 Cf Manuel DeLanda's attempt to devise a new form of realism for social entities whereby social entities will be treated as assemblages constructed through very special historical processes where language plays a role but not a constitutive role. See Manuel DeLanda, *A New Philosophy of Society: Assemblage Theory and Social Complexity* (Bloomsbury 2019).

31 The expression is from Jacques Derrida, *Parages* (Galilée 1986) 26.

32 See the remarks of Jacques Rancière, *La mésentente: Politique et philosophie* (La Fabrique 2025) 158.

33 The metaphor is from Jean Baudrillard, *Le crime parfait* (Galilée 1995) 19.

34 On the relationship between thing and structure, see ch 2, s 4.

35 Such a possibility is what Wilfrid Sellars criticizes in Wilfrid Sellars, *Empiricism and the Philosophy of Mind* (Harvard University Press 1997) (first published 1956) (where he claims that all awareness and knowledge are mediated by concepts, which are in turn embedded in language and social practices).

36 Bruno Latour has traced a similar regime of causality accompanying the idea of nature. See Bruno Latour, *Face à Gaïa* (La Découverte 2015) 94.
37 Bruno Latour has similarly shed light on the extent to which the concept of nature carries such a creationist narrative. See Bruno Latour, *Face à Gaïa* (La Découverte 2015) 94.
38 Cf the epistemological temporality at work in the regime of heterosexuality whereby the body signified as prior to signification is similarly an effect of signification. See Judith Butler, *Bodies That Matter: On the Discursive Limits of "Sex"* (Routledge 2011) xii–xv.
39 Thingness is a way to address the problem of evidencing what has come before or after human experience. If what comes before or after human experience comes with some thingly necessity, it can be proven without being experienced, perceived, observed, thereby solving a great deal of scientific and epistemological controversy. In that regard, see Quentin Meillassoux's attempt to reinvent Cartesian materialism and the possibility of an absolute without falling back into dogmatic metaphysics of naïve realism: Quentin Meillassoux, *Après la finitude: Essai sur la nécessité de la contingence* (Seuil 2006).
40 Maurice Merleau-Ponty, *Phénoménologie de la perception* (Gallimard 1945) 141.
41 Enrique Dussel, *Philosophie de la Libération* (PUF 2023) 178.
42 Ibid.
43 The expression is from Michel Serres, *Statues: Le second livre des fondations* (Champs 2014) 27–28.
44 Michel Serres, *Statues: Le second livre des fondations* (Champs 2014) 113.
45 See the remarks of Peter Berger and Thomas Luckmann, *The Social Construction of Reality: A Treatise in the Sociology of Knowledge* (Penguin Books 1967) 37.
46 Maurice Merleau-Ponty, *Phénoménologie de la perception* (Gallimard 1945) 384–85.
47 Enrique Dussel, *Philosophie de la Libération* (PUF 2023) 179.
48 Woosung Kang, 'Thing' (Oxford Research Encyclopedias: Literature, 23 February 2021) https://www.oxfordreference.com/ accessed 9 March 2026.
49 Herbert Marcuse, *One-Dimensional Man: Studies in the Ideology of Advanced Industrial Society* (Beacon Press 1964) ch 1 (who argues that concreteness, why dominates modern societies, has not made ideology disappear).
50 Bill Brown, 'Thing Theory' (2001) 28 *Critical Inquiry* 1, 8.
51 Cf the idea of an epistemology of the closet developed by Eve Kosofsky Sedgwick, *Epistemology of the Closet* (University of California Press 2008). Comp. also with the notion of epistemology of the secret put forward by Jean d'Aspremont, *The Epistemology of the Secret: International Law as Revelation* (CUP 2025).
52 Herbert Marcuse, *One-Dimensional Man: Studies in the Ideology of Advanced Industrial Society* (Beacon Press 1964) ch 4.
53 Bill Brown, 'Thing Theory' (2001) 28 *Critical Inquiry* 1, 1 (he writes that things "offer us a dry ground above those swirling accounts of the subjects, some place of origin unmediated by the sign, some stable alternative to the instabilities and uncertainties, the ambiguities and anxieties, forever fetishized by theory").
54 Tristan Garcia, *Forme et objet: Un traité des choses* (PUF 2011) 7–9 and 85.
55 On the idea that, in social sciences, thingification (reification), taxonomization and essentialization go together, see Manuel DeLanda, *A New Philosophy of Society: Assemblage Theory and Social Complexity* (Bloomsbury 2019) 27.
56 Martin Heidegger, *Qu'est-ce qu'une chose?* (Jean Reboul and Jacques Taminiaux trs, Gallimard 1971) 29.

57 Martin Heidegger, *Qu'est-ce qu'une chose?* (Jean Reboul and Jacques Taminiaux trs, Gallimard 1971) 37 and 39.
58 See this ch, s 1.5.
59 For another, but yet radically different, distanciation from originist thinking, see Jean d'Aspremont, *After Meaning: The Sovereignty of Forms in International Law* (Edward Elgar 2021).
60 On this traditional modern historical mindset, see Jean d'Aspremont, 'Critical Histories of International Law and the Repression of Disciplinary Imagination' (2019) 7 *London Review of International Law* 89–115. See also Jean d'Aspremont, *The Critical Attitude and the History of International Law* (Brill 2019); Jean d'Aspremont, 'Turntablism in the History of International Law' (2020) 22 *Journal of the History of International Law* 472–96.
61 Jacques Derrida, *Parages* (Galilée 1986) 178.
62 Isabelle Bishop, 'Everyday Hegemony: Reification, the Supermarket, and the Nuclear Family' (2004) 7 *Open Philosophy* 1. This is also the claim made by Herbert Marcuse. See Herbert Marcuse, *One-Dimensional Man: Studies in the Ideology of Advanced Industrial Society* (Beacon Press 1964) ch 4. In the same vein, see also Jean-François Bayart, *L'énergie de l'Etat: Pour une sociologie historique et comparée du politique* (La Découverte 2022) 172.
63 Jacques Derrida, *Parages* (Galilée 1986) 189.
64 Hannah Arendt, *The Human Condition* (2nd edn, University of Chicago Press 2018) 3–4. See also Bill Brown, *Other Things* (University of Chicago Press 2015) 155–62.
65 Jacques Rancière, *La mésentente: Politique et philosophie* (La Fabrique 2025) 48–49.
66 Ibid 51.
67 This aspect of thingness is further examined in ch 3.
68 On the idea that the question of production of human artefacts and human discourses is at the centre of modern thought, see Michel de Certeau, *L'écriture de l'histoire* (Gallimard 1975) 27–28. See also Roland Barthes, *Le bruissement de la langue: Essais critiques IV* (Seuil 1984) 63–69.
69 Michel Serres, *Statues: Le second livre des fondations* (Champs 2014) 208–09; Tristan Garcia, *Forme et objet: Un traité des choses* (PUF 2011) 7–9; Woosung Kang, 'Thing' (Oxford Research Encyclopedias: Literature, 23 February 2021) https://www.oxfordreference.com/ accessed 9 March 2026. Cf the Marxist concept of reification examined in this ch, s 3.6.
70 Achille Mbembe, *Critique de la raison nègre* (La Découverte 2013) 220 (speaking about the colonized-colonizer relationship). Cf the idea of "the disappearance of man" by Michel Foucault, *Les mots et les choses* (Gallimard 1966) 398 (where he argues that the concept of humanity and humanism as we understand them are relatively recent historical constructions that emerged in the 19th century, not timeless truths).
71 This notion of interpellation is borrowed from Louis Althusser, *Initiation à la philosophie pour les non-philosophes* (Presses Universitaires de France 2014) 228. See also Jean-Jacques Lecercle, *De l'interpellation: Sujet, langue, idéologie* (Éditions Amsterdam 2019) 19–26; Didier Eribon, *Principes d'une pensée critique* (Fayard 2016) 94–95; Frédéric Lordon, *Capitalisme, désir et servitude: Marx et Spinoza* (La Fabrique 2010) 28.
72 Cf Jean-Jacques Lecercle's argument that this hermeneutical phase is rather a moment of counter-interpellation. See Jean-Jacques Lecercle, *De l'interpellation: Sujet, langue, idéologie* (Éditions Amsterdam 2019) 97.
73 Cf Umberto Eco, *How to Spot a Fascist* (Richard Dixon and Alastair McEwen trs, Harvill Secker 2020) 17 (On the idea that, in fascism, the truth has already

been announced once and for all, and all we can do is continue interpreting its obscure message).

74 This distinction is most thoroughly developed in *Being and Time*, particularly in div I, ch 3 ('The Worldhood of the World'), ss 15–18 where Heidegger analyses the worldhood of the world and our everyday engagement with entities within it. See Martin Heidegger, *Being and Time* (Joan Stambaugh tr, SUNY Press 2010).

75 Ibid s 15.

76 Bruno Latour makes a similar argument when it comes to naturalizing modes of thinking whereby something is considered to be natural and part of nature. See Bruno Latour, *Face à Gaïa* (La Découverte 2015) 33–35. See also Herbert Marcuse's comments on how concreteness, which dominates modern societies, always entails a form of prescription: Herbert Marcuse, *One-Dimensional Man: Studies in the Ideology of Advanced Industrial Society* (Beacon Press 1964) ch 4.

77 See ch 3.

78 Cf Jean-François Bayart, *L'énergie de l'Etat: Pour une sociologie historique et comparée du politique* (La Découverte 2022) (for whom the formation of the State and the production of its concreteness are a form of abstraction).

79 This is the claim made by Herbert Marcuse. See Herbert Marcuse, *One-Dimensional Man: Studies in the Ideology of Advanced Industrial Society* (Beacon Press 1964) ch 4.

80 Gilles Deleuze and Félix Guattari, *Mille plateaux* (Éditions de Minuit 1980) 433–36 and 447–52. See also Gilles Deleuze and Félix Guattari, *L'Anti-Œdipe* (Éditions de Minuit 1972) 212–16. See also Gilles Deleuze, *Sur l'appareil d'Etat et la machine de guerre: Cours de novembre 1979–mars 1980* (Éditions de Minuit 2025) 22 and 123.

81 See this ch, s 3.6.

82 This abstraction of the commodity and its dialectical dimension has been compellingly exposed by Jacques Derrida. See Jacques Derrida, *Spectres de Marx* (Seuil 2024).

83 See this ch, s 2.5.

84 See this ch, s 2.3.

85 See this ch, s 1.6.

86 See this ch, s 1.3.

87 On the Kantian notion of the thing-in-itself, see ch 2, s 3.

88 On the idea that the thing-in-itself is a fiction, see Hans Vaihinger, *The Philosophy of "As If"* (Routledge 2021) 67.

89 This is a distinction made by Martin Heidegger, *Qu'est-ce qu'une chose?* (Jean Reboul and Jacques Taminiaux trs, Gallimard 1971). On that specific claim of Heidegger, see Bill Brown, *Other Things* (University of Chicago Press 2015) 24–32. See also Bill Brown, 'Things – In Theory' (Arcade, 2017) https://shc.stanford.edu/arcade/interventions/things-theory accessed 9 March 2026.

90 Jacques Derrida, *Parages* (Galilée 1986) 190.

91 Bill Brown, *Other Things* (University of Chicago Press 2015) 19.

92 Bill Brown, 'Thing Theory' (2001) 28 *Critical Inquiry* 1, 4.

93 Jean Baudrillard, *Le système des objets* (Gallimard 1968).

94 See this ch, s 1.3.

95 See e.g. Alfred North Whitehead, *The Concept of Nature* (Cosmo 2007) 3 (first published 1920). See the critical observations on the instability of the concept of nature by Bruno Latour, *Face à Gaïa* (La Découverte 2015) 32.

96 I owe this observation to Raphaële Xenidis.

97 On the ideas of naturalistic necessities and naturalized knowledge, see Judith Butler, *Gender Trouble: Feminism and the Subversion of Identity* (2nd edn,

Routledge 1990) 45. See also Judith Butler, *Notes Toward a Performative Theory of Assembly* (Harvard University Press 2018) 5, 40–41; Judith Butler, *Bodies That Matter: On the Discursive Limits of "Sex"* (Routledge 2011) xix; Silvia Federici, *Le capitalisme patriarcal* (La Fabrique 2019) 9, 20–29; Michel Foucault, *Phénoménologie et Psychologie 1953–1954* (Gallimard/Seuil 2021) 29; Étienne Balibar and Immanuel Wallerstein, *Race, nation, classe: Les identités ambigües* (La Découverte 2018) 50 and 62.

98 The invocation of "nature" as the ultimate truth-claiming criterion is a common feature of those discourses about the real. See generally Bruno Latour, *Science in Action: How to Follow Scientists and Engineers Through Society* (Harvard University Press 1987). Michel Foucault notes that the move to the scientistic age came with a forgetfulness that discourses about the real were first a philosophical invention. See Michel Foucault, *Leçons sur la volonté de savoir: Cours au Collège de France 1970–1971* (Seuil/Gallimard 2011) 50.

99 Bruno Latour, *Face à Gaïa* (La Découverte 2015) 33.

100 See the criticisms of organicism in social science by Manuel DeLanda's criticisms of organicism in social science: Manuel DeLanda, *A New Philosophy of Society: Assemblage Theory and Social Complexity* (Bloomsbury 2019) 9–25.

101 It is interesting to note that Marx referred to the organic composition of capital. See generally Karl Marx, *Capital: A Critique of Political Economy, Volume I* (Ben Fowkes tr, Penguin Classics 1990) ch 25. On this understanding of Marx, see Gilles Deleuze, *Sur l'appareil d'Etat et la machine de guerre: Cours de novembre 1979–mars 1980* (Éditions de Minuit 2025) 84.

102 Cf the idea that thingification entails naturalization developed by Isabelle Bishop, 'Everyday Hegemony: Reification, the Supermarket, and the Nuclear Family' (2004) 7 *Open Philosophy* 5.

103 In the same vein, see Matthew Dimick, 'Race and Reification' (2023) 31 *Historical Materialism* 69–105, 75.

104 Bruno Latour, *Face à Gaïa* (La Découverte 2015) 36–46.

105 See the remarks of Manuel DeLanda, *A New Philosophy of Society: Assemblage Theory and Social Complexity* (Bloomsbury 2019) 27.

106 Gayatri Chakravorty Spivak, *In Other Worlds: Essays in Cultural Politics* (Routledge 2006) xix, 119–22; Eve Kosofsky Sedgwick, *Epistemology of the Closet* (University of California Press 2008) 40–41; Jacques Derrida, *Spectres de Marx* (Seuil 2024) 12; Michel Foucault, *Leçons sur la volonté de savoir: Cours au Collège de France 1970–1971* (Seuil/Gallimard 2011) 246; Michel Foucault, *Dits et écrits, I (1954–1975)* (Gallimard 2001) 691 and 1685; Gilles Deleuze, *Proust et les signes* (PUF 1964) 109.

107 Roland Barthes, *Mythologies* (Éditions du Seuil 1957) 254; Peter Fitzpatrick, *The Mythology of Modern Law* (Routledge 1992) 10.

108 Martin Heidegger, *Qu'est-ce qu'une chose?* (Jean Reboul and Jacques Taminiaux trs, Gallimard 1971) 20.

109 Quentin Meillassoux, *Après la finitude: Essai sur la nécessité de la contingence* (Seuil 2006) 57 (speaking of 'nécessité réelle'). The official translation of "*nécessité réelle*" is "real necessity" (see Quentin Meillassoux, *After Finitude: An Essay on the Necessity of Contingency* (Ray Brassier tr, Continuum 2008) ch 2). I have better translated it by "necessity of the real". Cf the idea of "*effet du réel*" ('reality effect') of Roland Barthes: see Roland Barthes, 'Le discours de l'histoire' (1967) 6(4) *Social Science Information* 63, 74 (The "*effet du réel*" refers to the feeling that the form, order, and sequence of the past and the way in which the latter is narrated correspond to some kind of necessity).

110 Michel Serres, *Statues: Le second livre des fondations* (Champs 2014) 98.

111 On experience being the main source of knowledge since the advent of Modernity, see Michel Foucault, *Dits et écrits, I (1954–1975)* (Gallimard 2001) 758; François Jullien, *L'incommensurable* (L'Observatoire 2022) 182. See also François Châtelet, *Une histoire de la raison* (Seuil 1992) 127 and 130; Georges Canguilhem, *Idéologie et rationalité dans l'histoire des sciences de la vie* (Vrin 1977) 53; Arnaud Macé, *La matière* (GF Flammarion 1998) 23–25.
112 See generally Karl Popper, *Conjectures and Refutations: The Growth of Scientific Knowledge* (Routledge Classics 2002). See also Anthony Giddens, *The Consequences of Modernity* (Polity 1990) 40 and 176.
113 Umberto Eco, *How to Spot a Fascist* (Richard Dixon and Alastair McEwen trs, Harvill Secker 2020) 19–20.
114 Michel Serres, *Statues: Le second livre des fondations* (Champs 2014) 97.
115 See generally Bruno Latour and Steve Woolgar, *Laboratory Life: The Construction of Scientific Facts* (2nd edn, Princeton University Press 1986). On the idea of science and society being co-produced, see Sheila Jasanoff, 'The Idiom of Co-production' in Sheila Jasanoff (ed), *States of Knowledge: The Co-production of Science and Social Order* (Routledge 2004) 1; Sheila Jasanoff, 'Ordering Knowledge, Ordering Society' in Sheila Jasanoff (ed), *States of Knowledge: The Co-production of Science and Social Order* (Routledge 2004) 17.
116 Interestingly, this distinction between thingness and science is also very central in phenomenology where it plays a very distinct role. Since Husserl, phenomenology has called for a return to thingness, which is seen as a way to defeat scientific objectivism and return to the world prior to scientific knowledge. This does not mean rejecting science entirely, but rather questioning science's claim to provide the only or ultimate access to reality. Phenomenology seeks to recover this more fundamental level of experience that precedes scientific theorizing. On this point, see eg Maurice Merleau-Ponty, *Phénoménologie de la perception* (Gallimard 1945).
117 See ch 4, s 5.
118 Matthew Dimick, 'Race and Reification' (2023) 31 *Historical Materialism* 69–105, 70; Karen E Fields and Barbara J Fields, *Racecraft: The Soul of Inequality in American Life* (Verso 2022); Stuart Hall, *Race, éthnicité, nation: Le triangle fatal* (Éditions Amsterdam 2019) 28–46; Achille Mbembe, *Critique de la raison nègre* (La Découverte 2013) 61.
119 Martin Heidegger, *Qu'est-ce qu'une chose?* (Jean Reboul and Jacques Taminiaux trs, Gallimard 1971) 40.
120 It must be acknowledged that the great users of thingness in political discourse are sometimes annoyed by the competition of scientific facticity, which is why they seek to suppress the latter. See Stéphane Foucart, 'Donald Trump et Elon Musk plongent la science américaine dans un indescriptible chaos' *Le Monde* (24 February 2025).
121 See also Bruno Latour, *Face à Gaïa* (La Découverte 2015) 39–49.
122 Michel Serres, *Les Origines de la géométrie: Tiers livre des fondations* (Flammarion 2011). On the idea that it is movement in nature that first caught the attention and was the object of mathematization, which ultimately turns the mobile into immobile, see Henri Bergson, *Introduction à la métaphysique* (PUF 2011) 41; Henri Bergson, *Essai sur les données immédiates de la conscience* (Flammarion 2013) 224.
123 On the idea that mathematics constitutes a type of sovereign formalism, see Roland Barthes, *Le bruissement de la langue: Essais critiques IV* (Seuil 1984) 88; Jacques Derrida, *L'écriture et la différence* (Éditions du Seuil 1967) 35.
124 Michel Foucault, *Le Discours philosophique* (Gallimard/Seuil 2023) 80.

125 Michel Foucault, *Phénoménologie et Psychologie 1953–1954* (Gallimard/Seuil 2021) 28.
126 Quentin Meillassoux, *Après la finitude: Essai sur la nécessité de la contingence* (Seuil 2006) 171–72.
127 Michel de Certeau, *Histoire et psychanalyse entre science et fiction* (Gallimard 2016) 81; Henri Bergson, *Essai sur les données immédiates de la conscience* (Flammarion 2013) 224.
128 René Descartes, *Meditations on First Philosophy* (CUP 2017) Sixth Meditation 57–72; Quentin Meillassoux, *Après la finitude: Essai sur la nécessité de la contingence* (Seuil 2006) 16.
129 Quentin Meillassoux, *Après la finitude: Essai sur la nécessité de la contingence* (Seuil 2006) 172.
130 Jacques Derrida, *L'écriture et la différence* (Éditions du Seuil 1967) 35; Georges Canguilhem, *Idéologie et rationalité dans l'histoire des sciences de la vie* (Vrin 1977) 28.
131 For the sake of this book, "Marxian" refers to works based solely on what can be attributed to Marx and Engels, whilst "Marxist" refers to works that refer themselves to what can be ascribed to their followers and all those that have continued to unpack and develop their thoughts. See generally Sean Sayers, 'What Is Marxism?' (2021) 11 *International Critical Thought* 377–88.
132 See the very compelling and refined exposition of Marx's commodity fetishism provided by David Graeber, 'Fetishism as Social Creativity: Or, Fetishes Are Gods in the Process of Construction' (2005) 5(4) *Anthropological Theory* 407.
133 For useful terminological distinctions between thingification, alienation, reification, reism, and naturalism, see Frédéric Vandenberghe, 'La notion de réification: Réification sociale et chosification méthodologique' (1992) 103 *L'Homme et la société* 81–93. See also Douglas Litowitz, 'Reification in Law and Legal Theory' (2000) 9 *Southern California Interdisciplinary Law Journal* 401, 402; Tomonaga Tairako, 'Reification, Thingification, and Alienation in Marx's Economic Manuscripts' (2025) 55 *Hitotsubashi Journal of Social Studies* 1–39; Anselm Jappe, 'Aliénation, réification et fétichisme de la marchandise' in Vincent Chanson, Alexis Cukier and Frédéric Monferrand (eds), *La Réification: Histoire et actualité d'un concept critique* (La Dispute 2014) 65–84.
134 On the idea that the Frankfurt School did not share Lukács' belief that reification would be overcome by a proletarian revolution, see Douglas Litowitz, 'Reification in Law and Legal Theory' (2000) 9 *Southern California Interdisciplinary Law Journal* 401, 410. See also Vincent Chanson, 'La réification comme concept "épistémologique" chez Adorno' in Vincent Chanson, Alexis Cukier and Frédéric Monferrand (eds), *La Réification: Histoire et actualité d'un concept critique* (La Dispute 2014) 149–76.
135 On the idea that Marx's concept of commodity works as a spectre caught between the sensible and the suprasensible and constitutes a body without a body, see Jacques Derrida, *Spectres de Marx* (Seuil 2024) 236, 238–39.
136 According to Timothy Bewes, Marx used it twice in the three volumes of *Capital*. See Timothy Bewes, *Reification or The Anxiety of Late Capitalism* (Verso 2002) 5. See also Hanna Fenichel Pitkin, 'Rethinking Reification' (1987) 16 *Theory and Society* 263–93, 264.
137 See generally Georg Lukács, *Histoire et conscience de classe: Essais de dialectique marxiste* (K Axelos and J Bois trs, Éditions de Minuit 1960) (first published 1923) 109–56.

138 Axel Honneth, *Reification: A New Look at an Old Idea* (OUP 2008) 23. See also Susan Marks, 'Introduction' in Susan Marks (ed), *International Law on the Left: Re-examining Marxist Legacies* (CUP 2008) 1, 5–6.

139 See Nikos Foufas, *La critique de la réification chez Lukács* (L'Harmattan 2020) 39–42. See also Vincent Charbonnier, 'La réification chez Lukács' in Vincent Chanson, Alexis Cukier and Frédéric Monferrand (eds), *La Réification: Histoire et actualité d'un concept critique* (La Dispute 2014) 43–64.

140 Herbert Marcuse, *One-Dimensional Man: Studies in the Ideology of Advanced Industrial Society* (Beacon Press 1964) ch 3.

141 The expression is from Susan Marks, 'Introduction' in Susan Marks (ed), *International Law on the Left: Re-examining Marxist Legacies* (CUP 2008) 1, 5.

142 See however Tomonaga Tairako, 'Reification, Thingification, and Alienation in Marx's Economic Manuscripts' (2025) 55 *Hitotsubashi Journal of Social Studies* 1–39.

143 Cf the idea that modern critique is articulated around intellectual extractivism, see Laurent de Sutter, *Superfaible: Penser au XXIe siècle* (Climats 2023) 341.

144 This is a nuance famously introduced by Louis Althusser, who distinguishes between the (re)production of social reality by historical practices and the production of the knowledge of reality by theoretical practice. See Louis Althusser, *Pour Marx* (La Découverte 1996) 253–58 (first published 1965).

145 Hanna Fenichel Pitkin, 'Rethinking Reification' (1987) 16 *Theory and Society* 263–93, 273.

146 Peter Gabel, 'Reification in Legal Reasoning' (1980) 3 *Research in Law and Sociology* 25–51.

147 Timothy Bewes claims that reification is very central in Frantz Fanon's work to describe colonial relations. See Timothy Bewes, *Reification or The Anxiety of Late Capitalism* (Verso 2002) 69–72; Matthew Dimick, 'Race and Reification' (2023) 31 *Historical Materialism* 69–105; Achille Mbembe, *Critique de la raison nègre* (La Découverte 2013) 61 and 220. Cf Aimé Césaire's preference for "thingification" (chosification): Aimé Césaire, *Discourse on Colonialism* (Joan Pinkham tr, Monthly Review Press 2000) 42.

148 Hannah Arendt, *The Human Condition* (2nd edn, University of Chicago Press 2018) 93–96 and 139–44. On this aspect of Arendt's work, see Bill Brown, *Other Things* (University of Chicago Press 2015) 155–62 (note that Arendt does not idealize reification for the latter brings about violence as well as artificiality which, in turn, threatens to foreclose the sphere of politics and destabilize the very condition within which we attain our humanity).

149 Jean d'Aspremont, *After Meaning: The Sovereignty of Forms in International Law* (Edward Elgar 2021) 13; Jean d'Aspremont, *The Experiences of International Organizations: A Phenomenological Approach to International Institutional Law* (Edward Elgar 2023) viii.

150 Axel Honneth, *Reification: A New Look at an Old Idea* (OUP 2008) 18.

151 This is a point of Marxian thought that has been extensively discussed by Louis Althusser, *Pour Marx* (La Découverte 1996) 227–58, esp 253–58.

152 Georg Lukács, *Histoire et conscience de classe: Essais de dialectique marxiste* (K Axelos and J Bois trs, Éditions de Minuit 1960) (first published 1923). See also Axel Honneth's attempt to rehabilitate reification by means of the theory of recognition in Axel Honneth, *Reification: A New Look at an Old Idea* (OUP 2008). See also the attempt to reverse reification as a liberating concept by Timothy Bewes, *Reification or The Anxiety of Late Capitalism* (Verso 2002).

153 For a recent example of rehabilitation of the concept that remains bound by its Marxist premises, see Vincent Chanson, Alexis Cukier and Frédéric Monferrand (eds), *La Réification: Histoire et actualité d'un concept critique* (La Dispute 2014).
154 Martin Heidegger, *Qu'est-ce qu'une chose?* (Jean Reboul and Jacques Taminiaux trs, Gallimard 1971) 49–50.
155 Jean Baudrillard, *Le crime parfait* (Galilée 1995) 29 and 33.
156 See ch 5.

Chapter 2

Thingness then and now

It probably does not come as a surprise that the idea of thing has long been central in Western philosophical thought and has an extended history of heterogeneous meanings expressed through diverse terms that include object, substance, res, matter, monad, essence, etc.[1] This chapter surely is not the place to return to the immense variety of esoteric discussions that are found in ancient, pre-modern, and modern philosophy in relation to the concepts of object, substance, matter, monad, essence, thing, etc. and which are constitutive of the long philosophical tradition of engagement with the idea of thing.[2] Yet, a few considerations are warranted here with a view to situating thingness and thingification, as they are understood in this book, against this rich philosophical heritage whose sophistication sometimes sits uneasily with our contemporary frameworks of intelligibility.[3] The aim is not to provide a detailed linear chronology of the trajectory of the ideas of thingness and thingification over time but rather to offer a few pointers to apprehend their place and ramifications in a complex philosophical tradition with a view to showing that thinking in terms of thingness corresponds to a *precritical* type of epistemology.[4] In other words, this chapter situates the ideas of thingness and thingification in order to foreground their precritical dimension as well as their incommensurability with some of the main critical epistemologies that dominate contemporary humanities.[5]

First, the attention turns to the ancient and medieval philosophical heritage of the idea of thing, tracing the trajectory from Platonic participation and Aristotelian substance through the Latin concept of *res* to the medieval distinction between essence and existence, thereby situating the contemporary notion of thingness within a long tradition of philosophical inquiry (1). The chapter then examines the early modern distinction between primary and secondary qualities in the work of Descartes and Locke, showing how thingness, understood as a quality attached to what has necessary existence independent of perception and representation, echoes the material necessitarianism at the heart of this early modern framework (2). Subsequently, the analysis addresses the Kantian liquidation of philosophical thought about the

DOI: 10.4324/9781003753940-3

thing, demonstrating how the transcendental revolution rendered the very questions animating substance metaphysics philosophically illegitimate and inaugurated the era of constructivism and correlationism (3). The chapter then considers the relationship between thingness and structuralist thought, exploring possible parallels before showing that the structure, unlike the thing, remains a system of representation geared toward the elucidation of differential codes (4). Following this, the discussion turns to the concept of assemblage as developed in Science and Technology Studies, contrasting its dynamic, relational, and contingent epistemology with the fixity and monolithic character of thingness (5). Finally, the chapter concludes by foregrounding the fundamental incompatibility between thingness and Kantian philosophy, arguing that the contemporary invocation of thingness constitutes a return to precritical epistemology that repudiates more than two centuries of Kantian critical thought (6).

1. Ancient and medieval philosophy: Between essence and existence

Since at least Plato and Aristotle, a central philosophical problem has been how sensible particulars are able to be the way they are, that is, how they possess stable features or attributes. For Plato, this stability derives from participation in transcendent forms. In the *Phaedo*[6] and the *Republic*,[7] the forms constitute the truly real, while sensible particulars occupy an ontologically derivative status, caught between being and non-being. This participatory framework establishes a foundational dualism between the intelligible and the sensible, between essence and appearance, that would reverberate throughout the Western tradition. Aristotle, while retaining the vocabulary of essence, fundamentally reorients the inquiry. In the *Categories*,[8] he introduces substance as the primary category of being, that which is neither said of a subject nor present in a subject. For him, primary substances are individual things. Secondary substances are predicated of primary substances but remain ontologically dependent upon them. In the *Metaphysics*,[9] Aristotle deepens this analysis, identifying substance with the underlying subject that persists through change, while also associating it with form and essence. Interestingly, this tension between substance-as-subject and substance-as-form has generated interpretive difficulties have brought about numerous commentaries across centuries. Within this intellectual tradition, the thing – when it is not simply reduced to matter – has thus been conceived as substance (that which stands under) and that which supports attributes (that which exists in its own right rather than as a modification of something else). Substance accordingly names both the logical subject of predication and the ontological ground of persistence and identity.

In the Latin world, this Greek concern underwent a significant linguistic and conceptual reframing through the term *res*. Etymologically and in early usage, *res* names an affair, a matter at issue, or a concern (what is at stake in practical deliberation and legal dispute). The Roman legal tradition speaks of *res publica* (the public affair), *res mancipi* (things subject to formal transfer), and *res nullius* (things belonging to no one). Here, *res* carries a pragmatic, relational, and situational valence. It designates not abstract entities but matters of human concern, objects of transaction and contestation. With Lucretius and the Latin reception of Epicurean atomism, *res* begins to acquire a more explicitly philosophical sense as thing or entity. In *De Rerum Natura*,[10] Lucretius employs *res* to designate the fundamental constituents of reality – atoms and void – as well as the composite bodies they form. The title itself announces a new philosophical program: To give an account of the nature (*natura*) of things (*rerum*), where things are understood as material entities governed by natural laws rather than divine caprice. *Res* here approaches the Greek notion of beings, though it retains traces of its practical and juridical origins.

With Augustine, *res* is drawn decisively into the register of being, even as a constitutive ambiguity persists. In *De Doctrina Christiana*,[11] Augustine distinguishes between *res* (things to be enjoyed or used) and *signa* (signs that point to things), establishing a semiotic framework that would prove enormously influential. More fundamentally, Augustine inherits and transforms the neoplatonic hierarchy of being: God is the supreme being, the source and ground of all that exists.[12] Creatures possess being derivatively, by participation in divine being. Yet Augustine also introduces a crucial distinction between essence and existence, i.e. between what a thing is and that it is. This distinction, latent in Aristotle's differentiation between the what-it-is to the that-it-is, becomes explicit in the Latin tradition and receives its most rigorous formulation in the medieval period, particularly in Thomas Aquinas. For Aquinas, in all creatures essence and existence are really distinct. Indeed, a creature's essence does not include its existence, which must be received from an external cause.[13] In God alone are essence and existence identical.[14] In that intellectual tradition, the distinction between essence and existence thus underwrites the radical contingency of creatures and the absolute necessity of God.

The foregoing shows that the enduring ambiguity between being and beings, between essence and existence has been perpetuated in Western metaphysics. Martin Heidegger would later name this ambiguity the ontological difference – the difference between Being (*Sein*) and beings (*Seiendes*) – and argue that the entire history of Western metaphysics constitutes a forgetting of this difference, a reduction of being to the being of entities.[15] For Heidegger, the Latin translation of Greek philosophical terms represents not merely a linguistic shift but a fundamental transformation in the understanding of being, one that prepares the way for modern subjectivity and technological enframing.[16] Whether one accepts Heidegger's account of Western metaphysics or not, the trajectory from Platonic participation through

Aristotelian substance to Latin *res* and medieval *essence/existence* reveals a persistent philosophical preoccupation, namely how to account for the being of things, for their stability, identity, and intelligibility. As the next section will show, this question has remained alive in premodern philosophy.

2. The early modern organicists: The distinction between primary and secondary qualities

The trajectory from ancient substance metaphysics to medieval debates over essence and existence finds a significant new articulation in the early modern period, particularly through the work of René Descartes and John Locke. While both thinkers inherit the scholastic vocabulary of substance and attribute, they reconfigure it in ways that prove decisive for subsequent philosophy and that bear directly on the question of thingness as is understood here. The distinction between primary and secondary qualities, which emerges from their writings, represents a crucial moment in the history of Western philosophy, one that attempts to secure a domain of objective and mind-independent properties.

Descartes, in his *Meditations on First Philosophy*[17] and in the *Principles of Philosophy*,[18] develops a dualist epistemology in which extended substance (*res extensa*) and thinking substance (*res cogitans*) constitute the two fundamental kinds of being. Material bodies, for Descartes, are essentially extended: Their nature consists entirely in spatial dimensions – length, breadth, and depth – along with the modes of extension such as shape, size, position, and motion. These geometrical and mechanical properties belong to bodies *intrinsically*. They are what bodies truly are, independent of any perceiving subject. By contrast, sensory qualities such as colour, sound, taste, smell, and warmth do not inhere in bodies themselves but arise from the interaction between extended matter and the perceiving mind.

Although Descartes does not employ the precise terminology of primary and secondary qualities, the conceptual architecture is already in place. It is John Locke, however, who provides the canonical formulation in his *Essay Concerning Human Understanding*.[19] Locke distinguishes between qualities and ideas. Qualities are forces in objects to produce ideas in us, while ideas are the mental representations that result from the operation of those forces. Primary qualities – solidity, extension, figure, motion or rest, and number – are utterly inseparable from body. They belong to bodies however much they are divided or altered, and our ideas of them resemble the qualities themselves. Secondary qualities, by contrast, are nothing in the objects themselves but forces to produce various sensations in us by means of the primary qualities of their insensible parts. Colours, sounds, tastes, and odours do not exist in bodies as such; they are effects produced in perceiving subjects.

This distinction carries important epistemological implications. Primary qualities are endowed with what, in this book, is called thingness: They simply are, independent of any observer's perception, observation, representation, or discourse. They constitute the naked substance of the world, the objective furniture of reality that a well-trained rational mind can transparently and accurately apprehend. Extension, figure, and motion belong to bodies whether or not anyone perceives them. They are properties of the in-itself, features of things as they exist prior to and apart from any subjective encounter. Secondary qualities, by contrast, are relational and subject-dependent. They exist not in things themselves but in the subject's engagement with them. From such a perspective, to know the thing as it truly is, on this view, is to know its primary qualities, which requires keeping at bay the subjective accretions of sense experience and grasping the geometrical-mechanical structure that constitutes the thing's actual nature. According to such a framework, things are composed of properties-in-themselves that exist independently of any subject's relation to them, outside language, discourse, experience, and thought. The thing, for Descartes and Locke, is first and foremost naked substance, a configuration of primary qualities that enjoys uncontested validity and that, in principle, breaks out of the circle of discourse.[20] The rational subject, properly disciplined by method, can achieve unmediated access to this objective domain and, as a result, can know the world as it is.[21] This constitutes a form of dogmatic metaphysics[22] or organicism[23] articulated around the possibility of an absolute being, i.e. the extended thing with its primary qualities that exists necessarily and independently of how it is named, perceived, observed, or represented.[24]

It is against the background of such premodern philosophy that the contemporary invocation of thingness acquires its philosophical significance. To speak of thingness as a quality attached to what has necessary existence irrespective of how it is named, thought, perceived, or represented is to return to the conceptual framework of primary qualities of Descartes and Locke.[25] In fact, it is to posit a domain of objective properties that simply are, that exist independently of any subject's relation to them, that break out of the circle of discourse to make unmediated contact with the world. Said differently, the epistemological posture associated with thingness can be read as a return to the *precritical thought*,[26] one that is driven by a quest for the conditions necessary to make unmediated contact with the world, as is found in the work of Descartes or Locke. It is argued here that thingness, whenever it is invoked today, stands in direct continuity with the dogmatic metaphysics of the early modern distinction between primary and secondary qualities.

3. The modern liquidation of the in-itself: Constructivism and correlationism

The Cartesian and Lockean confidence in the possibility of grasping the naked substance of things through their primary qualities – a confidence that underwrites the very notion of thingness as has been theorized here – met its most formidable challenge in the critical philosophy of Immanuel Kant. With Kant, the ancient and early modern preoccupation with substance, essence, and the in-itself undergoes what can be described as a liquidation. The transcendental revolution inaugurated by the *Critique of Pure Reason*[27] does not merely modify or refine the inherited metaphysical vocabulary. It renders the very questions that animated substance metaphysics philosophically illegitimate. After Kant, the notions of substance, *res*, matter, monad, and essence cease to function as the engine of Western ontology.[28] The sophisticated inquiries into what composes the substance, into the primary qualities that constitute the thing as it is in itself, are not answered differently but are shown to be unanswerable in principle.

To understand why Kant can be considered the liquidator of metaphysical debates about the idea of the thing, it suffices to recall the central argument of transcendental idealism. For the philosopher of Königsberg, the thing-in-itself[29] is never knowable. For Kant, the thing-in-itself never stands in front of the subject, for it always is constructed by the subject, the latter being condemned to live in an always precarious and contingent world.[30] Said differently, human cognition is bounded by the *a priori* forms of sensibility – space and time – and by the categories of the understanding, such as substance, causality, and unity.[31] These forms and categories do not describe features of the world as it exists independently of the knowing subject. Rather, they constitute the conditions under which any object can appear to us at all. What one knows are objects as they are given in experience and structured by one's cognitive faculties. The thing-in-itself, the object considered apart from any relation to our sensibility and understanding, remains forever beyond the reach of human knowledge. It can be thought but it cannot be known. The essence of substance, its absolute validity, and its intrinsic properties are thus not items of possible knowledge anymore. This represents a decisive break with the Cartesian and Lockean framework. For Descartes and Locke, primary qualities belong to bodies as they are in themselves, independent of any perceiver. Kant denies precisely this possibility. The very qualities that Descartes and Locke took to be objective, intrinsic, and mind-independent turn out, on Kantian analysis, to be constituted by the subject's cognitive apparatus. There is no unmediated access to the naked substance of things, no transparent apprehension of primary qualities as they exist apart from experience. The thing-in-itself never stands in front of the subject as an object of direct cognition.

As is often forgotten, George Berkeley, whose work has been overshadowed by that of Kant, had already anticipated aspects of this critique, arguing in his *Treatise Concerning the Principles of Human Knowledge*[32] that primary qualities are no less mind-dependent than secondary ones. If secondary qualities exist only in the mind, Berkeley reasoned, so too must primary qualities, and the notion of material substance as a mind-independent substratum collapses into incoherence. It is true that Kant does not follow Berkeley into idealism of the Berkeleyan sort, but he shares Berkeley's rejection of the naïve realism that underwrites the primary/secondary distinction. The main difference is that Kant replaces Berkeley's subjective idealism with transcendental idealism: Objects can be empirically real but transcendentally ideal, meaning that their objectivity is constituted by the universal structures of human cognition rather than by mind-independent properties of things in themselves.

The consequences of this transcendental revolution for the question of thingness are profound. If the thing-in-itself cannot be known but only thought, then the very idea of thingness – understood as the quality attached to what has necessary material existence irrespective of how it is named, thought, perceived, or represented – becomes philosophically untenable. There is no breaking out of the circle of discourse, no unmediated contact with the world as it is in itself. The subject is condemned, as it were, to live within the bounds of possible experience, within a world that is always already structured by one's own cognitive conditions. The thing is never simply *in-itself* but always *with-the-subject*, always given through the mediation of language, discourse, representation, signification, thought, experience, sensibility, and culture. To put it in terms that would become canonical in twentieth-century philosophy, the only epistemology possible after Kant is *correlationist*.[33] That means that knowledge is determined by the correlation between the (thinking) subject and the (being) object. In such correlationist epistemology, one cannot verify whether one's ideas of primary qualities resemble the qualities themselves, for the qualities themselves, considered apart from our mode of apprehending them, are inaccessible. Since the modern transcendental revolution of Kant only the question of the correlation between the subject and the object remains.[34]

This correlationism entails a further consequence that bears directly on the status of thingness as is understood here. From the perspective of Kantian criticism, there can never be a contradiction between the thing-in-itself and its representation, for the simple reason that the thing-in-itself cannot be known but only represented.[35] Indeed, a contradiction requires two terms that can be compared; but if one of those terms – the thing as it is in itself – is in principle beyond the reach of knowledge, then no comparison is possible and no contradiction can arise. What one has are only representations, shaped by the forms of sensibility and the categories of the understanding.

It is for all these reasons that Kant is usually considered the founder of modern *constructivism*,[36] which constitutes the nemesis of thingness as is construed here. For Kant, being is neither given nor absolute but always constructed. The objects of experience are not simply found in a mind-independent world. They are constituted by the activity of the understanding. This constructivist turn simultaneously inaugurates the era of what is commonly called *critique and* de-absolutization.[37] Indeed, in the age in which all claims to knowledge must be subjected to scrutiny, in which the world we live in is always constructed, every claim about the world becomes open to critique, every supposed absolute is revealed as conditioned, every dogmatic metaphysics is exposed as transcending the bounds of possible experience.

The implications of Kantian constructivism for subsequent philosophy are immense. After Kant, the sophisticated notion of substance – which had animated inquiry from Aristotle through the scholastics to Descartes and Locke – is demoted to irrelevance, at least within the mainstream of critical thought. The thing, insofar as it is considered at all, is treated as a product of these mediating structures, not as a naked substance accessible to pure reason. Likewise, interrogations about the in-itself are left, as it were, to art and literature[38] as well as to those domains of human activity that do not claim cognitive access to reality but explore the textures of experience, the play of appearances, the resonances of meaning.

In sum, the legacy of Kantian epistemology, as it has been presented here, boils down to a philosophical landscape in which thingness, understood as the quality of what exists necessarily and independently of all subjective mediation, has no legitimate place. The precritical epistemology of Descartes and Locke – the belief in the possibility of knowing the primary qualities as the naked substance of things, graspable by a well-trained rational mind – is torn to pieces. Questions about what composes the substance, about the primary qualities that constitute the thing in itself, about the essence that underlies appearances are no longer the privileged site of philosophical inquiry. What remains is the correlation, the inescapable entanglement of subject and object, the recognition that one can never step outside one's cognitive conditions to grasp the thing as it is in itself. It follows that philosophy turns instead to questions of structure, of the conditions of possibility, of the forms through which experience is constituted. In the nineteenth and twentieth centuries, this turn is radicalized and diversified: The focus shifts to language, to discourse, to social and historical conditions of knowledge, and to the structures of signification as is examined in the next section.[39]

4. The thing and the structure: A deceptive kinship

It is relevant to share a few considerations on the possible thingness at work in structuralist thought, especially given the resounding success of structuralist modes of analysis in the social sciences and in the humanities in the 20th century, even after the poststructuralist revolution. One may indeed wonder whether, after its liquidation by Kantian constructivism, thingness resurfaced with the structuralist critique of the Kantian subject-object paradigm.

As is well known, structuralism, originally construed as a strand of linguistics and semiotics that emerged following Ferdinand de Saussure's *Course in*

General Linguistics published in 1916[40] has ramifications in a wide range of fields of study,[41] including anthropology,[42] literary critique,[43] the history of thought,[44] the theory of hermeneutics,[45] the history of myths and religions,[46] gender critique,[47] the study of affects,[48] critical legal theory,[49] and even Marxist philosophy.[50] Whilst there unsurprisingly are an immense variety of structuralist intellectual traditions, structuralism, for the sake of the following observations, is construed as boiling down to a type of synchronic method of analysis that focuses on the universality, permanence, and a-historical character of a given structure, system, language, or totality, in which the human subject is caught and no longer the focal point or cause thereof.[51] Indeed, according to structuralism as is understood here, the structure, rather than the agent or the subject, determines the availability of what can be thought, said, seen, and experienced.[52] From the perspective of structuralism, the subject and its agency are displaced by the structure,[53] which is what led Michel Foucault to famously claim that structuralism is the "death of the human" as a central epistemic object in social and human sciences.[54] The human subject can simply not constitute the origin[55] of what can be thought, said, seen, and experienced because, from the vantage point of structuralism, it is the structure that produces the subject and not the opposite.[56] To put it differently, structuralism amounts to the permanent negation of the foundational event[57] in favour of a permanent formal referencing system.[58]

If structuralism is so construed, it is tempting to draw a series of parallels between thingness and structuralist thought. Indeed, like thingness, structuralist thought tends to treat structures and systems of thought as real entities or real determining forces that determine human behaviour and thought.[59] From such a perspective, the structure and the thing can both be construed as monoliths that impose themselves on the subject, making the latter irrelevant. Structuralist thought accordingly resembles thingness in eclipsing the speaking observer who is deprived of their constituting role in relation to meaning and being. And, in doing so, structuralist thought and thingness both put in place synchronic epistemologies that obliterate the constructed and contingent character of the allegedly universal meaning or being they create in the present. This move is precisely what makes structuralism such an efficacious and popular mode of thinking: there never is a necessity to search for the origin or the foundation of the structure concerned. Thus, like thingness, structuralist thought is a very anti-foundationalist mode of thinking that stifles any possible need for the finding of origins or foundations. The structure is left hanging out of space, out of time, and out of agency, turning itself into the new autonomous, analysable, and governing thing that occupies the epistemic space once held by the human.[60]

It is submitted here that the foregoing is as far as the comparison between structuralist thought and thingness can go. Although structuralist thought rests on a synchronic epistemology that does away with the origin as well as the speaking subject, the very code of the structure must always be searched for. Indeed, thinking in structuralist terms is about breaking the code that is key to its systemic functioning.[61] Said differently, the quest imposed by structuralist thought is always a quest for revealing the code of the structure or the system.[62] This means that structuralist thought, *contrary to thingness*, is an inquisitory mode of thinking geared towards the elucidation of how the structure of the system constrains and enables. In fact, being structuralist is to find, elucidate, and reveal the code of the structure in the present.[63] In that regard, structuralist thought could not be more at loggerheads with thingness for which there never is anything to elucidate, let alone to comprehend. For thingness, the thing always is a given that is self-comprehended and self-signifying.

There is yet another fundamental distinction between structuralist thought and thingness which bars any further comparison. Although the former eclipses the speaking observer and comes close to thingifying the very notion of structure in a way that is reminiscent of an epistemology associated with thingness, it fundamentally remains a system of representation that negatively explains the production of signification through the differential relations between signs.[64] Structuralism is a way of thinking that explains meaning through relatively stable systems of relations (structures) that simultaneously generate and constrain representations (signs, texts, practices). Nothing could be more opposed to the representationlessness of thingness.

A final factor allows a distinction between thingness and the idea of structure. The structure is commonly thought of as a type of relation. But such a relation is neither natural nor organic, nor is it meant to have any thingly existence. The relation at work in the structure, as construed in structuralism, is primarily linguistic and logical,[65] thereby providing yet another reason for distinguishing thingness and the idea of structure.

5. Thingness in the age of assemblages: An epistemological regression

It is submitted in this penultimate section that thingness does not merely refute Kantian transcendental and correlationist philosophy based on the relation between the object and the subject for the sake of reviving a form of dogmatic metaphysics as well as the idea of primary qualities. When it is deployed in the 21st century, thingness also disparages the very extensive work carried out in the critical philosophy of science, and especially in Science and Technology Studies,[66] about the idea of *assemblage* by virtue of which the boundaries between human and the non-human, between the social and the natural, between the social and the scientific, between the thought and the object, between the being and the becoming, etc. are dissolved.

The concept of assemblage emerged as a radical reconfiguration in contemporary philosophy, most powerfully articulated in the work of Deleuze and Guattari,[67] where the term *agencement* invites one to conceptualize entities not as stable essences but as contingent arrangements of heterogeneous elements caught in perpetual processes of becoming. An assemblage, in Deleuzian terms, represents a complex constellation of heterogeneous elements – material objects, signs, expressions, bodies, actions, passions – that enter into relations of connectivity, creating provisional unities while preserving the distinctiveness of their components. Unlike totalizing systems or structures, assemblages operate through contingent, non-necessary connections. Assemblages exist at the intersection between contingency and structure, organization and change. This conceptual framework fundamentally challenges the Cartesian binaries that have dominated Western thought,[68] proposing instead a flat epistemology where human and non-human actants, material and discursive elements, exist not in hierarchical relation but in dynamic co-constitution. Through assemblage thinking, the world appears not as a collection of discrete objects awaiting human interpretation but as a complex fabric of relations where agency is distributed across networks that refuse simple categorization into nature versus society, human versus object, or scientific versus social domains. In short, assemblages offer a way to understand organization without appealing to essence, transcendence, necessary relations or fixity.

Such a dissolution of modern dualism through the idea of assemblage has been amplified in Bruno Latour's actor-network theory[69] and Sheila Jasanoff's concept of co-production,[70] both central to Science and Technology Studies' reconceptualization of socio-technical entanglements. From such a perspective, the assemblage manifests itself as a theoretical intervention that renders visible the intricate choreography through which supposedly autonomous domains – the scientific laboratory and the legislative chamber, the geological formation and the economic model, the bacterial culture and the cultural narrative – reveal themselves as always already intertwined, co-evolving, and mutually determining. In this framework, agency becomes redistributed, causality is rendered complex and non-linear, and the boundaries between supposedly distinct epistemological categories are exposed as performative achievements rather than reflections of any pre-existing natural order. Most recently, and in the very same vein, Manuel DeLanda, mobilizing the Deleuzian concept of assemblage, has proposed a "realist social ontology" in which the existence of institutional organizations, interpersonal networks and many other social entities, because they are approached as assemblage, are made conception-independent.[71]

Although the concept of assemblage, especially as it has been perpetuated in Science and Technology Studies, may at times perpetuate a form of belief in the thingness of things[72] while also dissolving the agency of the speaking observer like thingness does, it radically challenges the epistemology and philosophy at work in thingness as they have been exposed earlier in this book. In fact, the assemblage concept invites one to see the world not as composed of fixed objects with unchanging essences but as a dynamic field of becoming where provisional unities emerge and constantly transform through contingent connections between heterogeneous elements. This strikingly opposes the fixity that comes with thingness. Likewise, assemblages bring together elements of diverse types – linguistic, material, social, affective – without subordinating them to an organizing principle or homogenizing their differences. Indeed, in an assemblage, relations between components are not determined by their internal properties but emerge through their contingent connections. This radically contrasts with the idea of thingness which, for ensuring that material existence be taken for granted, is often construed as a monolithic whole. By the same token, assemblages, unlike thingness, rehistoricize the discourse and the knowledge as they constantly bring together components with entirely different histories, allowing for novel combinations and innovations that transcend historical necessity. These few contradictions between the concept of assemblage and that of thingness suffice to show that the type of materialism put forward by Science and Technology Studies, as is expressed through the concept of assemblage, remains very alien to the idea of thingness as it is understood here, thereby confirming the precritical atavism of the latter.

6. Concluding remarks: Death in Königsberg and the return to precritical thought

It has been one of the main claims of this chapter that nothing is more at loggerheads with Kantian correlationism and constructivism than the idea of thingness and the necessary material and self-signifying existence that comes with it. When mobilized in the twenty-first century, thingness buries more than two centuries of Kantian transcendentalism, effectively undoing the critical revolution that had seemed to settle, once and for all, the limits of human knowledge and the impossibility of unmediated access to the in-itself. It is important to stress that the contemporary embrace of thingness – which will be further discussed in the following chapter – represents not merely a modification or extension of post-Kantian thought but a wholesale repudiation thereof. To eliminate the speaking observer, to posit a domain of thingly properties that exist outside perception and representation, is to transgress the bounds of possible experience, to claim knowledge of what cannot in principle be known from the perspective of any Kantian epistemology. To invoke thingness as a quality that exists necessarily and independently of how it is named, thought, perceived, or represented is to resurrect precisely the dogmatic metaphysics that Kant sought to overcome, to return to a precritical epistemology that the transcendental turn had rendered philosophically untenable.[73] This chapter has simultaneously shown that thingness can hardly be reconciled with any philosophy that takes seriously the Kantian inheritance. This includes not only Kantian transcendentalism in its original form but also the diverse traditions that have developed in its wake, like structuralism and Science and Technology Studies.

This is not to say that Kantian epistemology cannot be questioned. As will be further discussed in the next chapter, the history of philosophy after Kant's transcendental revolution is, in large part, a history of attempts to overcome, modify, or challenge such critical inheritance. German Idealism, from Fichte through Schelling to Hegel, sought to overcome the dualism of phenomenon and noumenon, to think the absolute without falling back into precritical dogmatism. Phenomenology, from Husserl to Heidegger and beyond, sought to return to the things themselves while retaining the insight that things are always given to consciousness, always appearing within a horizon of meaning and intentionality.[74] Hermeneutics, from Gadamer to Ricoeur, emphasized the inescapability of interpretation, the situatedness of understanding, the fusion of horizons through which meaning is constituted.[75] These traditions do not simply repeat Kant but engage critically with his legacy, seeking to address its limitations while preserving its insights. But none of them returns to the precritical assumption that things possess self-signifying existence independent of all mediation and in the absence of a speaking observer. This is why it is fair to claim, then, that thingness's rejection of perception, its representationlessness, and its elimination of the speaking observer constitute a profoundly reactionary philosophical turn. Irrespective of its merits or perils, which will be further evaluated in subsequent chapters, espousing the epistemology that comes with the idea of thingness makes the modern mind travel back to precritical thought.

Notes

1 See the stellar history of the etymology of the word "res" and its relation with substance, essence, and existence provided by Giorgio Agamben. See Giorgio Agamben, *L'irréalisable* (Seuil 2025) ch 1 (trans of Giorgio Agamben, *L'irrealizzabile: Per una politica dell'ontologia* (Einaudi 2022)). On the intellectual heritage of the ancient and classical idea of substance, see Martin Heidegger, *Qu'est-ce qu'une chose?* (Jean Reboul and Jacques Taminiaux trs, Gallimard 1971) 44–45.
2 On these distinctions, see generally Arnaud Macé, *La matière* (GF Flammarion 1998); Tristan Garcia, *Forme et objet: Un traité des choses* (PUF 2011); Michel Serres, *Statues: Le second livre des fondations* (Champs 2014).
3 Tristan Garcia, *Forme et objet: Un traité des choses* (PUF 2011) 50.
4 See Quentin Meillassoux, *Après la finitude: Essai sur la nécessité de la contingence* (Seuil 2006) 16 and 22.
5 On the idea that Kantian correlationism remains the dominant epistemology nowadays, see Quentin Meillassoux, *Après la finitude: Essai sur la nécessité de la contingence* (Seuil 2006) 72.
6 Plato, *Phaedo* (David Gallop tr, OUP 2009) 99d–102a.
7 Plato, *Republic* (Christopher Rowe tr, Penguin Classics 2012) bks V–VII.
8 Aristotle, *Categories and De Interpretatione* (John Lloyd Ackrill tr, OUP 1963) chs 1–5.

9 Aristotle, *Metaphysics* (WD Ross tr, Jonathan Barnes rev, in Jonathan Barnes (ed), *The Complete Works of Aristotle: The Revised Oxford Translation*, vol 2 (Princeton University Press 1984)) bk VII.
10 Lucretius, *De Rerum Natura* (William Ellery Leonard tr, rev edn, University of Wisconsin Press 2008) bks I–II.
11 Augustine of Hippo, *De Doctrina Christiana* (Roger PH Green tr, OUP 1995) bk I, chs 2–4.
12 Augustine of Hippo, *Confessions* (Henry Chadwick tr, OUP 2008) bks VII and XI.
13 Thomas Aquinas, *De Ente et Essentia* (Armand Maurer tr, Pontifical Institute of Mediaeval Studies 1968) chs 4–5.
14 Thomas Aquinas, *Summa Theologiae* (Fathers of the English Dominican Province tr, CUP 2006) Prima Pars, qq 3–4.
15 Martin Heidegger, *Being and Time* (Joan Stambaugh tr, Dennis J Schmidt rev, State University of New York Press 2010) introd and div I.
16 Martin Heidegger, *Introduction to Metaphysics* (Gregory Fried and Richard Polt trs, Yale University Press 2014) chs 1–2.
17 René Descartes, *Meditations on First Philosophy* (John Cottingham tr, CUP 2017) med VI.
18 René Descartes, *Principles of Philosophy* (Valentine Rodger Miller and Reese P Miller trs, Kluwer Academic Publishers 1991) pt I, ss 48–70 and pt II, ss 1–25.
19 John Locke, *An Essay Concerning Human Understanding* (Peter H Nidditch ed, OUP 1979) bk II, ch 8.
20 The expression is from Wilfrid Sellars, who criticizes philosophers who think we can access a kind of pure, pre-conceptual experience that is not shaped by language, concepts, or social practices. See Wilfrid Sellars, *Empiricism and the Philosophy of the Mind* (Harvard University Press 1997) (first published 1956).
21 Jean-François Lyotard, 'Matière et temps' in *Matière et philosophie* (Editions du Centre Pompidou 1988) 37–47, 38.
22 Dogmatic metaphysics can be defined as the reliance on the possibility of an absolute that constitutes a real necessity and is validated through ontological evidence. See Quentin Meillassoux, *Après la finitude: Essai sur la nécessité de la contingence* (Seuil 2006) 58.
23 This is how Alfred North Whitehead describes those who tried to revive a pre-Kantian mode of thought. See generally Alfred North Whitehead, *Process and Reality* (corrected edn, The Free Press 1978).
24 For a contemporary survival of such material necessitarianism, see John Searle, *The Construction of Social Reality* (Penguin Books 1996).
25 For a different reading of Cartesian epistemology and the possibility of embracing a non-Cartesian materialism in the study of law, see Margaret Davies, *Law Unlimited: Materialism, Pluralism, and Legal Theory* (Routledge 2017). See also Giorgio Agamben's remarks on the ambiguity of the idea of the thing in Descartes: Giorgio Agamben, *L'irréalisable* (Seuil 2025) 77 (first published 2022).
26 The expression is from Quentin Meillassoux, *Après la finitude: Essai sur la nécessité de la contingence* (Seuil 2006) 16.
27 Immanuel Kant, *Critique of Pure Reason* (Paul Guyer and Allen W Wood trs, CUP 1998).
28 The expression is from Giorgio Agamben, *L'irréalisable* (Seuil 2025) 46.
29 Hans Vaihinger claims that, in the first edition of the *Critique of Pure Reason*, Kant calls the thing-in-itself a "mere idea" and that, therefore, it is not a hypothesis

but a fiction. See Hans Vaihinger, *The Philosophy of "As If"* (Routledge 2021) 67.

30 The metaphor is from Jean Baudrillard, *Le crime parfait* (Galilée 1995) 19.

31 See Martin Heidegger's description of Kantian epistemology: Heidegger, *Qu'est-ce qu'une chose?* (Jean Reboul and Jacques Taminiaux trs, Gallimard 1971) 38.

32 George Berkeley, *A Treatise Concerning the Principles of Human Knowledge* (Jonathan Dancy ed, OUP 1998) ss 9–15.

33 The expression is from Quentin Meillassoux, *Après la finitude: Essai sur la nécessité de la contingence* (Seuil 2006) 70.

34 Quentin Meillassoux, *Après la finitude: Essai sur la nécessité de la contingence* (Seuil 2006) 20. See also Giorgio Agamben, *L'irréalisable* (Seuil 2025) 98. An important attempt to break away from the distinction between the subject and the object has been offered by Martin Heidegger, *Being and Time* (Joan Stambaugh tr, State University of New York Press 2010).

35 Quentin Meillassoux, *Après la finitude: Essai sur la nécessité de la contingence* (Seuil 2006) 55–56.

36 Bruno Latour, *L'Espoir de Pandore* (Didier Gille tr, La Découverte 2007) 12–13.

37 The expression is from Quentin Meillassoux, *Après la finitude: Essai sur la nécessité de la contingence* (Seuil 2006) 18–19 and 62. Anthony Giddens has offered a different portrayal of Kantian epistemology, depicting it as inaugurating the era of reflexivity of which social sciences constitute a pillar. See Anthony Giddens, *The Consequences of Modernity* (Polity 1990) 40.

38 See Bill Brown, *Other Things* (University of Chicago Press 2015) 11; Paul de Man, *The Resistance to Theory* (University of Minnesota Press 1986) 10–11; Stanley Fish, 'With the Compliments of the Author: Reflections on Austin and Derrida' (1982) 8 *Critical Inquiry* 693–721, 696; Sarah Wasserman, 'Thing Theory 2017: A Forum' (Arcade, 2017) https://shc.stanford.edu/arcade/interventions/thing-theory-2017-forum accessed 9 March 2026.

39 See generally Bill Brown, *Other Things* (University of Chicago Press 2015) 12.

40 See generally Ferdinand de Saussure, *Course in General Linguistics* (Charles Bally and Albert Sechehaye eds, Open Court 1986). Cf Edward Sapir, *Language: An Introduction to the Study of Speech* (Ishi Press International 1921) 22.

41 On the wide ramifications of structuralist thinking across the humanities, see Jonathan Culler, *Literary Theory: A Very Short Introduction* (OUP 1997) 138. For some insights on why structuralist thought first emerged in relation to linguistics and anthropology, see Michel de Certeau, *Histoire et psychanalyse entre science et fiction* (Gallimard 2016) 226–27. On the contemporary fall from grace of structuralism in all such fields, see Etienne Balibar, *Passions du concept: Epistémologie, théologie et politique. Ecrits II* (La Découverte 2020) 215.

42 Claude Lévi-Strauss, *Structural Anthropology*, vol II (M Layton tr, University of Chicago Press 1976). See also Philippe Descola, *Par-delà nature et culture* (Gallimard 2005) 17.

43 See generally Roland Barthes, *L'aventure sémiologique* (Seuil 1985). See also Roland Barthes, *Le bruissement de la langue: Essais critiques IV* (Seuil 1984) 18 and 55. On the ambiguous relationship of Roland Barthes with structuralism, see Barthes, *Le bruissement de la langue* (Seuil 1984) 15. See also Roland Barthes, *Critique et vérité* (Seuil 1999) 54.

44 Foucault, like Barthes, had a very ambivalent relationship with structuralism. For some illustration of Foucault's repeated rejection of any espousal of a structuralist type of thinking, see Michel Foucault, *Dits et écrits*, vol I (1954–1975) (Gallimard 2001) 631, 844, 881 and 1077; Michel Foucault, *Dits et écrits*, vol II

(Gallimard 2001) 145, 467 and 1254; Noam Chomsky and Michel Foucault, *The Chomsky-Foucault Debate on Human Nature* (The New Press 2006) 147. See also Simeon Wade, *Foucault in California* (Heyday 2019) 101. For some illustrations of Foucault flirting with structuralism and of his regular uses of the concept of structure, see Michel Foucault, *Naissance de la clinique* (PUF 1963) 15–18 and 168; Michel Foucault, *Dits et écrits*, vol I (1954–1975) (Gallimard 2001) 426, 636, 679 and 685; Michel Foucault, *Dits et écrits*, vol II (Gallimard 2001) 1055; Michel Foucault, *Sécurité, territoire, population: Cours au Collège de France, 1977–1978* (Gallimard 2004) 109 and 186; Michel Foucault, *« Il faut défendre la société »: Cours au Collège de France, 1976* (Gallimard 1997) 44. On the relationship of Foucault with structuralism, see Paul Veyne, *Foucault: Sa pensée, sa personne* (Albin Michel 2008) 165. See also Etienne Balibar, *Passions du concept: Epistémologie, théologie et politique. Ecrits II* (La Découverte 2020) 127.

45 Stanley Fish, *Is There a Text in This Class?* (Harvard University Press 1980) 356; Paul Ricoeur, *De l'interprétation: Essai sur Freud* (Seuil 1965) 19–22.

46 Georges Dumézil, *L'Idéologie des trois fonctions dans les épopées des peuples indo-européens* (Gallimard 1968); Georges Dumézil, *Types épiques indo-européens: Un héros, un sorcier, un roi* (Gallimard 1971); Georges Dumézil, *Histoires romaines* (Gallimard 1973).

47 Judith Butler, *Gender Trouble: Feminism and the Subversion of Identity* (2nd edn, Routledge 1990) xxvi.

48 See generally Frédéric Lordon, *La société des affects: Pour un structuralisme des passions* (Seuil 2013).

49 See David Kennedy, 'Critical Theory, Structuralism and Contemporary Legal Scholarship' (1985–1986) 21 *New England Law Review* 209.

50 See eg Louis Althusser, *Être marxiste en philosophie* (Presses Universitaires de France 2015) 132–46 and 285–92.

51 Michel Foucault, *Entretiens radiophoniques 1961–1983* (Flammarion, Vrin, Ina 2024) 436.

52 Structuralism's exclusion of agency and historical contingency, as well as its turning a blind eye to social conditions of the production of signs, has been the object of very severe criticisms: Etienne Balibar, *Passions du concept: Epistémologie, théologie et politique. Ecrits II* (La Découverte 2020) 216; Philippe Descola, *Par-delà nature et culture* (Gallimard 2005) 170; Pierre Bourdieu, *Ce que parler veut dire: L'économie des échanges linguistiques* (Fayard 1982) 8–9 and 130; Michel Foucault, *Dits et écrits*, vol I (1954–1975) (Gallimard 2001) 1139; Noam Chomsky and Michel Foucault, *The Chomsky-Foucault Debate on Human Nature* (The New Press 2006) 147.

53 Michel Foucault, *Dits et écrits*, vol II (Gallimard 2001) 871; Etienne Balibar, *Passions du concept: Epistémologie, théologie et politique. Ecrits II* (La Découverte 2020) 219; David Kennedy, 'Critical Theory, Structuralism and Contemporary Legal Scholarship' (1985–1986) 21 *New England Law Review* 209, 249.

54 Michel Foucault, *Les mots et les choses: Une archéologie des sciences humaines* (Gallimard 1966) 398. See also Michel Foucault, *Entretiens radiophoniques 1961–1983* (Flammarion, Vrin, Ina 2024) 431–32 and 459–62.

55 Michel Foucault, *Dits et écrits*, vol II (Gallimard 2001) 590.

56 Etienne Balibar, *Passions du concept: Epistémologie, théologie et politique. Ecrits II* (La Découverte 2020) 221.

57 Jacques Derrida, *L'écriture et la différence* (Editions du Seuil 1967) 44.

58 On the idea that structure is a mechanism of permanent referencing, see Pierre Legendre, *Sur la question dogmatique en Occident: Aspects théoriques* (Fayard

1999) 141. See also Michel Foucault, *Entretiens radiophoniques 1961–1983* (Flammarion, Vrin, Ina 2024) 401.

59 Obviously, such self-representation of structuralism was blown away by post-structuralist critique. See eg Jacques Derrida, *L'écriture et la différence* (Editions du Seuil 1967). See also Jacques Derrida, *De la grammatologie* (Editions de Minuit 1967) 103; Jacques Derrida, *Marges de la philosophie* (Editions de Minuit 1972) 187–88.

60 In that sense, one could think that 'the famous death of the human' famously depicted by Foucault as epistemic object substituted an objectifying epistemology for a thingifying epistemology.

61 Pierre Bourdieu, *Ce que parler veut dire: L'économie des échanges linguistiques* (Fayard 1982) 13; see also Vincent Descombes, *Le Même et l'Autre: Quarante-cinq ans de philosophie française (1933–1978)* (Editions de Minuit 1979) 114–15.

62 David Kennedy, 'Critical Theory, Structuralism and Contemporary Legal Scholarship' (1985–1986) 21 *New England Law Review* 209, 269.

63 This quest for the code of the structure is even more conspicuous in Althusserian structural Marxism, whereby ideology is considered a structure that one ought to look for even if there is no way out of ideology. See Louis Althusser, *Pour Marx* (La Découverte 1996) 239–40 (first published 1965).

64 See eg Ferdinand de Saussure, *Course in General Linguistics* (Charles Bally and Albert Sechehaye eds, Open Court 1986) 119.

65 Michel Foucault, *Entretiens radiophoniques 1961–1983* (Flammarion, Vrin, Ina 2024) 439.

66 See generally Steven Shapin and Simon Schaffer, *Leviathan and the Air-Pump* (Princeton University Press 1985).

67 See Gilles Deleuze and Félix Guattari, *Mille plateaux: Capitalisme et schizophrénie* (Editions de Minuit 1980) ch 10. Cf Gilles Deleuze and Félix Guattari, *L'Anti-Cedipe* (Editions de Minuit 1972) ch 1.

68 Deleuze and Guattari's assemblage is positioned against several dominant philosophical traditions and not only Cartesianism. It stands against Hegelianism, as it rejects dialectical synthesis in favour of multiplicity and difference. It opposes structuralism, as it rejects fixed, determining structures in favour of contingent relations. It is against phenomenology, as it moves from consciousness-centred approaches towards distributed agency.

69 Bruno Latour, *Reassembling the Social: An Introduction to Actor-Network-Theory* (OUP 2005); Bruno Latour, *An Inquiry into Modes of Existence* (Harvard University Press 2013).

70 Sheila Jasanoff, 'The Idiom of Co-Production' in Sheila Jasanoff (ed), *States of Knowledge: The Co-Production of Science and Social Order* (Routledge 2004) 1. See also Sheila Jasanoff, 'Ordering Knowledge, Ordering Society' in Sheila Jasanoff (ed), *States of Knowledge: The Co-Production of Science and Social Order* (Routledge 2004) 13–45.

71 Manuel DeLanda, *A New Philosophy of Society: Assemblage Theory and Social Complexity* (Bloomsbury 2019).

72 See eg Sheila Jasanoff, 'Ordering Knowledge, Ordering Society' in Sheila Jasanoff (ed), *States of Knowledge: The Co-Production of Science and Social Order* (Routledge 2004) 13, 21.

73 In that sense, thingness amounts to 'the being of the Kantian thing-in-itself outside the spatiotemporal grid of experience, the perceptual apparatus that can only provide apprehension of the thing-for-us'. See Bill Brown, *Other Things* (University of Chicago Press 2015) 18.

74 Edmund Husserl, *Ideas Pertaining to a Pure Phenomenology and to a Phenomenological Philosophy: First Book* (Fred Kersten tr, Kluwer Academic Publishers 1983); Martin Heidegger, *Being and Time* (Joan Stambaugh tr, Dennis J Schmidt rev, State University of New York Press 2010).
75 Hans-Georg Gadamer, *Truth and Method* (Joel Weinsheimer and Donald G Marshall trs, Bloomsbury Academic 2013).

Chapter 3

The golden age of thingification

This chapter is premised on the idea that, in contemporary thought, the resort to thingification to affirm material necessities situated outside representation in order to immunise them from contestation has been gaining traction. Leaving aside the specific situation of legal thought and practice to which the next chapter will return, the following sections shed light on why thingification may be experiencing a new precritical golden age, or, more precisely, why the conditions of possibility for its resurgence have never been more favourable.

A first possible explanation for the new momentum of thingification may be a dissatisfaction with the modern Kantian epistemology and its constructivist foundations (1). A variant of that explanation lies in the possibility of what might be called a general fatigue with epistemological and hermeneutical debates about one's surrounding world and about which forms of existence the latter admits (2). Yet another reason for the success of thingification can be found in its supposed enabling and facilitation of communication about the world (3). It is also possible that debates about the Anthropocene and the climate crisis have accentuated the thingification of the human, thereby contributing to the dominance of thingifying discourses and epistemologies (4). Mention is penultimately made of the tension that some could possibly see arising between thingification and the dematerialization that accompanies the digitalization of human activities and products with a view to showing that, on the contrary, digitalization is exacerbating thingification processes (5). Finally, the attention turns to the dramatic return of specific forms of domestic and global modes of governance that have extensively resorted to thingification to efficaciously impose their own version of the world (6). This final explanation for the contemporary thriving of thingification will only be broached in this final section, receiving its full elaboration in a subsequent chapter.

1. The persistent disability of Kantian epistemology

It is submitted here that the growing resort to thingification in contemporary thought is being nurtured by the continuous dissatisfaction with the Kantian

DOI: 10.4324/9781003753940-4

legacy. Thingness and its affirmation of a necessary existence outside perception and representation, as well as its demotion of the speaking observer to irrelevance, are fundamentally anti-Kantian. It cannot be excluded that, in many instances, thingness is mobilized and produced through thingification processes precisely to bypass Kantian transcendentalism, constructivism, and correlationism.

Such contestation of the Kantian legacy would surely not be unprecedented.[1] In fact, it is not the first time that one seeks to unmake Kantian epistemology in favour of a return to dogmatic metaphysics. For instance, it is well known that Henri Bergson, who claims that Kant pushed symbolicism to an unbearable extreme,[2] tries to prove that the thing-in-itself can be immediately available to the speaking observer even if the thing-in-itself is always in the making and in movement.[3] For Bergson, a return to intellectual intuition, construed as a move to inhabit the infinite movement of what composes the world ought to be promoted in order to reach absolute knowledge.[4]

Heidegger should be mentioned here too, as he famously tries to unmake the distinction between object and subject through his notion of being-in-the-world as well as the abovementioned idea of ready-to-hand – that is, the primitive situation where objects are encountered as things that just exist as detached entities and where the relationship between subjects and objects has not even started to work.[5]

Another famous challenge to Kantian epistemology has been articulated by Alfred North Whitehead, who takes issue with Kant's limitation of direct knowledge to phenomena rather than things-in-themselves. Whitehead's critique centres on what he sees as Kant's problematic "mentalization" of reality, where the subject-object distinction creates an unbridgeable gulf between knower and known. Against this, Whitehead argues that actual entities – i.e. the fundamental constituents of reality – can be directly known through what he calls "prehension", a process that allows for immediate acquaintance with reality itself rather than mere representations. These entities are not things, but rather a process, i.e. a unit of becoming that constitutes the ultimate reality of the world. They are knowable precisely because they are constituted by the same fundamental process of prehension that characterizes our own experience, what Whitehead calls the "philosophy of organism".[6]

More recently, and possibly more compellingly, Bruno Latour challenges Kant's transcendentalism which placed the knowing subject at the centre of epistemology. For Latour, Kantian epistemology created an unbridgeable gap between human minds and the reality they attempt to understand, effectively trapping humans in what he mockingly refers to as the "mind-in-a-vat" predicament. Latour specifically criticizes Kant's form of constructivism which creates an artificial separation between the human subject and the external world, allowing a crippled despot now to reign over what is called the world of reality.[7] For Latour, the Kantian framework creates an epistemological prison where one can never access things-in-themselves but only one's representations of them, which leads to a fundamental impasse in understanding how science – which is the focus of attention of Latour – actually works in practice.[8]

An even more radical charge against Kantian epistemology has been provided by Jean Baudrillard.[9] He argues that, in the contemporary world, reality has been murdered and replaced by its simulation. For him, we have systematically replaced reality with its representations, simulations, and virtual constructions. What we experience as reality is actually a constructed hyperreality, i.e. a seamless web of signs, images, and simulations that have no referent in an original real world: A world where simulations (images, models, codes) do not just represent reality, but replace and precede it, making the distinction between reality and construction impossible. Baudrillard speaks of "the perfect crime" to qualify such eradication of the very possibility of distinguishing between reality and its construction, between the real and the representation of the real. Such crime is perfect because it leaves no evidence. Baudrillard's notion of crime thus refers to the destruction of the very distinction at the heart of Kant's epistemology, namely the thing-in-itself and the experience of such thing. As a result, the very question of an unknowable thing-in-itself turns irrelevant. In other words, because reality itself has been eliminated through simulation, then the entire Kantian project of grounding knowledge in the experience of the thing-in-itself has become obsolete. Notwithstanding the pushbacks that Baudrillard's argument has provoked,[10] what is most interesting in Baudrillard's repudiation of Kant's epistemology is that, for him, the latter was doomed from the start, as the real was always the child of disillusion,[11] and could only be a transitional stage.[12]

Mention must similarly be made of Giorgio Agamben who laments Kant's discontinuation of metaphysics and its demotion of ontology to irrelevance by invalidating the distinction between essence and existence. Agamben more specifically frames this Kantian turning point as an unfortunate watershed moment after which ontology is sidelined in favour of subject-object correlation, thereby disabling the distinctions (essence/existence, possibility/actuality, potentiality/act) through which the West had made reality intelligible and human action durably governable.[13]

An final source of dissatisfaction with Kantian constructivist epistemology, albeit of a different kind, is provided by decolonial theory, particularly in Enrique Dussel's reconstruction of modernity's origins.[14] In fact, Dussel argues that Kant's constructivism based on the relation between the knowing subject and the known object becomes historically plausible only within a geopolitical horizon produced by conquest, extraction, and racial ordering, so that the transcendental subject that "constructs" objectivity is itself an effect of a world-system. In Dussel's thesis that modernity begins in 1492, Europe's self-constitution as the privileged locus of enunciation is inseparable from the colonial relation through which the Americas are incorporated as exteriority and rendered available for classification, labour discipline, and resource extraction, a process that stabilizes the conceptual partitions later taken as self-evident in Kantian philosophy. For him, the distinction that separates the autonomous subject from an objectified environment – originally introduced by Descartes but refined and systematized by Kant – is grounded in the colonial situation which has produced superior and self-confident Europeans as bearers of rational social order as well as colonized peoples and colonized territories as nearer to nature, as resource, or as culturally particular material to be administered, thereby furnishing the background against which Kantian epistemology could appear.[15] In that sense, Kant is problematic not simply as an internal episode in Western epistemological debates, but as a canonical consolidation of a European-centred and colonial account of the world.

These few examples suffice to illustrate that Kantian epistemology, despite remaining dominant in the Western philosophical tradition, has attracted a great variety of objections.[16] To the extent that thingification processes put in place a severe repudiation of Kantian epistemology, they can accordingly be construed as building on (and continuing) a strong anti-Kantian tradition.[17]

2. Epistemological exhaustion and the aspiration for a simple life

The vigour of thingness in contemporary thought can simultaneously be understood as a collective retreat from the exhausting demands of perpetual existential and definitional interpretation. Surely, constructivism can never be the site of societal consensus.[18] This is why, after more than two centuries of being told that reality is merely a construction, that every object is a text to be decoded, and that the world is always plural and perspectival, a profound weariness seems to have settled over contemporary consciousness. This epistemological fatigue is nourished by a yearning for the solid, the given, the unquestionable, i.e. a world of things that simply are, existing in their brute materiality without requiring the endless labour of definitional debates and disagreements.

From this perspective, a turn toward thingness represents not mere intellectual laziness but could be interpreted as a form of self-preservation.[19] The (former) speaking observer, bombarded by an infinity of possible readings and representations for every encountered phenomenon, experiences what might be called an interpretive nausea,[20] i.e. a vertigo induced by too many conceptual frameworks, too many lenses through which to view the world. The refuge of thingness offers blessed simplicity.[21] This driver of the epistemology of thingness corresponds to what Timothy Bewes, in his attempt to rethink the notion of reification, has called the *thingitude* of modern capitalist societies, that is, the pull toward thing-like certainty, the desire for immediacy, solidity, and presence, the hunger for thing-like certainty in a world increasingly organized by abstraction, circulation, and representation.[22]

The success of this epistemological stance in contemporary thought simultaneously reflects a broader exhaustion with constructivism's infinite regress.[23] If everything is constructed, if there is no bedrock of reality beneath our representations, then one is condemned to float in a sea of competing narratives without anchor or orientation. Thingness provides that anchor, that is, the comforting belief that, beneath all our talk and theorizing, there exists a world of material things that persist regardless of what one says about them. This is not necessarily a return to naïve realism, but rather a strategic forgetting, a wilful blindness to the speaking observer's role in constituting the world. In choosing thingness, one chooses the possibility of rest, i.e. a respite from the tireless work of meaning-making that constructivism demands.

It is important to stress that this motivation behind the retreat into thingness carries within it a important irony[24] that reveals the inescapable nature of the epistemological predicament it seeks to escape. In choosing to inhabit a world of fixed, self-evident things, the speaking observer performs one final act of world-construction, that is, the construction of a world that denies construction itself. This ultimate gesture becomes simultaneously an act of self-annihilation. By refusing the burden of meaning-making and of representation, the speaking observer effectively renounces their constitutive capacity, transforming themselves from an active participant in reality's ongoing creation into a passive recipient of a pre-given world. The very capacity that defines them as a speaking observer – the ability to name and represent, and thereby bring forth worlds – is voluntarily surrendered in exchange for epistemological comfort. The simpler life they achieve is thus haunted by the spectre of a speaking observer who, in refusing to speak and represent, has rendered themselves mute.

3. Thingness as necessity for communication and action

Another factor instrumental in the contemporary vitality of thingification processes stems, not from philosophical naivety, but from an allegedly profound pragmatic utility. By treating the world as made of self-evident and self-signifying material entities with stable properties, thingness enables direct communication that bypasses the labyrinthine complexities of definitional inquiries. Short of thinking in terms of things, the world would just be a gigantic undifferentiated, undetermined, and unintelligible piece of matter.[25] In that regard, one can easily think of how inefficient communication would become if every utterance required one to acknowledge that the "thing" being referenced is actually a dynamic assemblage of relations, a temporary stabilization of processes, or a construct emerging from the intersection of human perception and material flux. Any simple statement from ordinary life would devolve into an elaborate philosophical meditation on what constitutes what is being addressed or talked about. From such a perspective, the thingness produced by thingification can thus be understood as operating as a kind of epistemological shorthand, one that makes coordinated action and shared understanding possible. Even critics of naive realism typically suspend their theoretical commitments when navigating daily life, implicitly acknowledging that thingness, whatever its philosophical limitations, remains indispensable for practical existence, including for human relations.[26] The same goes for more contemporary Kantian thinkers who acknowledge that, compelled thereto by reason of discursive thought, one must regard real existence as if things-in-themselves really existed.[27]

Interestingly, such a form of communicative pragmatism is already found in the work of Bentham in his famous theory of fictions. Indeed, Bentham makes a fundamental distinction between different types of entities that is central to his theory of fictions. He classifies *real entities* as physical objects existing in the material world that can be perceived directly through the senses, having actual existence independent of language and thought, such as physical objects, persons, and sensations. In contrast, *fictitious entities* are constructs of language with no physical existence but necessary for communication and thought, and are treaty grammatically as if they existed despite not being directly perceivable by the senses (examples include legal concepts like right, obligation, or property). The cornerstone of Bentham's approach is that, although fictitious entities do not physically exist, they remain necessary for language and reasoning (especially in law).[28]

The same pragmatism is supported by Bergson, who claims that our mind always seeks fixed buttresses and that thinking always starts from immobility and fixity.[29] For him, in ordinary life, it is normal to represent states as things, for our mind always substitutes discontinuity and fixity for what is always continuous and mobile.[30]

Giorgio Agamben must be mentioned here again. Indeed, in Agamben's horizon, the *res* is necessarily the presupposition of all discourse and of every statement about the world. For him, it is as a thing divided between essence and existence, possibility and actuality, that reality becomes intelligible, actionable, and governable. In that regard, he argues that the historical domination of the West, from scientific knowledge to the capacity to control and direct human action durably, has depended on this constitutive division of the thing, without which knowledge and praxis would lose their very object. Far from being a mere linguistic effect, the thing – to use the terminology of this book rather than Agamben's – produced by thingification is the very object that knowledge and praxis require, which is what support Agamben's abovementioned call for a return to a pre-Kantian epistemology in which the essence of substance becomes once again thinkable and operative.[31]

Although not seeking to back away from Kantian critical epistemology, a similar support for thingification as an enabler of knowledge and action can possibly be found in Anthony Giddens's account of modernity where he elevates what he calls 'trust' to a central epistemological tool. Indeed, for him, under a modern epistemology, trust functions as the enabling condition of intelligibility and action within time. In fact, trust, defined as confidence in the reliability of a person or system regarding specified outcomes, whether grounded in the probity or care of others or in the correctness of abstract principles, requires a world in which predicates are installed ahead of presence, so that actors can treat complex agencies and mechanisms as things whose essence and existence are sufficiently articulated to permit calculation and coordination. In our contemporary world, he claims, the reliance on abstract systems renders everyday security possible only by routinizing encounters with impersonal mechanisms and distant others, converting them into administrable things that can be trusted as stable supports of action. From Giddens's perspective, thingification can be deemed indispensable to the trust required by modernity, because it renders both persons and systems legible as things whose predicates can be relied upon across time and space, thereby sustaining the circular relation between knowledge, action, and governance.[32]

4. Thingness and the Anthropocene

The possible contemporary heyday of thingification can also be read against the backdrop of the Anthropocene and of the latter's discursive consequences. Indeed, this epochal designation[33] carries profound epistemological implications, for it reconfigures the relationship between human beings and the natural world in ways that intensify thingifying impulses and extend thingness even to human beings themselves.[34] Indeed, in the discourse about the Anthropocene, humans have often been turned into geological agents, a species-thing whose collective impact registers in ice cores, sediment layers, and atmospheric measurements. Dipesh Chakrabarty, in his influential essay on the climate of history, famously observes that the Anthropocene forces one to think of humans not merely as biological agents operating within ecosystems but as geological agents capable of altering the fundamental conditions of planetary existence.[35] This reconceptualization has significant consequences for how human beings understand themselves. To become a geological agent is to become a material force whose effects are measurable, quantifiable, and inscribed in the stratigraphic record. The human being, on this view, is no longer primarily a subject endowed with consciousness, intentionality, and moral responsibility – as is understood in mainstream modern philosophy, but a thing among things, a material entity whose existence is defined by its physical and chemical interactions with the Earth system.

Climate science necessarily reinforces this thingification by reducing human activity to quantifiable units. Carbon footprints, emission tonnages, consumption metrics, and ecological footprint calculations transform the complexity of human life into numerical values that can be aggregated, compared, and subjected to policy interventions. Each person becomes a thing that produces a measurable amount of waste, consumes a calculable quantity of resources, and occupies a specific ecological niche. Timothy Morton, in his work on "hyperobjects", argues that entities such as global warming are so massively distributed in time and space that they fundamentally alter our capacity to think about causality, agency, and responsibility.[36] In the face of such hyperobjects, the individual human subject appears diminished, reduced to a node in vast networks of material causation that exceed any possibility of comprehensive understanding or control. This scientific discourse has permeated popular consciousness, where one increasingly encounters oneself as a thing among things, not a transcendent subject observing an external world, but a material entity whose very existence is inseparable from cycles of extraction, consumption, and disposal.

The thingification processes that accompany the discourse about the Anthropocene admit, however, a major exception. Those who deny the changes to the climate are commonly prompted to contest the very material existence of those realities which scientists have sought to evidence. For climate sceptics, human activities and their consequences for the planet have no thingly existence and must therefore be refuted. For them, there is no such thing as climate change. De-thingifying human activities and their upshot is their way to fight scientific facts.[37] Naomi Oreskes and Erik Conway, in their study of the merchants of doubt, document how climate denial has been strategically deployed to undermine scientific consensus and to forestall political action on environmental issues.[38] The denial of climate change operates precisely by refusing to grant thingly status to the phenomena that climate science has documented, by insisting that global warming is not a thing but a construction, an artefact of flawed models and biased researchers. The foregoing is not without irony, for climate sceptics are often those who, in domestic politics, simultaneously resort to thingification processes most extensively to impose their views on the world and their policies.[39] The Anthropocene accordingly presents a paradoxical situation in which thingification is simultaneously intensified and contested. On the one hand, the ecological crisis encourages modes of thought that reduce human beings to geological agents, that quantify human activity in terms of carbon emissions and resource consumption, that dissolve the subject-object distinction in favour of a flat epistemology of things. On the other hand, the political contestation surrounding climate change simultaneously reveals the strategic and selective character of thingification processes.

5. Thingness exacerbated in the age of digitalization

More than thirty years ago, Jacques Derrida suggested that new digital technologies do not eliminate materiality but reconfigure it.[40] This resonates more powerfully today than ever, especially if one looks at the unprecedented digitalization of human activities and products from the vantage point of thingness and thingification. As one has come to inhabit an era characterized by processes of digitalization of a scale never witnessed before,[41] it seems that the resort to thingification has not merely survived but intensified. In fact, amidst such omnipresent digitalization processes, one can witness a burgeoning of thingness. The digital realm, rather than dissolving attachment to thingness, has created new territories for thingness to colonize.[42] Consider how one speaks of "digital assets", "data objects", or "virtual goods" – each term betrays the compulsion to conceptualize immaterial processes as concrete things. Social media posts become "content", algorithms become "tools", and even ephemeral interactions crystallize into "engagement metrics". This linguistic thingness is not necessarily a metaphorical convenience but can also be the expression of a cognitive attitude whereby thingness is granted to all phenomena that exist only as patterns of electrical impulses or magnetic orientations on servers. Perhaps most significantly, it can be said that digitalization has not replaced material culture but has created a parallel universe where thingification operates with even fewer constraints. In virtual worlds, cryptocurrencies, and NFTs, one witnesses the pure apotheosis of thingness. For instance, blockchains' very architecture embodies thingness par excellence, transforming abstract claims of ownership into immutable blocks that can be possessed, transferred, and hoarded like physical objects.

If this is the case, such amplification of thingness through digitalization can be said to occur through several mechanisms. First, the very act of digitization requires the parsing of continuous phenomena into discrete units – pixels, bits, packets – thereby imposing thing-like boundaries on formerly fluid experiences. Second, the digital economy's need for commodification transforms every aspect of online existence into tradable, ownable things: Personal data becomes an asset, attention becomes currency, and even relationships become quantifiable social capital. Third, interfaces with digital systems are deliberately designed to simulate physical manipulation of objects – one "drags" files, "drops" them into "folders", and "trashes" unwanted items – perpetuating thingified thinking even in immaterial spaces. Fourth, digital surveillance and data analytics create an unprecedented condition where humans simultaneously appear as biological things, digital things, and economic things. Everything, including humanity itself, comes to be construed as a thing to be measured, managed, monitored, or optimized.[43] In that sense, it can be claimed that the age of digitalization heralds not the dissolution of things but their multiplication across new dimensions of existence, confirming that thingness remains one of the most fundamental epistemological frameworks for engaging with the world, whether material or virtual.

6. The ease of governing a world composed of things

The contemporary multiplication of forms of authoritarian governance that no longer conceals itself may be yet another driver for the success of thingification processes. In fact, for a growing number of decision-makers, especially in the Global North, the systematic deployment of thingification offers a permanent and convenient tool of epistemological control, whereby pronouncements about people and the world are turned from contingent positions into immutable features of a reality presented as in-itself. When such governance speaks, it does not offer perspectives but allegedly names things that already exist in their full, unquestionable thingness. The border wall is not a policy choice but a thing that must be. The enemy is not a political construction but a thing with inherent properties of threat and otherness. The nation itself becomes thingified into a thing with fixed and unchangeable characteristics. As a result, whatever such decision-makers say, think, or experience always has a necessary existence in the world because it is a thing. What a speaking observer may perceive, observe, name, represent, etc. is absolutely irrelevant, for these authorities have monopolized the determination of what counts as a thing and what remains mere representation. The world simply is as is, and this "is-ness" coincides perfectly with whatever the authoritarian voice declares it to be. From such an authoritarian perspective, all the constructivist-minded observers should simply move on, as there is nothing to discuss or re-represent. The very possibility of alternative representations is foreclosed not through explicit censorship but through the more fundamental denial that there is anything to re-represent at all.

It is not totally surprising that authoritarian governance and thingification processes go together. Applied as a mode of governance, thingness reveals its potency and effectiveness: By presenting a world of fixed things rather than fluid meanings, decision-makers can universalize their own worldview while simultaneously pathologizing any attempt at critical re-representation as a form of delusion or denial of obvious reality. This is yet another reminder that thingness is a terribly efficacious way to represent the world[44] and to impose such representations on people. In the end, it is far easier to govern people through thingness than by reminding them that everything is constructed, including the political discourse itself. Constantly reminding citizens of the constructed nature of all political reality would invite precisely the kind of critical scrutiny and interpretive plurality that authoritarian governance, as will be further explored in a subsequent chapter,[45] resents and commonly seeks to foreclose.[46]

Notes

1 For a contemporary criticism of Kantian constructivism and a defence of realism, see John R Searle, *The Construction of Social Reality* (Penguin Books 1996).
2 Henri Bergson, *Introduction à la métaphysique* (Presses Universitaires de France 2011) 44.
3 Henri Bergson, *Introduction à la métaphysique* (Presses Universitaires de France 2011) 35–47.
4 Ibid 37–40.
5 See Martin Heidegger, *Being and Time* (Joan Stambaugh tr, State University of New York Press 2010) div I, ch 3.
6 Alfred North Whitehead, *Process and Reality* (corrected edn, The Free Press 1978) 153–56 (where he shows how his philosophy of organism opposes Kantian constructivism and distances himself from some of Kant's main dichotomies like that of the subject and object).
7 Bruno Latour, *Pandora's Hope: Essays on the Reality of Science Studies* (Harvard University Press 1999) 5.
8 By critiquing Kant, Latour attempts to break free from what he sees as artificial philosophical constraints and to develop actor-network theory to account better for how science and knowledge function in the world. See Bruno Latour, *Pandora's Hope: Essays on the Reality of Science Studies* (Harvard University Press 1999) ch 1.
9 Jean Baudrillard, *Le crime parfait* (Galilée 1995).
10 Jacques Rancière has argued that Baudrillard's framing misidentifies what is lost: The problem is not the disappearance of the real but the erasure of appearance – those gaps, disjunctions, and stagings through which different worlds can be set in relation and contested. The regime of total visibility, where everything is permanently presented as already identical to its image, suppresses the heterogeneity of appearance that enables political subjectivation – non-identitarian subjects who disrupt the sensible order by making separate worlds visible together. By equating reality with its simulated reproduction, the "all-visible" world leaves no space for the doubling and division that appearance performs; it thus forecloses politics understood as dissensus and instead tends towards a "police" logic of population management, where the count of parts matches the order of what is seen and sayable. In short, what Baudrillard reads as a loss of the real is, for Rancière, a loss of appearance and with it the conditions for genuine political emancipation. See Jacques Rancière, *La mésentente: Politique et philosophie* (La Fabrique 1995) 139–40.
11 Ibid 29, 73–74.
12 Ibid 96.
13 Giorgio Agamben, *L'irréalisable* (Seuil 2025) 100–02.
14 See generally CI Pinton, 'From Ego Conquiro to Ego Cogito: Dussel's Latin American History of Philosophy' (2025) 29 *RUDN Journal of Philosophy* 704–19. See also Philippe Colin and Lissell Quiroz, *Pensées décoloniales: Une introduction aux théories critiques d'Amérique Latine* (Zones 2023) 134.
15 See Enrique Dussel, *The Invention of the Americas: Eclipse of the Other and the Myth of Modernity* (Michael D Barber tr, Continuum 1995); Enrique Dussel, *Ethics of Liberation: In the Age of Globalization and Exclusion* (Eduardo Mendieta, Camilo Pérez Bustillo and Yolanda Angulo trs, Duke University Press 2013). See also Aníbal Quijano, 'Coloniality of Power, Eurocentrism, and Latin America' (2000) 1 *Nepantla: Views from South* 533–80.
16 See also Laurent de Sutter, *Superfaible: Penser au XXIe siècle* (Climats 2023). On the idea of the Kantian catastrophe, see Quentin Meillassoux, *Après la finitude:*

Essai sur la nécessité de la contingence (Seuil 2006) 186. One early objection came from Hegel himself. For instance, it is well known that Hegel came to repudiate the dualism of both Descartes and Kant by seeking to show that dualism is bound to be caught in idealism as only the idea provides the self with access to the thing-in-itself, idealism simultaneously enabling the possibility of absolute knowledge. For an interpretation of Hegel, see Jean Hyppolite, *Logique et existence* (Presses Universitaires de France 1952).

17 For an early 20th-century attempt to vindicate and push further Kantian epistemology, see Hans Vaihinger, *The Philosophy of "As If"* (Routledge 2021) (first published 1911). See also Wilfrid Sellars, *Empiricism and the Philosophy of the Mind* (Harvard University Press 1997) (first published 1956) (Sellars is sometimes called a "neo-Kantian" because he agrees with Kant that experience is conceptually structured and that there is no "raw" given to serve as the foundation of knowledge; yet he moves beyond Kant by making language and social practices central to conceptual activity).

18 Bruno Latour, *Face à Gaïa* (La Découverte 2015) 31.

19 On the idea that concreteness relieves us from unnecessary abstraction, see Bill Brown, 'Thing Theory' (2001) 28 *Critical Inquiry* 1, 1. See also Herbert Marcuse, *One-Dimensional Man: Studies in the Ideology of Advanced Industrial Society* (Beacon Press 1964) ch 4.

20 Cf Francis Ponge, 'My Creative Method' in Francis Ponge, *The Voice of Things* (Beth Archer tr and ed, McGraw-Hill 1972) 93 ('Ideas give me a queasy feeling, nausea' whereas 'objects in the external world… delight me').

21 Cf Barthes, who speaks of the happiness of clarity. See Barthes, *Mythologies* (Editions du Seuil 1957) 254.

22 Timothy Bewes, *Reification, or The Anxiety of Late Capitalism* (Verso 2002) xiv–xv.

23 On the idea that Kantian epistemology always condemned thought to infinite regress, see Quentin Meillassoux, *Après la finitude: Essai sur la nécessité de la contingence* (Seuil 2006) 25.

24 I owe this observation to Rebecca Mignot-Mahdavi.

25 Tristan Garcia, *Forme et objet: Un traité des choses* (PUF 2011) 46.

26 See eg Maurice Merleau-Ponty, *Phénoménologie de la perception* (Gallimard 1945) 348.

27 Hans Vaihinger, *The Philosophy of "As If"* (Routledge 2021) 69.

28 Jeremy Bentham, *Bentham's Theory of Fictions* (CK Ogden ed, Routledge 2007); Philip Schofield, Jean-Pierre Cléro and Christian Laval (eds), *Jeremy Bentham, De l'ontologie et autres textes sur les fictions* (Editions du Seuil 1997); Christian Laval, *Jeremy Bentham: Le pouvoir des fictions* (PUF 1994). I owe this whole observation to an exchange with Guillaume Tusseau. It must be noted that Bentham's theory of fictions, which remains grounded in a very modern epistemology, should not be understood as promoting a thingification move. For Bentham, legal fictions never carry any fixed existence outside representation. He only claims that they should be evaluated based on their practical consequences. On the contrary, his theory of fictions is meant to show that fundamental concepts in law, politics, and ethics are linguistic constructs rather than natural entities, which usefully anticipates later developments in analytical philosophy and linguistic theory.

29 Henri Bergson, *Introduction à la métaphysique* (Presses Universitaires de France 2011) 35–36.

30 Ibid 36.

31 Giorgio Agamben, *L'irréalisable* (Seuil 2025) 44, 101 and 108.

32 Anthony Giddens, *The Consequences of Modernity* (Polity 1990) 26–36 and 113.
33 The concept was first proposed by Paul Crutzen and Eugene Stoermer in 2000 and subsequently elaborated in geological, ecological, and humanistic scholarship. See Paul J Crutzen and Eugene F Stoermer, 'The "Anthropocene"' (2000) 41 *Global Change Newsletter* 17–18.
34 Sarah Wasserman, 'Thing Theory 2017: A Forum' (Arcade, 2017) https://shc.stanford.edu/arcade/interventions/thing-theory-2017-forum accessed 9 March 2026.
35 Dipesh Chakrabarty, 'The Climate of History: Four Theses' (2009) 35(2) *Critical Inquiry* 197–222, 206–12.
36 Timothy Morton, *Hyperobjects: Philosophy and Ecology after the End of the World* (University of Minnesota Press 2013) 1–24.
37 See the remarks of Bruno Latour, *Face à Gaïa* (La Découverte 2015) 37–40.
38 Naomi Oreskes and Erik M Conway, *Merchants of Doubt: How a Handful of Scientists Obscured the Truth on Issues from Tobacco Smoke to Global Warming* (Bloomsbury Press 2010) 169–215.
39 See ch 5 below.
40 Rather than seeing the digital as eliminating materiality, Derrida contends that it reconfigures our relationship with material presence, absence, and archival practices. Derrida characterizes digital presence as spectral a priori, neither fully present nor absent. This spectral quality does not mean immateriality but rather a different kind of materiality that challenges binary oppositions between presence and absence, material and immaterial. See Jacques Derrida, *Mal d'Archive: Une impression freudienne* (Éditions Galilée 1995); Jacques Derrida, *Papier Machine: Le ruban de machine à écrire et autres réponses* (Éditions Galilée 2001).
41 Bill Brown, *Other Things* (University of Chicago Press 2015) 12–13; Jean Baudrillard, *Le crime parfait* (Galilée 1995).
42 Derrida argues that the digital archive creates new forms of materiality that differ from traditional paper archives but still maintain material presence through different infrastructures and storage mechanisms. More generally, Derrida argues that the digital trace is material but in ways that differ from conventional understanding – it exists as electrical patterns, magnetic alignments, or optical encodings rather than ink on paper. See Jacques Derrida, *Mal d'Archive: Une impression freudienne* (Éditions Galilée 1995); Jacques Derrida, *Papier Machine: Le ruban de machine à écrire et autres réponses* (Éditions Galilée 2001).
43 Cf. the claim of Bruno Latour according to whom human societies have been turned into objects whilst nature has become the active subject. See Bruno Latour, *Face à Gaïa* (La Découverte 2015) 97.
44 On the idea that thingness is a representationless mode of representation, see ch 1, s 1.3 above.
45 See ch 1, s 1.3 above.
46 Cf Hannah Arendt, *The Human Condition* (2nd edn, University of Chicago Press 2018) 248–325 (on the idea that it is far easier to act under conditions of tyranny than it is to think).

Chapter 4

Figures of legal thingification

This chapter makes the claim that law is both an artisan and a beneficiary of thingness.[1] Law thingifies itself and thingifies what it addresses: The State, the people, sex, race, nature, and culture.[2] In each instance, law performs, reiterates, and secures a necessary being-in-the-world by attributing thingness to itself and what it encounters in a way that excludes perception, forecloses the speaking observer, annuls representation, collapses agency into self-causation, installs ancestrality, and effaces the discursive labour that produces it. What is more specifically at stake here is how law produces thingly entities that present themselves as being-in-themselves, anterior to perception, outside representation, self-caused, ancestral, and self-effacing. What matters the most here is that the upshot of such legal thingification processes is not simply the creation of a catalogue of thingly entities but a regime of prescription (an imperative of acknowledgement) where the "is" concomitantly becomes a "must be". From such perspective, law emerges as a privileged machinery of thingification that puts in place a precritical epistemology: It makes things that are, and in the same gesture, makes the very fact of their being extra-discursive and uncontestable. As a result, dissent is relocated from the question of existence to peripheral matters of application and scope. In other words, the "is" of the legal thing is never just the report of a fact; it is the establishment of a necessity.

To account for this precritical condition of law and the projection of an image of law as machinery of thingification, the current chapter adopts Roland Barthes' *figure* as its basic unit of exposition.[3] The choice for figures of thingification rather than cases, instances, or illustrations is meant as an anti-encyclopaedic stance that nourishes neither taxonomic ambition nor descriptive comprehensiveness. Indeed, I only intend to expose, in this chapter, a sequence of fragments of legal thingification processes, thereby leaving them in a continuous variation and deprived of a single final meaning.[4] This is meant to resist the common scholarly temptation to stabilize, synthesize, and exhaust. Such a focus on figures of legal thingification simultaneously aligns with one of the book's core claims, namely that the production of thingness is

DOI: 10.4324/9781003753940-5

always self-effacing, and what effaces itself cannot be captured by an exhaustive encyclopaedic description.

The focus is on thingification and not thingness, for I am concerned here with the process of production of thingness and the routinized discursive practices that compose it. Because thingness is an epistemological and discursive attribute,[5] then the exposition that follows must zero in on the processes that generate it. Centring thingification also has the advantage of laying bare one of the normative claims that runs throughout this book. Focusing on thingification insists that, because thingly necessity is always manufactured, it can always be unmade or resisted.[6]

Before embarking on the exposition of seven figures of legal thingification, three important observations are necessary. First, it is of the utmost importance to distinguish between, on the one hand, the idea that law thingifies what it encounters, and, on the other hand, the general and – now – well-accepted idea that *law is performative* in that it constitutes its object. The point made here is that thingification is a more specific, more determinate modality of law's performativity. The performativity thesis, and the speech act theory[7] it commonly builds on, is well known. In the context of legal thought, performativity names the capacity of legal discourse and practice to constitute the social realities to which law applies.[8] This means that, rather than addressing a pre-given world, law participates in making the very subjects, objects, spaces, domains of application, problems, and relations that it governs or addresses.[9] In other words, legal operations are said to generate institutions, identities, statuses, and problems, simultaneously making the world legible to legal intervention.[10] In contrast, the claim about thingness is that law not only constitutes what it encounters but also awards a thingly quality to what it constitutes: A quality of necessary being-in-the-world that presents itself as independent of perception, language, discourse, and representation, and that effaces the speaking observer. To say it differently, thingification does more than constitute. It awards necessity, installs ancestrality, collapses agency into self-causation, excludes perception, forecloses the speaking observer, annuls representation, and effaces the labour of production. In this sense, thingification is a species of performativity, but it is not equivalent to it. It is more specific, more radical, more violent because it overlays constitution with a further epistemic attribute: It confers the status of necessary being, excludes the speaking observer, forecloses critique, and masks the constitutive operation that produced this state of affairs.

Second, it goes without saying that this chapter's exposition of several figures of legal thingification is far from being exhaustive. As law thingifies all the way, plenty of other figures could have been provided. In fact, one can immediately think of how law comes to thingify poverty, development, under-development, the Third World, the cyber, the digital, artificial intelligence, etc. The study of these other instances of thingification is left for subsequent inquiries, for exhaustion is not necessary to show the extent to which law is a big thingifying apparatus.

A third observation is warranted on the need to refrain from classifying too rigidly the seven figures of thingness that are exposed in the following sections. The seven figures exposed in this chapter as well as the way and order in which they are presented are not supposed to form a system. The following simply and modestly sketches a topography of legal thingification across key domains of modern governance. Each figure isolates a few recurrent discursive operations by which law produces necessary beings and installs the imperative of acknowledgement, while simultaneously dehistoricizing, depoliticizing, and abstracting. The figures of legal thingification exposed here concern law itself (1), the State (2), the people (3), sex (4), race (5), nature (6), and culture (7). In each figure, the discussion foregrounds some of the effects of thingness – contemplation, differentiation, dehistoricization, depoliticization, dehumanization, interpellation, prescription, and abstraction – and shows how law orchestrates them. This chapter ends with an observation on how thingification contributes to law's discursive efficacy (8).

An ultimate remark on the style adopted in this chapter is in order. The following sections will draw extensively on the works of many scholars and thinkers from a great variety of fields within the humanities and critical theory. I deliberately foreground such works in the discussion to highlight the intellectual companions that enable me to make the claims I make here. This is not because they have explicitly and directly discussed the extent to which law thingifies what it encounters, let alone because they have used the terminology of thingness and thingification. Rather, it is because their engagement with questions of materiality provides a very solid pillar for what I am trying to do here that they must be explicitly included in the discussion, and not simply relegated to footnotes.

1. Law

The central claim advanced in this first section is that any legal discourse begins by thingifying itself. Before projecting thingness onto the world it governs, law confers upon itself the status of a thing. It frames its own rules, doctrines, sources, practices and institutions as endowed with thingly materiality, thereby harvesting the discursive and epistemological effects of thingness. Through this initial self-thingification, law stabilizes itself as a necessary being-in-the-world and equips itself with a repertoire of effects, i.e. independence from perception, the cancellation of the speaking observer, representationlessness, originary causation, lineage, and self-effacement.

This self-thingification process is most tangible in the long-standing lawyers' preoccupation with the question of the nature of law. Asking what law is, what composes it, and what its essence might be presupposes the very thingliness it purports to disclose. In fact, one ordinarily inquires into the nature of something only after one has staged the thingness of law.[11] The metaphor of the "body of law" that is so commonly used in such scholarly works is yet another expression of the thingness permeating them. The same goes for the many studies about the nature of international law[12] that populate the international legal literature.

The commonplace image of law as a system of rules similarly projects some kind of thingness by picturing law as a kit of well-defined building blocks.[13] This is the case with the well known Hartian distinction between primary and secondary rules,[14] and all its many variants,[15] which enact rules as the main thingly composites of law. Legal education cements this impression by presenting the rules of contracts, torts, criminal law, and procedure as durable components, cultivating a felt sense that rules have body-like persistence and can be carried from case to case. In civil law traditions, codification elevates this posture into a material practice. The code's spine, numbered articles, and official commentary coalesce into a single artefact, a self-signifying being that appears to speak through article numbers and headings without needing external representation.[16] In the common law world, the American Law Institute's Restatements similarly condense the common law into an authoritative corpus, a thing that can be possessed, cited, and transported across jurisdictions.[17] The structuring creates not just intelligibility but corporeality: The law appears to possess skeleton and flesh.[18] Similar rulist approaches are witnessed in connection with international law and thus come to project an image of the latter as a concrete assemblage of well-defined building blocks called rules. It is, for instance, very common to portray the doctrines of sources, of interpretation, of responsibility, of jus cogens, and of statehood as constituting corpora made of actual rules.[19]

Interestingly, once rules are staged as composites, bindingness can be narrated as a thingly property that attaches to those composites when certain indicators are met. In domestic public law, for instance, the constitution's binding force is presented as a quality inherent to the inscriptional formalities (seal, date, and formal promulgation) which are meant to carry the norm's bindingness.[20] Even where intent is significant, as in contract formation, one captures the *animus* through signatures, seals, delivery, and other materialities that translate intention into things, thereby reinforcing the representationlessness of the binding quality once inscribed.[21] The adjudicative rhetoric that a court "finds" a contract or 'gives effect' to a statutory provision relies on the felt independence of a thingly quality.

As these qualities accrete, legal orders themselves come to be portrayed as bodily wholes endowed with identity, hierarchy, and continuity. The very idea of the legal system thingifies a horizon within which the system is described as a being-without-a-witness.[22] The notion that a system has closure – that it contains its own criteria for validity and provides its own foundations – further serves to depict law as a self-sufficient organism.[23]

One of the most revealing expressions of law self-thingification is probably found in the metaphor of the sources of law, which makes law appear as something that jumps, quite literally, out of a fountain. In fact, speaking of sources of law summons an image of law whereby the latter springs from certain apertures. This hydraulic picture naturalizes the production of law as if legal norms were fluids that issue from pre-given mouths.[24] The fountain suggests a being-in-itself: The spring is there and it flows even without a witness. It connotes self-signifying being: The flow announces its own origin. As a result, no external representation is necessary because the emanation marks the source. The metaphor of the sources of law also evokes a self-caused and ancestral being: The spring is imagined as primordial, feeding successive streams without itself being produced. When scholars debate whether soft law, unilateral acts, or resolutions qualify as sources, they are, figuratively, arguing about whether a new spout belongs in the fountain's stonework. The very idea of an "emerging source" leverages the hydrological metaphor even further.

It is submitted here that, in international law, self-thingification not only recurs but intensifies. It suffices to look at the extent to which customary international law is incessantly described as a "matter of facts", i.e. state practice accompanied by *opinio juris*,[25] suggesting a material actuality that appears to persist without an observer.[26] The language of "crystallization" and "formation" furthers the sense of custom formation as a material becoming. Treaties are similarly approached as things. The insistence on authenticated texts, the equality of languages, certified copies, annexes, and maps presents meaning and force as inscribed in artefacts that can be handled, stored, and reproduced.[27] The textual apparatus – preambles, definitions, operative clauses, final clauses – reads like a chassis with fitted components. Consolidated treaty series, official repositories, and subject-matter codifications further materialize treaty law into a library of binders and databases. The archival materiality – e.g. the registered number, the United Nations Treaty Series citation – acts as the treaty's tag, making its legal existence palpable as a thing. Even when intent (*animus contrahendi*) is emphasized, the law immediately recaptures intent through inscriptions.[28]

Most remarkable in international law is that practice itself frequently acquires the status of a thing, i.e. it is awarded thingness and thereby treated as a necessary being-in-the-world that can be relied upon without further mediation. Indeed, whether for customary norm-making or interpretative purposes, practice is treated as a self-signifying being: It is said to speak to meaning or to norm-creation without passing through the vicissitudes of representation. It is configured as a being-without-a-witness: It is presumed to be there, to endure and to operate irrespective of the speaking observer. Customary international law, which has already been mentioned, offers the most explicit theatre of this thingification of practice. Indeed, state practice is routinely described as the "material component" of customary norms.[29] It is often approached as if it materially existed outside the projected standards and putative prescriptions that shape the apprehension of state conduct and give it a specific form of intelligibility.[30] This is how practice is configured as an a-perception: It is said to be available to observers without requiring that the observer traverse the layered representational and institutional mediations that produce and frame intelligible conduct. The same thingification process is at work in treaty interpretation through "subsequent practice". The International Law Commission's 2013–2018 study on subsequent agreements and subsequent practice codifies this gravitational pull by formatting practice as a thing that can "establish the agreement of the parties regarding the interpretation".[31] In such treatments, practice is awarded a being-in-itself that is presumed to stabilize meaning. The speaking observer does not vanish, but the discursive and epistemological work that constructs practice as an object is effaced so that practice can be relied upon like an exterior self-signifying thing.

Although already occasionally mentioned, legal hermeneutics warrants a closer look here, for it is the theatre where far more fundamental processes of thingification are orchestrated. It is submitted here that, in legal hermeneutics, the quality of being a thing is not merely affixed to auxiliary techniques but installed at the core of the interpretive scene itself: Both the object and the product of interpretation are awarded thingness. On the one hand, the text is instituted as a *corpus*, i.e. an inert, anonymous being-in-itself whose necessary material existence precedes and survives any speaking observer. The text is a body. It can be handled, weighed, collated. This gives the hermeneutic enterprise its raw materiality. On the other hand, the very meaning sought is configured as a thing in the thing, a self-signifying deposit presumed to reside within the textual body and to be extracted by a mechanism that cancels the interpreter's agency. The interpretive act is accordingly configured as a mechanism that extracts a thingly entity – meaning – from another thingly entity – the text. In this double operation, hermeneutics activates many of the discursive and epistemological effects of thingness. The meaning becomes mind-independent. It is in the text, a necessary being-in-the-world that exists irrespective of any particular interpreter's perception. To apprehend legal hermeneutics in this light is to see it not as a mere toolkit but as a factory of thingness, i.e. an apparatus that first manufactures both text and meaning as things and then validates its own operations by proclaiming that it has merely uncovered what was always already there.[32]

Similar thingification processes can be seen at work in the critical discourses. Even those that are most attentive to the performativity of law and the constituting force of legal discourse[33] are not spared by thingification. Indeed, when they set out to disclose hidden agendas, ideologies, structures, structural biases, patriarchy, phallo-centrism, imperialism, capitalism, managerial rationalities, or security logics, these discourses frequently install what they target as a thing in the thing: A hidden deposit presumed to inhabit the legal corpus and to work within it. The object of critique is thereby regularly endowed with thingness and treated as a necessary being-in-the-world whose existence does not depend on the speaking observer's perception. The very success of critique in identifying patterned recurrences and deep-seated regularities often hinges on granting its object the quality of thingness and installing it as a thing that works behind thingly law and thingly practices. Such thingification is particularly visible in Marxist critique of law where capitalism operates as a thing-without-a-witness that is produced or coded by law,[34] in feminist jurisprudence where patriarchy or phallo-centrism is sometimes cast as a deposit that speaks from within the doctrinal corpus and institutional routines,[35] in critical race scholarship when whiteness is treated as an inhering property that structures legal doctrine from the inside,[36] in postcolonial and Third World approaches to international law where imperialism is often configured as an interior thing that inhabits the legal concepts of sovereignty, development, trusteeship, and civilization,[37] in indeterminacy critique where indeterminacy functions as the name of the thingly interiority of a corpus that possesses a material, albeit undisciplined, plenitude,[38] and in critical histories of law that construe archives and old texts as ancestral bodies.[39]

It is important to point out that none of the scholars concerned imply that critics claim an external vantage point or that they deny their status as speaking observers. They do not deny discursivity. On the contrary, much of this scholarship explicitly acknowledges its embeddedness in language and in the very objects it studies. The point is different: In order to make their objects of critique intelligible and tractable, these scholars often confer upon them the attributes of thingness. Hidden agendas, ideologies, structures, structural biases, patriarchy, phallo-centrism, imperialism, capitalism, managerialism, security logics, algorithmic governance, and legal traditions are thereby installed as things that inhabit the legal corpus, as if their necessary existence preceded their articulation. This is how critique, in its most incisive operations, becomes a theatre where the objects it targets are thingified.[40]

A final observation is in order with a view to give this figure of thingification a bit more contour. It is of the utmost importance to insist that the attribution of thingness to law, to its doctrines, its rules, its practices, its critique, etc. does not extinguish interpretive life but rather cohabits with, and often intensifies, scenes of divergence and contestation. As argued in Chapter 1,[41] the speaking observer, albeit sidelined as to the existence of the thing, returns through quarrels over scope and consequences. In the context of the legal discourse, lawyers routinely install doctrines and practices as beings-in-themselves that can be relied upon as if they signified by themselves, but they do not cease to dispute what these beings say, what they contain, and what follows from them. In adjudication and scholarship, for instance, entire controversies revolve around whether the supposed self-signifying being has in fact been properly ascertained as such. Debates over sources and evidence are replete with conflicts about whether a rule, a doctrine, or a practice can credibly be exhibited as a being-in-itself or whether the dossier that purports to reveal it is the outcome of contestable curatorship. Far from signalling an end to interpretive debate, thingification sets the stage on which interpretation proliferates.

2. The State

This section discusses how law thingifies the State. The idea that the State comes with some thingly materiality is common.[42] The claim made here is more specific in that it is argued here that the thingness of the State is a product of law itself. The legal concept of State is even one of the most obvious figures of how law thingifies what it encounters. Such thingification is also one that is as crucial for law as the thingification of law which was discussed in the previous section. Indeed, when law thingifies the State, it simultaneously thingifies its object as well as its own foundation and origin. Said differently, the thingification of the State matters a great deal for law because the State is not merely an entity that law addresses but constitutes the framework that law presupposes as the condition of its own validity and operation. Law's thingification of the State should thus be considered as having two inseparable effects. First, it consolidates the object "State" by organizing offices, jurisdictions, procedures, and archives, thereby stabilizing the State as a legible, enduring thing. Second, it consolidates law's own foundations and origin by locating the sources, forms, and validity-conferring operations within that very institutional thing.

The coupling of law and the State, and the common idea that the State is the natural habitat of legality, are commonly traced back to the Gregorian Revolution in the 11th century whereby the centralization and systematization of canon law created a bureaucratic legal order grounding in law a state-like apparatus capable of generating, transmitting, and enforcing norms.[43] In doing so, canon law rendered the Church a durable corporate person, legible through names, offices, files, procedures, while staging that corporate body as the site and source of law's foundations.[44] It is since then that law and the State have been enjoying a deep kinship, one that manifests itself in the thingification of the latter by the former.

It is conspicuous that, across constitutional law and administrative law, legal discourse stages the State as a being-in-itself, independent of perception, such necessary materiality being continuously enacted in legal forms and institutional routines that thingify the State and its many facets. The result is a domestic scene in which the State presents itself as a necessary, prior, and thingly materiality. Constitutional law and administrative law can be seen as enabling a dense and extensive thingification of the State. Files, permits, registries, and chains of command enact the being-without-a-witness. The apparatus continues when any particular observer leaves the scene. Property registries are exemplary. When the cadastre records ownership, the State appears as an impersonal, continuing author of rights that exist irrespective of perception.[45] The routine of the registry and files is the very site where the State's self-effacing being is performed. The procedures that produce the State's presence vanish behind their outputs.

These patterns are amplified in international law, where the legal form condenses dispersed agency into an anthropomorphized being-in-itself that acts as one.[46] This is particularly tangible in the law of statehood which comes to be discussed and argued as if it were simply about the ascertainment of a pre-existing thing.[47] The Montevideo criteria – permanent population, defined territory, government, capacity to enter into relations with others – are routinely presented as describing a mind-independent State-thing. The Montevideo criteria are treated as descriptors and thresholds – population, territory, government, capacity – that organize perception to see the State as a composite object whose parts can be checked off, inspected, and then deemed to have coalesced into a thing.[48] Such thingly materiality awarded to the State and its components is reinforced by the mainstream understanding of the act of recognition, at least in mainstream approaches to the matter, which is not itself performative and constitutive of statehood but only declaratory of a pre-existing thingly reality.[49] From such a perspective, the State is said to exist prior to and independently of the speaking observer's recognition. Recognition is thus construed as a mirror raised to a pre-given materiality and is stripped of performativity.[50]

Another example of the thingification of the State by international law can be found in the rules related to the defence of territorial integrity and the inviolability of borders. In fact, such rules thingify statehood by treating territory as a self-standing, impermeable body whose integrity appears prior to, and outside, representation. In particular, the UN Charter's prohibition on the threat or use of force against the territorial integrity or political independence of any state[51] and its collective security framework[52] stabilize territory as a necessary substrate of State being.[53] Likewise, albeit from a radically different perspective, feminist critiques have compellingly shown how this doctrinal edifice about territorial integrity thingifies the State by erecting territory as an impenetrable male body, casting sovereignty as a masculinized protector whose hardened exterior secures an ostensibly vulnerable interior.[54] Thus, the legal veneration of territorial integrity naturalizes a corporeal metaphor (closure, inviolability, penetration) that projects borders as morally sacrosanct membranes and thereby consolidates the State's self-signifying materiality.[55]

The State is not the only institution that is being thingified by law. Law regularly attributes thingness to courts, parliaments, administrations, governments, and international organizations which it presents as necessary beings-in-the-world whose materiality imposes itself.[56] Yet, the discussion of how law thingifies the State that has been provided in this section suffices to capture how such production of institutional thingness by law operates.

A final observation is in order. It goes without saying that the idea of the State as a thing has been extensively contested in the literature. Many have shown that the State's apparent materiality is always produced. For instance, Herbert Marcuse argues that universals like "the Nation", "the State", "the Constitution", "the Party", present themselves as if they possessed necessary material existence independent of perception, representation, agency, and history, but this is the outcome of thingification rather than a material given.[57] The tangibility of such institutions arises because legal-administrative discourse formats, authorizes, and materializes them through texts of law and their consequences, appointments and salaries, imperatives, sanctions, procedures, and ultimately the infrastructures and weapons systems they command. In the same vein, Benedict Anderson has famously provided an account of the devices that make the nation-State imaginable as a pre-given entity by congealing abstraction into durable materialities that then appear original.[58] Together, these lines of critique show that the State's supposed necessary materiality is an achievement of discourses. The point made in this section is that law is one of these discourses at the service of producing the thingness of the State.

3. The people

Social contract theories have long rehearsed a scene in which a legal instrument constitutes the very community said to have authored it, staging an inaugural moment where the people are constituted as a being-in-itself by virtue of a pact that is at once presupposed and produced. It is submitted here that each of the canonical variants of the social contract[59] enacts the discursive operation that this book calls thingification: An act of speech and writing installs the people as being-without-a-witness by making the pact's signature and formulae the locus of a self-caused being. In the very moment of foundation, representation is annulled: The inaugural text is presented as if the people were already there. What appears as necessity is a discursive and epistemological montage through which thingness is conferred upon the people.[60]

Unsurprisingly, domestic constitutional law commonly institutionalizes this montage. It thingifies the people whose life it claims to organize and from whom it claims to emanate, presenting the constitutional text as both trace and cause of a necessary being-in-the-world. Indeed, the preamble "We the People" is staged as a self-signifying utterance that both speaks and installs the subject who speaks. Jacques Derrida's famous reflections on declarations of independence capture this montage with precision: The performative that declares independence does not simply record a pre-existing subject but produces, by signature and proclamation, that which it claims to represent. In other words, the signature of the representatives of the United States of America attests to a people that is not there before its attestation.

The performative "we declare" constitutes the "we", and the "we" retroactively authorizes the declaration, a circular temporality in which the origin is both presupposed and produced.[61]

Constitutional jurisprudence reinforces this annulment of representation by treating popular sovereignty as a self-caused being that repeats itself through elections, referenda, and amendments. Judicial invocations of the constituent body invariably present the people as an ancestral being, transmitting an essence from foundation to present, even though that essence is a doctrinal curation. The being-in-itself of the people is further staged by selective inclusion and exclusion that are then effaced as administration. The being-without-a-witness that the people appears to be is sustained by registries, censuses, and identity documents that function as archives which do not merely record but produce the object they enumerate, while hiding their productive force.[62] The representationlessness that constitutional discourse claims is a way of cancelling the role of language and naming in constituting the object.[63]

The creation of a thingly people by domestic law was also witnessed in States born of decolonization. During anti-colonial struggle, unity could be built around a single horizon, i.e. the fight against the colonizer. Once independence was attained, that unifying parameter disappeared, leaving newly independent States with the necessity to produce a people that could bear the weight of culture, language, history, and destiny. Clifford Geertz captures this predicament with acuity as he shows that the new States faced integrative revolutions, compelled to create national communities from deeply plural societies in which primordial attachments of kinship, language, region, and religion exerted powerful centrifugal force.[64] In this setting, constitutions, legal texts, flags, national anthems, and standardized languages functioned as self-signifying artefacts through which the State could posit a being-in-itself (the people) as if its materiality were given rather than produced. Homi Bhabha's account of nation narration similarly underscores how postcolonial nations are narrated into being through pedagogical and performative time, where repetition produces the impression of a self-caused people whose everyday practices are folded into a homogeneous national time.[65]

International law also provides an example of how law can constitute a thingly ancestral entity. This is particularly the case in relation to the right to self-determination of peoples. Here, "peoples" are posited as bearers of a right whose addressees are States, and whose realization is narrated as a process through which an abstract collective is installed as a being-in-itself. Crucially, and as is well known, the restrictive definition embedded in General Assembly Resolution 1541 (XV) on principles for determining when a territory is non-self-governing sharply delimited the remit of the thingly "people" contemplated by the Charter's decolonization regime. By tying the status of non-self-governing territory to concrete criteria – geographical separation and distinctness in ethnic and cultural characteristics – the Resolution shaped a narrow class of collectivities eligible to be treated as "peoples" for the purpose of decolonization, thereby stabilizing the category by reference to colonial administrative units.[66] The legal discourse thus posited the people as a presence without presence, but then immediately circumscribed which collectivities could inhabit that presence, effecting a self-effacing selection. The decolonization framework prioritized certain colonial territorial units over other claimants, reasserting that the "people" is a carefully designed construct within positive law.[67]

The foregoing should suffice to show the extent to which the preambles that refer to the people, the judgements that ventriloquize a collective will, the right to self-determination, the archive of censuses, and electoral rolls all are instruments of thingification. To recognize the discursive production of thingness is not to deny the efficacy of the people, but to re-situate the efficacy of such speech acts within the apparatuses that create their appearance as necessary beings-in-the-world. And the result is always the same: Interpretive controversies do not abate but they migrate. Debates over who is the people, who counts in referenda, whose voices are included in constituent assemblies, how narrowly Resolution 1541 should be construed in delimiting the remit of Charter-era self-determination, testify that thingness is not the end of interpretation but a condition for its multiplication. The very stability of the people is staged, contested, and restaged across the legal texts, rituals, doctrines, and archives that bestow thingness upon it, ensuring that the law's most central subjects remain simultaneously claimed as necessary and performed.

4. Sex

With an emphasis on international law, this section makes the claim that law has long served as a site where sex is stabilized as a being-in-itself, endowed with necessary material existence that appears to arise outside perception, outside representation, and outside contestation. I develop this claim in two steps. First, I draw on feminist theory – especially Judith Butler, along with intersectional and Marxist-feminist scholarship – that has shown how sex is materialized through heteronormative discourses and socio-economic organization. These authors do not use the language of thingification, but their analyses closely approach the argument here: That law renders sex a being-in-itself, a being-without-a-witness, by projecting a fixed, intelligible substance that seems to speak for itself.[68] Second, I turn to international legal instruments, principally the Convention on the Elimination of All Forms of Discrimination against Women (CEDAW), alongside regional instruments, to show how, through definitional choices, binary grammars, and programmatic techniques, law codifies sex as an already-known category and consolidates its thingness.

The starting point is the insight that sex is neither a purely biological datum nor a mere linguistic construction. Rather, sex acquires a sedimented materiality through regulatory norms, institutional practices, and technoscientific and economic apparatuses that produce bodies as intelligible matter. Judith Butler's account remains foundational. In *Bodies That Matter*, Butler argues that sex is materialized through the reiterative citation of regulatory ideals. The body's matter is not a pre-discursive substrate but the effect of norm-governed processes that exclude and abject what they cannot assimilate, securing the appearance of naturalness through repetition.[69] Earlier, in *Gender Trouble*, she had destabilized the sex/gender distinction by showing how the naturalness of sex is itself an effect of discourse.[70] Importantly for the argument here, Butler does not deny materiality. She relocates it. The matter of sex is not outside representation. It is condensed through social, legal, and epistemic practices that give sex its apparent solidity. This is precisely where the analysis nears the claim of thingification made here: Regulatory discourse produces a sexed body that looks like a self-standing thing – fixed, pre-given, and self-explanatory – thereby obscuring the witnessing labour, institutional scaffolds, and exclusions that materialize it.

Intersectional feminists sharpen this point by showing how sex is co-constituted with race, class, sexuality, disability, and migration status, such that the putative universal subject of "woman" is a normative projection that makes some lives legible and others peripheral. Kimberlé Crenshaw's classic interventions demonstrate how anti-discrimination frameworks presuppose a unitary subject and thereby miss compounded harms; the legal subject is stabilized through categorical silos that erase simultaneity and interdependence.[71] Shreya Atrey presses this further at the doctrinal level, showing how intersectional discrimination challenges the legal architecture that presumes fixed axes of identity and thus thingifies the subject it purports to protect.[72] These accounts make visible how the figure "woman" functions as a presence without presence: A universal placeholder whose content is supplied and policed by institutional sightlines and interpretive routines.

Marxist-feminist scholarship complements this point by situating sex in the circuits of social reproduction and capitalist accumulation. Silvia Federici's historical materialism traces how witch hunts, enclosure, and the disciplining of women's bodies were key to the production of a reproductive labour force. The sexed body is organized as a site of accumulation and control.[73] Nancy Fraser's analysis of "crisis of care" ties the gendered organization of social reproduction to political-economic regimes, showing how law and policy naturalize feminized care labour as a background condition, stabilized through familial and heteronormative norms.[74] In both accounts, sexed materiality appears as an effect of institutionalized relations (labour markets, welfare States, kinship regulations) that congeal difference into thingified divisions. Again, the argumentative arc approaches what this book means by thingification: Sex is rendered a thing-like substrate that grounds and justifies allocations of labour and dependency, even though it is actively produced by these arrangements.

Queer, trans, and intersex scholarship similarly uncovers how binary sex categories are stabilized and enforced by medico-legal techniques that present themselves as plain observation of pre-given facts. Anne Fausto-Sterling's work demonstrates the variability of sex characteristics and the role of bio-clinical protocols in policing the binary.[75] Dianne Otto's interventions within international law expose how treaty bodies and reporting practices gradually "read in" gender identity, yet do so within an inherited binary grammar that reaffirms the very distinctions under contestation.[76] Across these lines of inquiry, sex appears not as a passive referent but as an effect of classificatory labour (medical, bureaucratic, legal) that confers thingness by coding, measuring, and enforcing.

These theoretical strands converge on three propositions that are key for the argument here. First, that sex has material force. Second, that materiality is organized and condensed through discursive, institutional, and economic practices; and third, that the result is an object-like appearance (a self-signifying being) that occludes the practices of production and the voices of those whose lives do not fit the mould. This is thingification as is understood here. Again, the authors cited above do not claim that law literally turns sex into a physical object but they compellingly show how law participates in a metaphysics of presence, establishing sex as a being-in-itself that seems to pre-exist representation. The present claim extends that insight: Law's techniques of definition, categorization, measurement, and enforcement consolidate sex's thingness.

It is submitted here that the Convention on the Elimination of All Forms of Discrimination against Women (hereafter CEDAW) is the paradigmatic site where sex's thingness is organized and produced. The Convention centres "women" as the subject of protection against discrimination, defining discrimination "against women" and building obligations around that subject across public and private spheres.[77] Feminist international lawyers applauded the extension into the so-called private sphere and the challenge to formalist equality, yet they also warned that CEDAW presupposes a unitary, ostensibly universal category "women" and cements binary sex assumptions. Charlesworth, Chinkin, and Wright's canonical critique shows how the architecture of the treaty rests on a prior intelligibility of "woman" that is then protected, rather than problematized.[78] In a subsequent intervention, Charlesworth and Chinkin demonstrate how the remedy of anti-discrimination, while practically vital, risks reifying the categories it deploys when it presumes fixed subjects rather than interrogating the co-constitution of sex, gender, and hierarchies.[79]

The operative grammar of CEDAW simultaneously exemplifies a being-without-a-witness. Article 5(a) calls on States to modify "social and cultural patterns of conduct of men and women", thereby adopting "men" and "women" as binary givens to be rebalanced, rather than opening the question of how those categories are produced and policed.[80] Reporting practice has often treated sex as biological and binary, a lens that entrenches a particular intelligibility rather than making visible sex variance and non-binary embodiments. Protective provisions around maternity – temporary special measures under Article 4(2) and employment protections under Article 11(2) – have been criticized for reinscribing maternalism and biological essentialism, naturalizing reproductive roles as the axis of womanhood.[81] The point is not to deny the need for protections. It is to register the cost of a binary grammar that channels remedy through the very categories whose thingness is under critique. As Dianne Otto argues, expansionary interpretations that incorporate sexuality and gender identity remain constrained by a textual architecture that stabilizes sex difference as a primary, knowable referent.[82]

To its credit, the CEDAW Committee has developed interpretive guidance that moves beyond essentialism. General Recommendation No. 28 recognizes intersectionality and articulates core obligations under Article 2 that address structural discrimination.[83] General Recommendation No. 33 on access to justice and General Recommendation No. 35 on gender-based violence against women amplify attention to institutional barriers and structural harms.[84] Yet, as critics note, these interpretive moves continue to operate within a treaty architecture that posits "women" as a unitary subject and presupposes a binary epistemology, thereby perpetuating a metaphysics of self-signifying being that the Committee can only mitigate but not dissolve entirely.[85]

Parallel dynamics are visible in regional regimes. The Council of Europe's Istanbul Convention on preventing and combating violence against women and domestic violence is rightly celebrated for a robust due diligence framework – criminalization, protection orders, coordinated policies – yet its titular and textual centring of "women" and "domestic violence" risks marginalizing non-binary and transgender persons where implementation remains tied to narrow sex categories.[86] Critics also note a carceral tilt that can eclipse structural socio-economic measures, revealing how sexed harm is channelled into penal categories that consolidate a legible victim-perpetrator dyad, itself a technique of thingification that prioritizes what can be policed over what can be transformed.[87] The African Union's Maputo Protocol similarly extends protections and rights in vital ways while anchoring them in a binary subject that can narrow the horizon of intelligibility unless operationalized with intersectional attention.[88]

The structure of rights protection across these instruments also deploys managerial techniques (definitions, indicators, targets) that translate sexed lives into governable objects. State reporting under CEDAW, for instance, often relies on sex-disaggregated statistics, compliance checklists, and programmatic benchmarks that render visible only what is countable, thereby reinforcing a template of the sexed human as an administrative unit. The move from norm to metric is not a benign step. It is a materializing operation that gives sex the consistency of a thing by aligning protection with measurability. This is not an argument against data. It is rather a reminder that datafication selects and confirms a particular epistemology of sex, one in which being-in-itself coincides with what the apparatus can see.

This short overview of some of the main international legal instruments protecting women illustrates the extent to which law's treatment of sex as a pre-given referent installs a being-in-itself that appears to precede witnessing. The witness – the situated interpreter, the embodied subject whose life exceeds the template – is always displaced by a grammar that makes sex speak as if it were self-caused. Butler's materialization thesis, Crenshaw's intersectionality, Federici's and Fraser's accounts of social reproduction, Fausto-Sterling's bioclinical critique, and Otto's doctrinal interventions converge on a shared insight: Sex is material because it is made. International human rights law, when it defines, classifies, and enforces sex as an already-known category, does not merely reflect that making. It amplifies it. This corresponds precisely to what this book means by the legal production of thingness.

5. Race

With a similar emphasis on international legal instruments, this section makes the claim that law thingifies race, colour, and ethnic origin. This section draws on critical literature that interrogates race, colour, and ethnic origin, but does not distinguish systematically between these three concepts. For didactic reasons, it uses race as a generic term. The choice is didactic, for it allows the focus to remain on processes of ossification, fixation, and reification while acknowledging that these terms can diverge in meaning and operation across contexts and authors.[89]

At this preliminary stage, it should also be emphasized that the claim that race is constituted by discourse is obviously not new. Such a claim is at the very heart of the many existing rich critical histories of the concept of race, especially of those works that have shown that race has been produced by imperial technology in the Americas in the 16th century.[90] It is also a claim at the heart of the extensive critical literature that more specifically takes issue with how race has been ossified, reified, and fixed through discursive and epistemological operations across empire, capital, and governance.[91] Although it does not use the vocabulary of thingification, some of this literature must be mentioned here for it provides insightful groundwork for the claim made here about the thingification of race.

The part of such literature that grapples with reification, fixation, and ossification of race is of particular relevance here because it commonly takes as its starting point that race is commonly endowed with an unquestionable concreteness. Matthew Dimick underscores precisely this paradox by showing that constructionist accounts often mischaracterize a socially constituted category as if it were a self-sufficient natural thing, such that even careful social explanations silently harbour a residual thingness treated as necessary being.[92] Dimick does not use the vocabulary of thingification; nonetheless, his analysis comes close to the understanding developed here by clarifying how discursive practice confers the qualities of necessary being on race. Karen E Fields and Barbara J Fields extend this point by demonstrating that, although the biological non-correspondence of race has been amply established, discourse and institutional practices persist in treating race as a biological thing – an envelope, a membrane – thus sustaining a regime of signification that evacuates language by positing race as self-signifying, *hors langue*, outside representation.[93] They do not employ the term thingification either, but their argument is closely aligned with it: Social processes conjure race's necessary biological dimension at loggerheads with the scientific invalidation of biological race, reattaching race to bodies as if they were inherited, time-insensitive properties. The mechanism creates a discursive necessity: Race, as thing, imposes itself on the speaking observer as if mind-independent, and it comes to signify by itself and to cause itself.

Achille Mbembe's analysis of modern racial imagination is also germane for understanding how race functions as an outer casing that replaces being, life, and language, stratifying into a membrane and hardening into a shell. Mbembe does not use the concept of thingification, yet his claims converge with the question of thingification examined here. He traces how people of African origin are converted into living ore, extracted for value, and subjected to an economy of sensation, pointing to an ancestral being rendered commodity and to a self-effacing apparatus of extraction that leaves only the thing to appear. This is precisely how the envelope substitutes for being and language, and how race becomes self-signifying and self-caused, annihilating the sign, as if the signifier and signified had vanished and only the fixed corporeality remained.[94]

This critique of reification similarly resonates through early postcolonial thought. Frantz Fanon, for instance, dissected the moment of petrification when the Black subject is hailed, named, and ossified by the white gaze, a moment where a living, relational subject becomes a thing, reduced to an epidermal schema, a colour, a smell, a sum of sensations.[95] Fanon does not use the term thingification, but his analysis closely approaches it: The thingifying interpellation displaces the speaking observer and cancels language in the production of a self-signifying race. Stuart Hall, in describing race as a floating signifier, insists that it is not a biological property; yet he also shows how discourses fix and freeze race into administrative and cultural grids that purport merely to describe it.[96] Hall does not employ the vocabulary of thingness, but his account demonstrates how institutional practices turn fluid signification into fixed membranes for governance, thereby approximating the modes of being described here.

Compelling insights on the constitution of race by law can also be found in contemporary critical race theories even if they do not specifically engage with the thingification of race. Indeed, these scholarly works have shed light on the legal grammar that makes race become an administrable object – counted, reported, benchmarked – thus consolidating taxonomies, privileging state self-reporting and formal equality, depoliticizing structural and colonial racial orders, and channelling contestation into technocratic compliance metrics. For instance, David Theo Goldberg argues that modern liberal states manage race through law, statistics, and policy; race becomes a managerial object in the racial state, whose rationality requires classification, enumeration, and audit, making race self-signifying and self-caused – a datum that appears to naturalize itself through repeated cycles of reporting.[97] Goldberg does not use the concept of thingification, but his analysis aligns with it: Legal and bureaucratic practices confer on race the qualities of being-in-itself and self-signifying being. Charles W Mills situates international and domestic order within a racialized structure of domination; non-discrimination frames that proceed as if race were a discrete attribute risk reifying race as a property, eliding its relational and historical production.[98] Mills does not employ the vocabulary of thingness, yet his diagnosis converges with the idea that law conjures race's necessary existence as an object to which rights attach. Ian Hacking's notion of "making up people" explains how official categories co-produce the kinds they classify, initiating looping effects that stabilize identities as if they were self-caused beings; Hacking does not speak of thingification, but his account maps onto the self-caused and self-signifying modes of being central to this framework.[99]

The theoretical apparatus that has been provided by all the authors cited here now allows one to better appreciate thingification processes enabled by law, and especially by the International Convention on the Elimination of All Forms of Racial Discrimination (hereafter ICERD). Indeed, the Committee on the Elimination of All Forms of Racial Discrimination (hereafter CERD)'s General Recommendation No. 8 on identification provides, in substance, that the identification of persons as "belonging to a particular racial or ethnic group" shall be based on self-identification by the individual if different from the identification by others or by authorities, but in practice, the treaty body also relies on state census categories and administrative designations to monitor compliance.[100] The move is telling: Identity is promised as self-identification, yet governmental enumerations and reporting cycles stabilize the set of categories as if they were beings-in-themselves. General Recommendation No. 30 on discrimination against non-citizens normalizes status distinctions that are routinely racialized ("differential treatment based on citizenship or immigration status will constitute discrimination if the criteria for such differentiation... are not applied pursuant to a legitimate aim, and are not proportional to the achievement of this aim") but the operationalization of "non-citizen" as a protected slot thingifies alienage and national origin as administrative kinds.[101] Socio-legal studies of treaty-body practice – e.g. on indicators – show how state self-reporting, lists of issues, and General Recommendations transform lived relations into measurable objects, where "discrimination" becomes a checklist and identity a coded variable.[102] It has also been claimed that the CERD periodic review mechanism privileges state narrative; the Committee's concluding observations often request disaggregated data by race, ethnic origin, national origin, and citizenship status, thereby consolidating taxonomies whose repetition makes identity appear self-caused, ancestral, and *hors langue*, because the curatorial apparatus of data production is effaced in the name of necessary monitoring.[103]

These criticisms of ICERD and CERD are compelling and warrant great attention. They point to a legal grammar that stabilizes race as an administrable object, privileges formal equality, and depoliticizes structural and colonial orders that have produced the categories and the measures. Yet they do not strictly amount to criticisms of thingification. Their focus is primarily on managerialism, formalism, and depoliticization. Thingification by ICERD and related instruments goes even further. It is not only that the legal grammar consolidates categories. It is that the law makes race into a being-in-itself, a being-without-a-witness, a self-signifying being, a self-caused being, an ancestral being, and a self-effacing being. This means that CERD's discursive and epistemological operations attribute to race the qualities of necessary material existence independent of perception, representation, and language. Race, within this apparatus, appears as a presence without presence, a membrane that substitutes for life and for the speaking observer's relation to language, calcifying into a second epistemology. The legal category becomes the envelope, the audit and the report become the membrane, and the repetition of identification and disaggregation becomes the calcification. The apparatus that generates this effect – census, registry, administrative typology, indicator – dissolves into invisibility, leaving the thing to signify by itself, *hors langue*, as if it did not need the work of representation.

Additional illustrations of how ICERD thingifies race can be provided. Mention can be made of Article 1 that defines "racial discrimination" as "any distinction, exclusion, restriction or preference based on race, colour, descent, or national or ethnic origin" which has the purpose or effect of impairing the enjoyment of rights. This definitional clause appears modest, merely condemning behaviour. Yet its grammar presupposes, and thereby reproduces, the existence of race, colour, descent, and origin as stable attributes that can be identified and administered. Here again, the thingness is not asserted. It is performed. When CERD requests disaggregated data by "race, colour, national or ethnic origin", it demands that States supply the envelope within which persons are sorted.[104] In General Recommendation No. 8, the Committee asserts that "identification with a particular racial or ethnic group shall, if no justification exists to the contrary, be based upon self-identification by the individual concerned", yet immediately, the need to monitor progress and to ensure non-discrimination entails reliance on census categories, police files, immigration statuses, and administrative labels. The promise of self-identification does not eliminate the curatorial apparatus; rather, it presupposes it, codifies it, and makes it circulate, and as it circulates, identity becomes self-signifying: The category speaks for itself in the file, the table, the chart. The being-without-a-witness is here the disappearance of the speaking observer's relation to the subject; the category stands in place of language. In General Recommendation No. 30 on discrimination against non-citizens, the Committee speaks of "citizenship" and "immigration status" as bases for differential treatment that may constitute discrimination. But in the operationalization of "non-citizen", "foreigner", "alien", we encounter the ancestral being: National origin and alienage are treated as inherited, time-insensitive properties that attach to bodies and biographies, as if they were self-caused and independent of the political economy of borders, imperial histories, and mobility regimes.[105] Across these treaty-body practices, the repetition of identification and disaggregation reattaches race and origin to bodies, reinstating a biological dimension through the routines of measurement and enforcement.

At this stage, an important objection against the finding made in this section must be addressed. In fact, it could be asserted that ICERD does not thingify race but rather condemns discriminatory *behaviour*, leaving race un-thingified. In other words, behaviour thingifies, while ICERD de-thingifies by resisting and prohibiting. It must be acknowledged that such a reading of the Convention is not unwarranted. Yet, it is submitted here that the Convention's condemnation of behaviour continues to be articulated through a grammar that presupposes racial categories as pre-given classes. It must do so to make discrimination intelligible and justiciable. From such a perspective, behaviour is condemned by reference to things that are treated as necessary beings-in-the-world. The Convention's denunciation operates by inviting the speaking observer – the judge, the official, the monitor – to withdraw from representation and to let the category speak: Race appears as self-signifying, as the envelope that substitutes for life and language. The same goes for the apparatus that enforces the Convention – periodic reports, lists of issues, General Recommendations, country visits – which cannot avoid hiding the thingifying labour (census-making, category negotiation with communities, administrative standardization), leaving the thing's presence to appear independent of perception. The discursive necessity of enforcement accordingly produces thingness. Thus, the law participates in thingification not by directly asserting that race exists as a material entity, but by staging race as the necessary material yardstick through which discrimination is ascertained, monitored, and resisted.

A final observation is in order as to how the thingification of race compares to the thingification of sex that has been studied in the previous section. It is argued here that the thingification of race does not operate in the same way as the thingification of sex. In that respect, Judith Butler usefully cautions against analogical thinking: Power must be understood to work fundamentally differently with respect to racism, homophobia, and misogyny.[106] In the vocabulary adopted here, the modes of being produced by thingification – being-in-itself, being-without-a-witness, self-signifying being, self-caused being, ancestral being, self-effacing being – do not map identically across race and sex. The envelope of race substitutes for being in a manner that calcifies into a second epistemology whereas the discursive production of sex involves different materializations of the body, different relations to language, and different operations of performativity. In the racial register, the self-signifying thing demands silence and invisibility, a command bound to colonial policing of sight and voice. In the sex register, performativity works by reiteration of norms that materialize bodies in and through language, making representation and citation central to the production of what appears as naturalized sex. Race's ancestral being is tethered to blood, origin, descent, and nationality; sex's ancestral being, insofar as it is produced, operates through genealogies of kinship and reproduction that are differently legalized. The legal grammar of anti-discrimination law, in enumerating protected grounds, tends to analogize race and sex as listable objects but the discursive and epistemological production of thingness differs.

6. Nature

The present section argues that law thingifies nature, the environment, Earth, and the planet. Here too, for didactic reasons, it uses nature as a generic term and does not distinguish systematically between nature, the environment, Earth, and the planet. To appreciate how law has come to thingify nature, one must briefly return to social contract imaginaries that provided the first systematized exteriorization and stabilization of nature. In that respect, Michel Serres argues that the idea of social contract excluded nature from the circle of obligation, relegating it to a background against which the human negotiates rights and property, thereby prefiguring legal architectures that treat Earth as an inert estate and the environment as a governable surround.[107] Bruno Latour's critique of modern thought similarly shows how nature is made the realm of mute objects subject to impersonal laws while culture is construed as the sphere of subjects, meanings, and politics.[108] Isabelle Stengers deepens such projection by tracing how nature is now usually invoked as an authoritative outside that silences divergent modes of relating and knowing, thereby disciplining nature into a field of expert administration.[109] For all such thinkers, social contract imaginaries and modern thought have construed nature as an exterior domain that is stabilized as if it possesses a necessary materiality that precedes and exceeds witnessing, representation, and politics.[110]

Externalization of nature, as demonstrated by the abovementioned thinkers, locates it outside the human and, thus, outside law. Yet, it is argued here that law not only sustains such externalization, but also further isolates nature from perception, language, representation, and agency. Indeed, according to the argument made here, law always stabilizes nature as an administrable substrate that is divisible, scalable, and measurable as if it constituted a self-signifying, self-caused, and ancestral being that is independent of representation.[111]

Domestic environmental statutes illustrate how nature becomes self-signifying through the work of law. The United States Clean Air Act defines air pollutants, sets national ambient air quality standards, and establishes compliance mechanisms that render air a measurable object whose legal existence is tied to codified thresholds.[112] The environment here appears as a being-in-itself that persists beyond witness, for the legal identity of ambient air is authenticated by the metric that measures it. Environmental impact assessment regimes similarly translate nature into quantified harms and mitigations, thereby turning nature into a self-signifying entity through thresholds and matrices.[113]

Biodiversity law similarly approaches nature through lists and targets. The Convention on Biological Diversity defines biological diversity and mandates national strategies, with the Aichi Targets and the Kunming–Montreal Global Biodiversity Framework translating nature into coverage percentages and outcome indicators.[114] In this rendering, nature becomes a self-effacing being as the apparatus of mapping, criteria, and negotiation withdraws behind the percentage that appears to speak for nature. Species protection regimes such as the Convention on International Trade in Endangered Species of Wild Fauna and Flora similarly convert negotiated science into legal listings that function as self-signifying facts. Indeed, appendix status appears to mirror biological status.[115] Water law similarly renders nature as made of divisible flows and entitlements. The United Nations Convention on the Law of the Non-Navigational Uses of International Watercourses, for instance, codifies principles of equitable and reasonable use and no significant harm that translate river basins into allocable units, presenting hydrological cycles as beings-in-themselves that signify distribution through the very metrics that partition them.[116]

Mention must also be made here of international climate law which scales the planet as a legally governable geobody. In fact, the United Nations Framework Convention on Climate Change initiates a legal grammar that invites planetary metrication.[117] The Paris Agreement particularly codifies a global temperature goal along with cycles of nationally determined contributions and monitoring, reporting, and verification systems.[118] The planet simultaneously appears to enunciate a limit – although the latter is a negotiated artefact co-produced by science, justice claims, and legal compromise.[119] Carbon accounting systems under the Paris Agreement framework similarly translate emissions into commensurable units, consolidating the environment as an administrable substrate and Earth as a self-caused being whose natural sinks and sources are treated as ontic givens rather than representational constructs.[120]

It must be emphasized that such legal thingification of nature is not unqualified. Indeed, recent invocations of the rights of nature possibly denote a counter-gesture that interrupts such legal thingification processes. For instance, Ecuador's 2008 Constitution recognizes the rights of nature to exist, persist, maintain, and regenerate its vital cycles.[121] Jurisprudence such as Los Cedros enjoined mining concessions by grounding standing and substantive review in nature's own rights, foregrounding a relational epistemology that situates the forest not as an object but as a subject whose degradation is cognizable as a rights violation.[122] Colombia's Constitutional Court has recognized the Atrato River as a subject of rights with guardianship structures combining state and community representatives.[123] It must be acknowledged that the justificatory grammars in these experiments challenge the self-effacing invisibility of the abovementioned legal thingification processes by explicitly naming guardianship, tikanga, and community witness as constitutive of legal being. Instead of a being-without-a-witness, nature is accordingly re-situated as a being-with-witness, with procedures that reinscribe representation and testimony at the heart of legality. Indigenous scholarship further anchors this turn as it shows that relational ontologies in which Earth and the planet are kin or ancestor confound the nature/culture divide and resist the purification that underwrites thingification.[124] Earth jurisprudence and wild law theorists similarly advocate a reorientation of legal subjectivity and obligation toward Earth community.[125] Insofar as they reinstall a witness, foreground relational ontologies that disallow the purification of nature and culture, and shift the referent of law from an object to a subject in relation, the allocation of rights to nature can be read as interrupting thingification.

It remains that the externalization of nature – long diagnosed by critiques of the social contract theories and modern thought – continues to be furthered by the legal thingification of nature that is enabled by the abovementioned contemporary legal instruments through categories, metrics, and compliance. The debate on the rights of nature simply shows that countermoves are possible, but their capacity to de-thingify depends on whether they actually reinstall witness, maintain revisability, and refuse the self-effacing erasure of thingness.

7. Culture

Law does not only thingify nature. It also thingifies what modern epistemologies commonly oppose to nature, namely culture, conferring upon it thingness and positing it as a necessary being-in-the-world that appears mind-independent.[126] It must be acknowledged right away that the idea that culture is given some materiality through discursive and institutional processes is far from being unheard of. Indeed, even in orthodox strands of modern thought, culture is commonly construed as having been invented, selected, and staged, often by the modern nation-State anxious to give itself a body and a foundation that appear anterior to politics. Mainstream and critical literatures converge on this point. For instance, Benedict Anderson shows how imagined communities are produced through print-capitalism, bureaucratic routines, and commemorative practices that conjure a sense of shared culture as if it were primordial.[127] For their part, Eric Hobsbawm and Terence Ranger famously document how traditions that appear ancient are frequently invented to provide cultural continuity for modern polities.[128] The same goes for Walter Mignolo's demonstration of how non-European primitive traditions were objectified by the colonizers so as to be located in a remote backward time in order to ensure that European epistemology remains the locus of enunciation of knowledge.[129] Mention can also be made of Clifford Geertz's interpretive anthropology that treats culture as webs of significance spun by humans, always interpretive and contested, never simply given.[130] Postcolonial and decolonial critiques likewise emphasize that culture is invented within imperial and colonial apparatuses. For instance, Frantz Fanon exposes the colonial imposition and reification of "native culture" in the service of domination.[131] Edward Said similarly demonstrates how "oriental culture" is produced as an object of knowledge by colonial discourse.[132]

The thingification of culture by law, which is examined in this section, carries a further, specific effect not captured by the abovementioned recurrent recognitions that culture is given materiality by discursive and institutional processes. The difference lies in the fact that the legal attribution of thingness permits culture to be presented as a unified, coherent whole. The impression of unity is a discursive achievement of thingification. By installing culture as a self-signifying corpus, law suppresses internal heterogeneity, dissent, and contradiction, arranging signs and practices into an apparently seamless totality. Legal discourse on culture makes this unity appear mind-independent and prior to the speaking observer. Indeed, as will be illustrated in the following paragraphs, constitutional preambles, heritage statutes, minority-protection clauses, and cultural-exception doctrines turn multiplicity into objects whose alleged coherence then polices authenticity, fidelity, and tradition rather than exposing composite, contested production.

It must be conceded that such a thingifying role of law has already been noted in the literature. For instance, Louis Althusser's theory of *Ideological State Apparatuses* helps explain how school, media, and law interpellate subjects into a national culture that appears to signify itself.[133] Likewise, John R Searle's account of institutional facts clarifies how declarations (including legal acts) create social objects and convert practices into unitary cultures.[134] In the same vein, Stuart Hall shows that legal regimes fix culture in lists and definitions, transform a dynamic field into a coherent thing whose boundaries are treated as self-evident while erasing hybridity and internal difference.[135]

While the thingification of culture by law has already been studied in the literature, it remains relevant to provide some concrete examples here. Within domestic law, the thingification of culture is both overt and subtle. Constitutions commonly refer to "national culture", "heritage", "tradition", and "civilization" as foundational sources of identity and authority, thereby installing culture as a self-signifying being that appears to authorize law rather than to be authorized by it. The preamble often becomes the theatre of an ancestral being: A narrative of origins that transmits an essence forward in time, stabilizing culture as a necessary, mind-independent corpus that stands outside perception and representation. Spain's Constitution declares that public authorities shall "promote and safeguard Spain's cultural heritage",[136] and creates a regime of *bienes de interés* cultural where listing confers objective status and triggers duties of preservation.[137] France's *Code du patrimoine* constructs national treasures and imposes export controls that presuppose a cultural corpus belonging to the nation beyond the speaking observer's contestation.[138]

International law pursues this process by universalizing particular images of culture and giving them legal fixity. The Constitution of UNESCO charges the organization with contributing to peace and security by promoting collaboration among nations through education, science, and culture, grounded in the belief that "since wars begin in the minds of men, it is in the minds of men that the defences of peace must be constructed".[139] Culture thereby becomes an object that can be inventoried, exchanged, and elevated so that peace may ensue. On the one hand, UNESCO's emphasis on cultural diversity and the free flow of ideas gestures toward culture as created, shared, and debated; on the other, its programming and standard-setting stabilize culture as a corpus to be listed, safeguarded, and transmitted, conferring upon culture the attributes of being-in-itself and an ancestral being. The 1954 Convention for the Protection of Cultural Property in the Event of Armed Conflict defines "cultural property" as property of great importance to the cultural heritage of every people and mandates respect and protection.[140] Here, culture is transmuted into a protected matter that exists apart from the multiplicity of practices and interpretations: A self-signifying being whose importance appears intrinsic, even though its qualification as "of great importance" is the product of expert and diplomatic determination. The Blue Shield emblem and special protection regimes instantiate self-effacing being: The marks and manuals promise neutrality, while the classificatory criteria and geopolitical hierarchies behind listing and protection are displaced from view.[141]

The 1970 UNESCO Convention on the Means of Prohibiting and Preventing the Illicit Import, Export and Transfer of Ownership of Cultural Property similarly frames culture as national patrimony whose integrity must be preserved by States.[142] By defining categories of protected cultural property and empowering restitution, the Convention consolidates culture as a sovereign object, i.e. a being-without-a-witness that belongs to a body politic independently of the speaking observers whose practices made these objects significant.[143] The 1972 Convention concerning the Protection of the World Cultural and Natural Heritage advances a catalogue of outstanding universal value (hereafter OUV), codified through the World Heritage List.[144] OUV functions as a self-signifying reason: Once inscribed, a site's value appears as a presence without presence – self-evident, mind-independent – while the dossiers, expert missions, and committee politics that authored its value are turned into a self-effacing background.[145] Repetition across periodic reporting and reactive monitoring yields self-caused being. Each cycle reenacts the site's OUV, making the category seem to cause itself by repetition.

The 2003 Convention for the Safeguarding of the Intangible Cultural Heritage (hereafter ICH) could be construed as resisting the thingification of culture by shifting attention from objects to practices, representations, expressions, knowledge, and skills recognized by communities.[146] Yet the ICH regime also produces a thingly necessity. Indeed, once a practice is nominated and inscribed on the Representative List or the List in Need of Urgent Safeguarding, it acquires a stabilized identity, an authorized description, and a safeguarding plan. What was fluid and improvisational becomes a definitional corpus with guardians, often redirected towards staged performances to satisfy listing criteria and tourism economies.[147] The community is cast as custodian of a tradition that must be preserved rather than as author of ongoing reinterpretation. The idiom of "transmission from generation to generation" further installs ancestral being, while inscription imparts self-signifying being. The element constitutes heritage because it is inscribed as such. The Operational Directives and expert bodies that filter nominations operate as self-effacing beings. In fact, the curatorial apparatus disappears behind community consent and universal recognition.[148] The 2005 Convention on the Protection and Promotion of the Diversity of Cultural Expressions supplements this architecture by affirming States' rights to adopt measures to protect and promote cultural expressions.[149] Diversity becomes a policy object whose safeguarding is assumed to preserve pluralism; yet diversity, once codified, functions as a self-signifying index that can conceal the selection of which expressions count and which do not, particularly in interaction with trade and intellectual property regimes.[150]

The foregoing should suffice to show that international cultural heritage law installs culture as a being-in-itself by presenting cultural value as mind-independent, prior to perception and judgement. It enthrones culture as being-without-a-witness by withdrawing the speaking observer (the communities, critics, practitioners) and substituting committees, criteria, and lists that purport to register what is already there. It treats culture as a self-signifying being. Labels like OUV, ICH elements, national treasures, and patrimony operate as reasons that require no further mediation. It produces culture as a self-caused being. Repetition across treaties, listings, and jurisprudence generates the impression that cultural value is self-generating, as the same categories iterate and confirm themselves. It constructs culture as an ancestral being. Invocations of tradition, transmission, and authenticity supply a lineage that confers necessity, i.e. what must be preserved because it comes from before.[151] And it masks the curatorial labour through self-effacing being: The classificatory labour, expert adjudications, and bureaucratic routines vanish behind the narrative of universality.[152]

Obviously, and to return to the consideration made at the start of this section, such stabilization and fixation of culture are profoundly anti-modern in the sense that it repudiates a core commitment of modern critical thought, i.e. that culture is a practice of signification authored by human beings within history, not a thing-in-itself. This is precisely what Clifford Geertz objects to when he criticizes social sciences for handling culture as if it were an entity in itself, reified and law-like, rather than webs of significance to be interpreted.[153] Such objection, however, is not limited to the thingification of culture but applies to all those legal thingification processes that have been examined in this chapter.

8. Concluding remarks: A thingifying apparatus of outstanding discursive efficacy

This chapter has argued that law continuously taps into the simplicity and efficacy provided by thingness. It has shown the dramatic extent to which law thingifies itself and thingifies what it addresses: The State, the people, sex, race, nature, and culture. The foregoing has further shown that thingifying what it encounters is not a contingent habit of legal discourse but is at the heart of how law does its work. One could even say that law is a large thingifying apparatus, perhaps the most accomplished of all, one that turns representations into thingly entities bearing the stamp of necessary being. The ambition of the chapter has not been to produce a catalogue of things produced by the legal discourse but to shed light on some fragments of discursive operations through which law converts representations into entities that present themselves as being-in-themselves, anterior to perception, outside representation, self-caused, ancestral, and self-effacing. From such perspective, law emerges both as an artisan and a beneficiary of thingness. It makes the things that are, and in the same gesture, makes their being appear pre- and extra-discursive, relocating dissent from the question of existence to peripheral matters of application and scope. The result is the juxtaposition of two regimes of prescription, namely law's primary corpus of do's and don'ts and law's imperative of acknowledgement in which the "is" has become "a must be".[154]

Law's extensive tapping into thingness and thingification should not be a surprise. Short of thingifying itself and what it encounters, law would be deprived of its efficacy and reduced to an ethereal discourse floating without purchase on the world it seeks to address. Thingness grants law its grip. It is the means by which legal utterance ties itself to what it posits as necessary, grounding itself by first making a ground. One could even say that thingness is a condition of legal force. It is what allows the latter to ground itself in the world and intervene therein. Contingency is displaced and law can go on doing what it does. For law, the attraction of thingness also lies in its simplicity. It offers an easy epistemic shortcut by which law can lay hold of the world. Without much effort, thingness economizes disagreement and produces the impression that law intervenes in a world of stable entities that are outside representation.

The finding about law's extensive resort to thingness is surely not groundbreaking, although it is being expressed here through a novel conceptual apparatus. Indeed, the discursive move examined in this chapter had already been lucidly observed in Bruno Latour's study of the *Conseil d'État* where he emphasizes that lawyers always begin to speak by transforming the world into a set of inscriptions, that is, into files amenable to handling. In other words, before any legal intervention, the world is made legible and that legibility is immediately recast as necessity. From such a perspective, law's thingifying apparatus whose fragments have been examined in this chapter can thus also be construed as an inscription apparatus: The necessary being of the legal object is the afterlife of law's scriptural labour that effaces its own performativity beneath the object's self-signification.[155]

This chapter has aimed to shed light on some key figures of law's thingification processes. The examination provided here lays the groundwork for the more ambitious endeavour pursued in the rest of this book. Because legal thought and practice are marked by extensive recourse to thingification processes, the grammar thereof must be further scrutinized. This is what the next chapter will do. I will show that, even if law is both artisan and beneficiary of thingness, such discursive move can echo darker ways of thinking. Indeed, the simplicity, the foreclosure of the speaking observer, the internalization of causality, the installation of lineage, and the effacement of productive labour can resonate with authoritarian epistemologies that privilege inevitability over contingency and unanimity over dissent. The next chapter directly confronts this resonance. What follows particularly interrogates the shadows that accompany thingness. Law's extensive use of thingification, if left unscrutinized, can reproduce the very closures that authoritarian knowledge entails.

Notes

1 For a very opposite understanding of law, one which construes law as being articulated around dematerialized and dephysicalized ideas, see Margaret Davies, *Law Unlimited: Materialism, Pluralism, and Legal Theory* (Routledge 2017) 30.

2 The claim that law commonly thingifies an outside and creates a "false concrete" around itself is not new. See Peter Gabel, 'Reification in Legal Reasoning' (1980) 3 *Research in Law and Sociology* 25, 27 (who speaks of reification rather

than thingification). See also Susan Marks, 'Introduction' in Susan Marks (ed), *International Law on the Left: Re-examining Marxist Legacies* (CUP 2008) 1, 6 and 14.

3 Roland Barthes, *Le Neutre: Cours au Collège de France, 1977–1978* (Seuil 2023).

4 Ibid 57.

5 See supra ch 1.

6 This will be the object of a subsequent chapter. See ch 6.

7 JL Austin, *How to Do Things with Words* (OUP 1962) lectures I–V; John R Searle, *The Construction of Social Reality* (Free Press 1995) chs 1–3. See also Peter L Berger and Thomas Luckmann, *The Social Construction of Reality: A Treatise in the Sociology of Knowledge* (Penguin 1967).

8 Pierre Bourdieu, 'The Force of Law: Toward a Sociology of the Juridical Field' (1987) 38 *Hastings Law Journal* 814–53; Bruno Latour, *The Making of Law: An Ethnography of the Conseil d'État* (Polity 2010) chs 1–3.

9 Cornelia Vismann, *Files: Law and Media Technology* (Stanford UP 2008) chs 1–2; Alain Pottage and Martha Mundy (eds), *Law, Anthropology, and the Constitution of the Social: Making Persons and Things* (CUP 2004); Robert Cover, 'Nomos and Narrative' (1983) 97 *Harvard Law Review* 4–68.

10 On the performativity of international law, see Frédéric Mégret, 'Is International Law Addressing Problems of its Own Making?' in David Lefkowitz and Andreas Follesdal (eds), *Philosophy and International Law: Contestations and Extensions* (forthcoming); Jean d'Aspremont, 'A Worldly Law in a Legal World' in Andrea Bianchi and Moshe Hirsch (eds), *International Law's Invisible Frames: Social Cognition and Knowledge Production in International Legal Processes* (OUP 2021) 110–23; Janis Grzybowski and Martti Koskenniemi, 'International Law and Statehood: A Performative View' in Robert Schuett and Peter MR Stirk (eds), *The Concept of the State in International Relations: Philosophy, Sovereignty and Cosmopolitanism* (Edinburgh UP 2015) 23–47; D Van Den Meerssche, 'International Organizations and the Performativity of Measuring States: Discipline through Diagnosis' (2018) 15(1) *International Organizations Law Review* 168–201.

11 For two famous examples, see HLA Hart, *The Concept of Law* (2nd edn, OUP 1994); Ronald Dworkin, *Law's Empire* (Harvard UP 1986).

12 On debates about the nature of international law, see Miodrag A Jovanović, *The Nature of International Law* (CUP 2019); David Armstrong, Theo Farrell and Hélène Lambert, 'The Nature of International Law' in David Armstrong, Theo Farrell and Hélène Lambert, *International Law and International Relations* (2nd edn, CUP 2012) 9–37; Anna Södersten and Dennis Patterson, 'The Nature of International Law' in Dennis Patterson and Anna Södersten (eds), *A Companion to European Union Law and International Law* (John Wiley & Sons 2016) 16–25; Daniel Bethlehem, 'The End of Geography: The Changing Nature of the International System and the Challenge to International Law' (2014) 25 *European Journal of International Law* 9; Hugh Thirlway, 'The Nature of International Law and the Concept of "Sources"' in Hugh Thirlway, *The Sources of International Law* (2nd edn, OUP 2019); Philip Allott, 'Language, Method and the Nature of International Law' (1971) 45 *British Yearbook of International Law* 79; WW Willoughby, 'The Legal Nature of International Law' (1908) 2 *American Journal of International Law* 357.

13 See Susan Marks, 'Introduction' in Susan Marks (ed), *International Law on the Left: Re-examining Marxist Legacies* (CUP 2008) 1, 6.

14 HLA Hart, *The Concept of Law* (2nd edn, OUP 1994).

15 See eg Frederick Schauer, *Playing by the Rules* (OUP 1991).
16 John Henry Merryman, *The Civil Law Tradition* (3rd edn, Stanford UP 2007) ch 5; Franz Wieacker, *A History of Private Law in Europe* (OUP 1995) ch 8.
17 American Law Institute, *Restatement (Second) of Contracts* (1981).
18 There are, of course, huge jurisprudential problems with the idea of "rule-ness" or "rulism". See generally Cass R Sunstein, *Legal Reasoning and Political Conflict* (OUP 1996) 130–35. In particular, the "rule-ness" of the "rule of recognition" is contested. See Frederick Schauer, *Playing by the Rules* (Clarendon Press 1991) 199; see also Frederick Schauer, 'Amending the Presuppositions of a Constitution' in Sanford Levinson (ed), *Responding to Imperfection: The Theory and Practice of Constitutional Amendment* (Princeton Press 1995) 145, 150–51; Frederick Schauer, 'Is the Rule of Recognition a Rule?' (2012) 3(2) *Transnational Legal Theory* 1; AWB Simpson, 'The Common Law and Legal Theory' in AWB Simpson (ed), *Oxford Essays in Jurisprudence* (OUP 1973) 77.
The authority or "rule-ness" of the constraints on interpretation is equally contested. If construed as rules by mainstream international legal scholarship, such constraints on content-determination interpretation correspond to what Owen Fiss calls "disciplining rules": see Owen M Fiss, 'Objectivity and Interpretation' (1982) 34 *Stanford Law Review* 739. See contra Stanley Fish, 'Fish v Fiss' (1984) 36 *Stanford Law Review* 1325, 1336. See also George Letsas, 'Strasbourg's Interpretive Ethic: Lessons for the International Lawyer' (2010) 21 *European Journal of International Law* 509, 534; Fuad Zarbiyev, *Le discours interprétatif en droit international contemporain* (Pedone 2015) 28–35; Andrea Bianchi, 'The Game of Interpretation in International Law: The Players, the Cards, and Why the Game is Worth the Candle' in Andrea Bianchi, Daniel Peat and Matthew Windsor (eds), *Interpretation in International Law* (OUP 2015) 34–57, 35–36. The debate about rulist thinking is not limited to legal scholarship and includes all the humanities. See, for example, the use of the idea of rules by Michel Foucault: Michel Foucault, *Naissance de la biopolitique: Cours au Collège de France (1978–1979)* (Gallimard/Seuil 2004) 37. On the imperialistic dimension of rulist thinking, see China Miéville, *Between Equal Rights: A Marxist Theory of International Law* (Pluto Press 2005) 66–74, 318–19.
19 I have discussed all these instances of rulism elsewhere. See Jean d'Aspremont, *International Law as a Belief System* (CUP 2017) 56.
20 Joseph Raz, *Practical Reason and Norms* (2nd edn, OUP 1999) ch 1; Andrei Marmor, *Social Conventions* (Princeton UP 2009) ch 6.
21 E Allan Farnsworth, *Farnsworth on Contracts* (4th edn, Wolters Kluwer 2019) §§ 3.1–3.7.
22 Neil MacCormick, *Institutions of Law* (OUP 2007) chs 1–3.
23 I have studied this elsewhere. See Jean d'Aspremont, *International Law as a Belief System* (CUP 2017).
24 On the distinction between thingification and naturalization, see ch 1, s 3.2.
25 See International Law Commission, *Identification of Customary International Law, with Commentaries* (2018).
26 This claim about the thingification of customary international law in international legal thought and practice would have deserved to be inserted and fully developed in my study of the patterns of thought at work in the discourse about customary international law. Yet, this is a thought that had not yet matured at the time of my work on customary international law. See Jean d'Aspremont, *The Discourse on Customary International Law* (OUP 2021).
27 Vienna Convention on the Law of Treaties (adopted 23 May 1969, entered into force 27 January 1980) 1155 UNTS 331 (VCLT) arts 10–16, 31–33.

28 *Aegean Sea Continental Shelf* (Greece v Turkey) (Judgement) [1978] ICJ Rep 3, para 96; Kal Raustiala, 'Form and Substance in International Agreements' (2005) 99 *American Journal of International Law* 581; Duncan Hollis, 'Why State Consent Still Matters: Non-State Actors, Treaties, and the Changing Sources of International Law' (2005) 23 *Berkeley Journal of International Law* 1; Jean d'Aspremont, 'Bindingness' in Jean d'Aspremont and Sahib Singh (eds), *Concepts for International Law: Contributions to Disciplinary Thought* (Edward Elgar 2019) 67–82. See also Jean d'Aspremont, 'Current Theorizations About the Treaty' in DB Hollis (ed), *The Oxford Guide to Treaties* (OUP 2020) 46–58. For indicators used to build this *animus*, see Anthony Aust, *Modern Treaty Law and Practice* (CUP 2007) 33–37; Jan Klabbers, *The Concept of Treaty in International Law* (Kluwer 1996) 68–89; Oscar Schachter, 'The Twilight Existence of Nonbinding International Agreements' (1977) 71 *American Journal of International Law* 296–304, 296–97.

29 International Law Commission, 'Draft Conclusions on Identification of Customary International Law' (2018) *Yearbook of the International Law Commission* vol II, pt 2, conclusion 6; *Delimitation of the Marine Boundary in the Gulf of Maine Area* (Canada v United States of America) (Judgement) [1984] ICJ Rep 246, 269 para 111 ("A body of detailed rules is not to be looked for in customary international law which in fact comprises a limited set of norms for ensuring the co-existence and vital co-operation of the members of the international community, together with a set of customary rules whose presence in the opinio juris of States can be tested by induction based on the analysis of a sufficiently extensive and convincing practice, and not by deduction from preconceived ideas").

30 For some critical thoughts on the notion of practice constitutive of customary international law, see Jean d'Aspremont, *The Discourse on Customary International Law* (OUP 2021).

31 International Law Commission, *Draft Conclusions on Subsequent Agreements and Subsequent Practice in Relation to the Interpretation of Treaties, with Commentaries* (2018) conclusion 4.

32 It has been argued that the Christian hermeneutical tradition provides the decisive ancestry of traditional hermeneutics when it comes to treating its textual authorities as a corpus juris and to extracting a thingly deposit from that parent body. This logic has arguably passed into later civil and common law hermeneutics. See Pierre Legendre, *L'Amour du Censeur: Essai sur l'ordre dogmatique* (Seuil 2005) 80–98; Pierre Legendre, *L'empire de la vérité: Introduction aux espaces dogmatiques industriels* (Fayard 1983) ch I; Pierre Legendre, *Leçons VI: La fabrique de l'homme occidental* (Fayard 1996) ch 2.

33 For an overview of that stream of the international legal literature, see Fleur Johns, 'Critical International Legal Theory' in JL Dunoff and MA Pollack (eds), *International Legal Theory: Foundations and Frontiers* (CUP 2022) 3, 133; BS Chimni, 'New Approaches to International Law: The Critical Scholarship of David Kennedy and Martti Koskenniemi' in *International Law and World Order: A Critique of Contemporary Approaches* (CUP 2017) 246–357; José María Beneyto and David Kennedy, *New Approaches to International Law: The European and the American Experiences* (Springer 2013); David W Kennedy, 'A New Stream of International Law Scholarship' (1988) 7 *Wisconsin International Law Journal* 1; DZ Cass, 'Navigating the Newstream: Recent Critical Scholarship in International Law' (1996) 65 *Nordic Journal of International Law* 341–84.

34 Evgeny B Pashukanis, *The General Theory of Law and Marxism* (Barbara Einhorn tr, Transaction 2002) ch 2; Louis Althusser, *Pour Marx* (La Découverte

1996) 227–49 and 253–58 (first published 1965); Katerina Pistor, *The Code of Capital* (Princeton UP 2019); Jacques Rancière, *La Leçon d'Althusser* (La Fabrique 2011) 154–57.

35 Catharine A MacKinnon, *Toward a Feminist Theory of the State* (Harvard UP 1989) ch 8; Carol Smart, *Feminism and the Power of Law* (Routledge 1989) ch 1.

36 Cheryl I Harris, 'Whiteness as Property' (1993) 106 *Harvard Law Review* 1707, 1713–23; Kimberlé Williams Crenshaw, 'Race, Reform, and Retrenchment: Transformation and Legitimation in Antidiscrimination Law' (1988) 101 *Harvard Law Review* 1331, 1376–86.

37 Antony Anghie, *Imperialism, Sovereignty and the Making of International Law* (CUP 2005) chs 1–2; Sundhya Pahuja, *Decolonising International Law: Development, Economic Growth and the Politics of Universality* (CUP 2011) chs 1–2.

38 Duncan Kennedy, 'Form and Substance in Private Law Adjudication' (1976) 89 *Harvard Law Review* 1685, 1741–51; Mark Tushnet, 'Defending the Indeterminacy Thesis' (1996) 16 *Quinnipiac Law Review* 339, 343–51; Roberto Mangabeira Unger, *The Critical Legal Studies Movement* (Harvard UP 1986) ch 1.

39 Martti Koskenniemi, *The Gentle Civilizer of Nations: The Rise and Fall of International Law 1870–1960* (CUP 2001).

40 On the idea that some minimal materiality is necessary for critique to do its job, see ch 6.

41 See ch 1, s 1.2.

42 For some remarks on how the State is thought of as a machine, see Jacques Rancière, *La mésentente: Politique et philosophie* (La Fabrique 2025) 48; cf Gilles Deleuze, *Sur l'appareil d'État et la machine de guerre: Cours de novembre 1979–mars 1980* (Les Éditions de Minuit 2025) 22 and 123; Gilles Deleuze and Félix Guattari, *Mille plateaux* (Les Éditions de Minuit 1980) 433–36, 447–52; Gilles Deleuze and Félix Guattari, *L'Anti-Œdipe* (Les Éditions de Minuit 1972) 212–16; Martti Koskenniemi, 'What Should the International Lawyer Learn from Karl Marx?' in Susan Marks (ed), *International Law on the Left: Re-examining Marxist Legacies* (CUP 2008) 30, 33–35.

43 Harold J Berman, *Law and Revolution: The Formation of the Western Legal Tradition* (Harvard UP 1983) chs 5–7 (esp 85–119, 199–256); Jean-François Bayart, *L'Énergie de l'État: Pour une sociologie historique et comparée du politique* (Fayard 2022) 17–58, 201–49.

44 Pierre Legendre, *L'Empire du vrai: Introduction aux espaces dogmatiques industriels* (Fayard 1983) ch 2, 63–112; Pierre Legendre, *Leçons VI: La fabrique de l'homme occidental* (Fayard 1996) 41–78.

45 See Max Weber's analysis of rational-legal domination which captures this impersonal, rule-bound order that "exists" beyond the individuals who staff it, fabricating an objective-seeming necessity. See Max Weber, *Economy and Society* (University of California Press 1978) vol 1, ch III; ch XI.

46 On the history of the anthropomorphization of the state in international law, see Jean d'Aspremont, 'The Doctrine of Fundamental Rights of States and Anthropomorphic Thinking in International Law' (2015) 4(3) *Cambridge Journal of International and Comparative Law* 503. On anthropomorphic thinking at work in the expression of opinio juris, see Jean d'Aspremont, *The Discourse on Customary International Law* (OUP 2021), Chapter 5.

47 On the idea of the state as pre-existing international law, see eg Lassa Oppenheim, *International Law: A Treatise, vol 1: Peace* (2nd edn, Longmans, Green & Co

1912) 264, para 209; Dionisio Anzilotti, *Corso di diritto internazionale, vol 1* (Athenaeum 1928) 154–55; Gaetano Ruiz, 'L'État dans le sens du droit des gens et la notion de droit international' (1975) 26 *Österreichische Zeitschrift für Öffentliches Recht und Völkerrecht* 3–63, 265–406; James Crawford, *The Creation of States in International Law* (2nd edn, OUP 2006) 23; Arbitration Commission of the Peace Conference on the Former Yugoslavia (Badinter Commission), 'Conference on Yugoslavia Arbitration Commission: Opinion No 1' (1992) 3 *European Journal of International Law* 178. On the similar idea that the creation of states is a 'thingly' process, see also Charles de Visscher, *Les effectivités du droit international public* (A Pedone 1967) 34; Georges Abi-Saab, 'Cours général de droit international public' (1987) 207 *Recueil des cours* 9, 68; and Opinion No 1 of the Badinter Commission, 29 November 1991: 'the existence or disappearance of a state is a question of fact' (English translation in (1992) 3 *European Journal of International Law* 182).

48 James Crawford, *The Creation of States in International Law* (2nd edn, OUP 2006) chs 1–3.

49 Ibid 93. See also Christopher J Borgen, 'The Language of Law and the Practice of Politics: Great Powers and the Rhetoric of Self-Determination in the Cases of Kosovo and South Ossetia' (2009) 10 *Chicago Journal of International Law* 1, 12–13; John Dugard and David Raic, 'The Role of Recognition in the Law and Practice of Secession' in Marcelo Kohen (ed), *Secession: International Law Perspectives* (CUP 2006) 94, 110.

50 Hersch Lauterpacht's contrary insistence – recognition as constitutive and a matter of duty – had the advantage of exposing better the performative machinery otherwise effaced. See Hersch Lauterpacht, *Recognition in International Law* (CUP 1947) chs 1–2.

51 UN Charter art 2(4).

52 UN Charter arts 24–25, ch VII.

53 *Military and Paramilitary Activities in and against Nicaragua* (Nicaragua v United States of America) (Merits) [1986] ICJ Rep paras 202–11; *Armed Activities on the Territory of the Congo* (DRC v Uganda) (Judgement) [2005] ICJ Rep paras 148–65; *Legal Consequences of the Construction of a Wall in the Occupied Palestinian Territory* (Advisory Opinion) [2004] ICJ Rep paras 87–101, 149–51; *Alleged Violations of Sovereign Rights and Maritime Spaces in the Caribbean Sea* (Nicaragua v Colombia) (Judgement) [2022] ICJ Rep paras 86–103.

54 Hilary Charlesworth and Christine Chinkin, *The Boundaries of International Law: A Feminist Analysis* (Manchester UP 2000) chs 1 and 7; Hilary Charlesworth, Christine Chinkin and Shelley Wright, 'Feminist Approaches to International Law' (1991) 85 *American Journal of International Law* 613–45.

55 Complementing this analysis, Gail Lythgoe's account of the "rebirth of territory" shows how contemporary international law and global governance practices re-centre territorial logics through everyday administrative and security techniques – mapping, surveillance, jurisdictional zoning – that render territory an apparently pre-given object rather than a historically produced assemblage. See Gail Lythgoe, *The Rebirth of Territory in International Law: Space, Governance, and the Legal Imagination* (CUP 2024); Gail Lythgoe, 'Reimagining Territory in International Law' (2022) 35 *Leiden Journal of International Law* 247–67.

56 In some earlier work, I have tried to debunk the thingification of international organizations by promoting what I have called a phenomenological approach to international organizations. See Jean d'Aspremont, *The Experiences of International Organizations: A Phenomenological Approach to International Institutional Law* (Edward Elgar 2023); Jean d'Aspremont, 'Is an International

Organization a Thing?' 22 *International Organizations Law Review* (forthcoming 2026).

57 Herbert Marcuse, *One-Dimensional Man: Studies in the Ideology of Advanced Industrial Society* (Beacon Press 1964) 229–30.

58 Benedict Anderson, *Imagined Communities* (Verso 2006).

59 See e.g. Thomas Hobbes, *Leviathan* (Richard Tuck ed, CUP 1996) ch 17, 120–23; John Locke, *Two Treatises of Government* (Peter Laslett ed, CUP 1988) *Second Treatise* §§ 95–99; Jean-Jacques Rousseau, *The Social Contract* (Victor Gourevitch ed, CUP 1997) bk I, ch 6.

60 See Jacques Rancière, *La mésentente. Politique et philosophie* (La Fabrique 2025) 163–65. In this register, Benedict Anderson's insight that communities are "imagined" because members will never know most of their fellow members yet conceive of a deep, horizontal comradeship, is directly relevant: The nation is a product of print capitalism, calendrical time, and ritual forms that make an abstract people appear as a palpable, necessary being. See Benedict Anderson, *Imagined Communities* (Verso 2006) 6–7, 37–46.

61 Jacques Derrida, 'Declarations of Independence' (1986) 7(1) *New Political Science* 7–15, 8–12 and 13–14.

62 Michel Foucault, *The Archaeology of Knowledge* (Routledge 2002) ch 2.

63 See Benedict Anderson's work on the technologies of nationhood – print-languages, museums, censuses, maps – which exposes the self-effacing being that makes the people seem to pre-exist the discursive machinery that brings it forth, Benedict Anderson, *Imagined Communities* (Verso 2006) 163–85.

64 Clifford Geertz, *The Interpretation of Cultures* (Basic Books 1973) chs 9–12 (esp 'The Integrative Revolution') 255–310.

65 Homi K Bhabha, *Nation and Narration* (Routledge 1990) 1–7, 204–11; Frantz Fanon, *The Wretched of the Earth* (Richard Philcox tr, Grove Press 2004) 119–65, 166–205; Partha Chatterjee, *Nationalist Thought and the Colonial World* (University of Minnesota Press 1986) 38–52; Partha Chatterjee, *The Nation and Its Fragments* (Princeton UP 1993) 3–13.

66 UNGA Res 1541 (XV) (15 December 1960) Principles IV–IX.

67 Antonio Cassese, *Self-Determination of Peoples* (CUP 1995) 50–67, 101–42; James Crawford, *The Creation of States in International Law* (2nd edn, OUP 2006) 126–65.

68 This critique has also been made outside feminist critique. See Timothy Bewes, *Reification, or The Anxiety of Late Capitalism* (Verso 2002) 4.

69 Judith Butler, *Bodies That Matter: On the Discursive Limits of "Sex"* (Routledge 1993) 1–23, 28–57.

70 Judith Butler, *Gender Trouble: Feminism and the Subversion of Identity* (Routledge 1990) 6–14, 133–41.

71 Kimberlé Williams Crenshaw, 'Demarginalizing the Intersection of Race and Sex' (1989) *University of Chicago Legal Forum* 139–67, 149–57; Kimberlé Williams Crenshaw, 'Mapping the Margins: Intersectionality, Identity Politics, and Violence against Women of Color' (1991) 43(6) *Stanford Law Review* 1241–99, 1244–55.

72 Shreya Atrey, *Intersectional Discrimination* (OUP 2019) 1–31, 124–35.

73 Silvia Federici, *Caliban and the Witch: Women, the Body and Primitive Accumulation* (Autonomedia 2004) 61–117, 163–200.

74 Nancy Fraser, *Fortunes of Feminism: From State-Managed Capitalism to Neoliberal Crisis* (Verso 2013) 209–31.

75 Anne Fausto-Sterling, *Sexing the Body: Gender Politics and the Construction of Sexuality* (Basic Books 2000) 3–13, 45–77.

76 Dianne Otto, 'Queering Gender [Identity] in International Law' (2015) 33(4) *Nordic Journal of Human Rights* 299–318, 302–11.
77 Convention on the Elimination of All Forms of Discrimination against Women (adopted 18 December 1979, entered into force 3 September 1981) 1249 UNTS 13 (CEDAW) arts 1, 2, 5, 11 and 16.
78 Hilary Charlesworth, Christine Chinkin and Shelley Wright, 'Feminist Approaches to International Law' (1991) 85 *American Journal of International Law* 613–45, 625–36.
79 Hilary Charlesworth and Christine Chinkin, *The Boundaries of International Law: A Feminist Analysis* (Manchester UP 2000) 211–40.
80 CEDAW, 1249 UNTS 13, art. 5(a).
81 CEDAW, 1249 UNTS 13, arts. 4(2), 11(2); Catharine A MacKinnon, 'Are Women Human?' in Catharine A MacKinnon, *Are Women Human? And Other International Dialogues* (Harvard UP 2006) 41–77, 48–57; Joanne Conaghan, *Law and Gender* (OUP 2013) 182–95.
82 Dianne Otto, 'Lost in Translation: Re-scripting the Sexed Subjects of International Human Rights Law' in Anne Orford (ed), *International Law and Its Others* (CUP 2006) 318–56, 332–44.
83 Committee on the Elimination of Discrimination against Women, General Recommendation No 28 on the Core Obligations of States Parties under Article 2 of the Convention (16 December 2010) UN Doc CEDAW/C/GC/28, paras 16–18 and 31–34.
84 Committee on the Elimination of Discrimination against Women, General Recommendation No 33 on Women's Access to Justice (3 August 2015) UN Doc CEDAW/C/GC/33, paras 8–15 and 51–59; Committee on the Elimination of Discrimination against Women, General Recommendation No 35 on Gender-Based Violence against Women (14 July 2017) UN Doc CEDAW/C/GC/35, paras 9–21 and 24–29.
85 Shreya Atrey, *Intersectional Discrimination* (OUP 2019) 124–35; Dianne Otto, 'Queering Gender [Identity] in International Law' (2015) 33(4) *Nordic Journal of Human Rights* 299–318, 311–17.
86 Council of Europe Convention on Preventing and Combating Violence against Women and Domestic Violence (opened for signature 11 May 2011, entered into force 1 August 2014) CETS No 210 (Istanbul Convention) arts 3–5 and 18–22; Alexandra Timmer, 'Judging Stereotypes: What the European Court of Human Rights Can Do to Address Sexist Stereotypes' (2015) 33(4) *Nordic Journal of Human Rights* 369–84, 372–78; Francesca Bettio and Anna Bottazzi, 'The Istanbul Convention and Gender-Based Violence: Challenges of Implementation' (2021) 28(2) *Social Politics* 453–77, 460–68.
87 Nicola Lacey, 'Feminist Legal Theory and the Rights of Women' in Heikki Pihlajamäki and others (eds), *The Oxford Handbook of European Legal History* (OUP 2018) 912–33, 925–30; Tina Søreide and Siri Gloppen, 'Gender-Based Violence and the Law: A Critical Review' (2021) 76 *Crime, Law and Social Change* 179–97, 185–92.
88 Protocol to the African Charter on Human and Peoples' Rights on the Rights of Women in Africa (adopted 11 July 2003, entered into force 25 November 2005) arts 2, 4 and 14; Johanna Bond, 'International Intersectionality: A Theoretical and Pragmatic Exploration of Women's International Human Rights Violations' (2003) 52 *Emory International Law Review* 71–90, 80–88.
89 On the shift from "race" to "ethnicity" in the critical discourse, especially by the diasporas, see Stuart Hall, 'Cultural Identity and Diaspora' in Jonathan Rutherford (ed), *Identity: Community, Culture, Difference* (Lawrence & Wishart

1990) 222–37; Stuart Hall, 'New Ethnicities' in David Morley and Kuan-Hsing Chen (eds), *Stuart Hall: Critical Dialogues in Cultural Studies* (Routledge 1996) 441–49; Stuart Hall, 'The Question of Cultural Identity' in Stuart Hall, David Held and Tony McGrew (eds), *Modernity and Its Futures* (Polity Press/Open University 1992) 273–325.

90 Aníbal Quijano, 'Coloniality of Power, Eurocentrism, and Latin America' (2000) 1(3) *Nepantla: Views from South* 533–80 (esp 534–43); Sylvie Laurent, *Capital and Race: The History of a Modern Hydra* (Polity Press forthcoming 2026); Mahmood Mamdani, *Citizen and Subject: Contemporary Africa and the Legacy of Late Colonialism* (Princeton UP 1996); Mahmood Mamdani, *Define and Rule: Native as Political Identity* (Harvard UP 2012) 13–42; Mahmood Mamdani, *Neither Settler nor Native: The Making and Unmaking of Permanent Minorities* (Harvard UP 2020) ch 2, 49–86; Karen E Fields and Barbara J Fields, *Racecraft: The Soul of Inequality in American Life* (Verso 2022); WEB Du Bois, *The Souls of Black Folk* (AC McClurg 1903); Stuart Hall, 'Race, Articulation and Societies Structured in Dominance' in *Sociological Theories: Race and Colonialism* (UNESCO 1980) 305–45; Cedric J Robinson, *Black Marxism: The Making of the Black Radical Tradition* (UNC Press 1983; revised edn 2000) 36–90; Fernando Coronil, *The Magical State* (University of Chicago Press 1997) ch 4, 153–97; Deborah A Thomas, *Exceptional Violence* (Duke UP 2013) intro, 1–26.

91 For some remarks on the role of law in the ossification of identity on the basis of colour as held outside symbolic mechanisms, see Jacques Rancière, *La mésentente: Politique et philosophie* (La Fabrique 2025) 158–61.

92 Matthew Dimick, 'Race and Reification' (2023) 31 *Historical Materialism* 69–105, 76–79.

93 Karen E Fields and Barbara J Fields, *Racecraft: The Soul of Inequality in American Life* (Verso 2022) 17–23, 95–113, 176–83, 189–93.

94 Achille Mbembe, *Critique of Black Reason* (Duke UP 2017) 1–10, 28–35, 117–24.

95 Frantz Fanon, *Black Skin, White Masks* (Charles Lam Markmann tr, Grove Press 1967) 9–14 and 89–119.

96 Stuart Hall, 'The Work of Representation' in Stuart Hall (ed), *Representation: Cultural Representations and Signifying Practices* (Sage/Open University 1997) 13–74; Stuart Hall, 'The Spectacle of the "Other"' in Hall (ed), *Representation: Cultural Representations and Signifying Practices* (Sage/Open University 1997) 223–90.

97 David Theo Goldberg, *The Racial State* (Blackwell 2002); David Theo Goldberg, *Are We All Postracial Yet?* (Polity 2015) 87–112, 145–70.

98 Charles W Mills, *The Racial Contract* (Cornell UP 1997) 11–40, 72–99.

99 Ian Hacking, *Historical Ontology* (Harvard UP 2002) chs 2 and 9; Ian Hacking, *The Social Construction of What?* (Harvard UP 1999) chs 7 and 10.

100 Committee on the Elimination of Racial Discrimination, General Recommendation No. 8: Identification with a particular racial or ethnic group, 1990; see also General Recommendation No. 14: Definition of discrimination, 1993.

101 Committee on the Elimination of Racial Discrimination, General Recommendation No 30 (2004) paras 2–4.

102 Sally Engle Merry, *The Seductions of Quantification* (University of Chicago Press 2016) 3–15 and 129–56; Sally Engle Merry, Kevin E Davis and Benedict Kingsbury (eds), *The Quiet Power of Indicators* (CUP 2015).

103 See eg Makau Mutua, *Human Rights: A Political and Cultural Critique* (University of Pennsylvania Press 2002) 86–92.

104 See CERD concluding observations across multiple states; cf Committee on the Elimination of Racial Discrimination, General Recommendation No 9: The Application of Article 8 of the Convention (1990).
105 Committee on the Elimination of Racial Discrimination, General Recommendation No 30 (2004) paras 2–4 and 10–12.
106 Judith Butler, *Bodies That Matter* (Routledge 2011) 1–23.
107 Michel Serres, *Le Contrat naturel* (François Bourin 1990) 21–49; Michel Serres, *Le Mal propre: Polluer pour s'approprier* (Le Pommier 2008) 13–38.
108 Bruno Latour, *Nous n'avons jamais été modernes: Essai d'anthropologie symétrique* (La Découverte 1991) 25–52; Bruno Latour, *Politiques de la nature: Comment faire entrer les sciences en démocratie* (La Découverte 1999) 51–98.
109 Isabelle Stengers, *Cosmopolitiques VII: Pour en finir avec la tolérance* (La Découverte/Les Empêcheurs de penser en rond 1997) 13–36; Isabelle Stengers, *Au temps des catastrophes: Résister à la barbarie qui vient* (La Découverte 2009) 45–72.
110 See also Philippe Descola, *Par-delà nature et culture* (Gallimard 2005) 63–94, 115–54.
111 Sheila Jasanoff, *The Fifth Branch: Science Advisers as Policymakers* (Harvard UP 1990) 1–23; Sheila Jasanoff (ed), *States of Knowledge: The Co-production of Science and Social Order* (Routledge 2004) 1–22; Sheila Jasanoff, 'Technologies of Humility' (2007) 450 *Nature* 33.
112 42 USC §§ 7408–7410; 40 CFR pt 50.
113 National Environmental Policy Act, 42 USC §§ 4321–4370h; Council on Environmental Quality Regulations, 40 CFR pts 1500–1508; Directive 2011/92/EU (as amended by Directive 2014/52/EU) [2014] OJ L124/1 arts 3–5.
114 Convention on Biological Diversity (adopted 5 June 1992, entered into force 29 December 1993) 1760 UNTS 79 arts 2 and 6; CBD COP10 Decision X/2 (29 October 2010); Kunming–Montreal Global Biodiversity Framework, CBD/COP/DEC/15/4 (19 December 2022).
115 Convention on International Trade in Endangered Species of Wild Fauna and Flora (adopted 3 March 1973, entered into force 1 July 1975) 993 UNTS 243 arts II–IV; Council Regulation (EC) No 338/97 [1997] OJ L61/1.
116 Convention on the Law of the Non-Navigational Uses of International Watercourses (adopted 21 May 1997, entered into force 17 August 2014) arts 5–7.
117 United Nations Framework Convention on Climate Change (9 May 1992) UN Doc FCCC/INFORMAL/84 art 1(2).
118 Paris Agreement (adopted 12 December 2015, entered into force 4 November 2016) UN Doc FCCC/CP/2015/10/Add.1 arts 2(1)(a), 4 and 13.
119 IPCC, *Global Warming of 1.5°C* (2018) Summary for Policymakers.
120 UNFCCC, Decision 18/CMA.1 'Modalities, Procedures and Guidelines for the Transparency Framework' (2018).
121 Constitución de la República del Ecuador (2008) arts 71–74.
122 Corte Constitucional del Ecuador, Sentencia No. 1149-19-JP/21 (1 December 2021, 36–49).
123 Corte Constitucional de Colombia, Sentencia T-622/16 (10 November 2016).
124 María Valeria Berros and Nicolás Espejo Yaksic (eds), *Perspectivas latinoamericanas sobre derechos de la naturaleza* (Tirant lo Blanch 2020) 19–47; Karin van Marle and Louis J Kotzé, 'Earth Jurisprudence and Rights of Nature: The Emergence of a New Legal Paradigm' in Louis J Kotzé and Duncan French (eds), *Sustainable Development, Global Governance and the Law* (Edward Elgar 2018) 139–60.
125 Cormac Cullinan, *Wild Law: A Manifesto for Earth Justice* (Siber Ink 2002) 51–83; Thomas Berry, *The Great Work* (Bell Tower 1999) 104–24.

126 It is noteworthy that Lawrence Rosen speaks about the "crystallization" of culture by law and by that he means that law condenses and stabilizes cultural meanings. See Lawrence Rosen, *Law as Culture* (Princeton UP 2006) 4–6.
127 Benedict Anderson, *Imagined Communities* (Verso 2006) 1–46.
128 Eric Hobsbawm and Terence Ranger (eds), *The Invention of Tradition* (CUP 1983) intro 1–14; Eric Hobsbawm, 'Mass-Producing Traditions: Europe, 1870–1914' in Eric Hobsbawm and Terence Ranger (eds), *The Invention of Tradition* (CUP 1983) 263–307.
129 Walter Mignolo, 'Delinking: The Rhetoric of Modernity, the Logic of Coloniality, and the Grammar of Decoloniality' (2007) 21 *Cultural Studies* 449–514, 472.
130 Clifford Geertz, *The Interpretation of Cultures* (Basic Books 1973) 3–30.
131 Frantz Fanon, *Les Damnés de la terre* (Maspero 1961) 209–45.
132 Edward W Said, *Orientalism* (Pantheon 1978) 31–49, 201–25.
133 Louis Althusser, 'Idéologie et appareils idéologiques d'État' in *Positions* (Éditions Sociales 1976) 67–125.
134 John R Searle, *The Construction of Social Reality* (Free Press 1995) 27–52.
135 Stuart Hall, 'The Question of Cultural Identity' in Stuart Hall, David Held and Tony McGrew (eds), *Modernity and Its Futures* (Polity Press/Open University 1992) 287–302.
136 Constitución Española art 46.
137 Jesús Prieto de Pedro, *Patrimonio Cultural: Concepto y Régimen Jurídico* (Civitas 1996) 45–68.
138 Code du patrimoine arts L111-1 and L111-2; Pierre-Laurent Frier and Jean-Baptiste Donnier, *Droit du patrimoine culturel* (Dalloz 2015) 93–121.
139 UNESCO Constitution (adopted 16 November 1945, entered into force 4 November 1946) Preamble.
140 Convention for the Protection of Cultural Property in the Event of Armed Conflict (The Hague Convention) (adopted 14 May 1954, entered into force 7 August 1956) arts 1–4; Roger O'Keefe, *The Protection of Cultural Property in Armed Conflict* (CUP 2006) 74–105.
141 Lyndel V Prott and Patrick J O'Keefe, *Law and the Cultural Heritage* (vol 1, Professional Books 1984) 237–61.
142 Convention on the Means of Prohibiting and Preventing the Illicit Import, Export and Transfer of Ownership of Cultural Property (adopted 14 November 1970, entered into force 24 April 1972) arts 1–7; John Henry Merryman, 'Two Ways of Thinking About Cultural Property' (1986) 80 *American Journal of International Law* 831–53, 842–50.
143 Patty Gerstenblith, *Art, Cultural Heritage, and the Law* (Carolina Academic Press 2019) 259–314.
144 Convention Concerning the Protection of the World Cultural and Natural Heritage (adopted 16 November 1972, entered into force 17 December 1975) arts 1–11; Operational Guidelines, paras 49–53.
145 Francesco Francioni, 'World Heritage Convention' in Francesco Francioni and Martin Scheinin (eds), *Cultural Heritage, Cultural Rights, Cultural Diversity* (OUP 2008) 17–36, 24–30; Lucas Lixinski, *Intangible Cultural Heritage in International Law* (OUP 2013) 35–44.
146 Convention for the Safeguarding of the Intangible Cultural Heritage (adopted 17 October 2003, entered into force 20 April 2006) arts 2–14.
147 Lucas Lixinski, *Intangible Cultural Heritage in International Law* (OUP 2013) 78–105; Valdimar Tr Hafstein, *Making Intangible Heritage* (Indiana UP 2018) 41–67.
148 Janet Blake, *International Cultural Heritage Law* (OUP 2015) 127–51.

149 Convention on the Protection and Promotion of the Diversity of Cultural Expressions (adopted 20 October 2005, entered into force 18 March 2007) arts 5–6; Sabine von Schorlemer and Peter-Tobias Stoll, *The UNESCO Convention on the Protection and Promotion of the Diversity of Cultural Expressions* (Springer 2012) 3–29.
150 Mira Burri, *Public Service Broadcasting 3.0* (Routledge 2015) 46–61.
151 Barbara Kirshenblatt-Gimblett, *Destination Culture* (University of California Press 1998) 149–77.
152 Laurajane Smith, *Uses of Heritage* (Routledge 2006) 11–29; Lucas Lixinski, 'Selecting Heritage: The Interplay of Art, Politics and Identity' (2011) 22 *European Journal of International Law* 81–100, 86–94.
153 Clifford Geertz, *The Interpretation of Cultures* (Fontana Press 1993 [1973]) 9–10, 14–17.
154 In an earlier work, I had already shown that international legal thought and practice commonly rest on a partition between international law and the world to which it applies, and that this partition is itself an effect of discourse that law produces and polices. What was then at stake was to exhibit how law shapes the world while grounding itself in that world. See Jean d'Aspremont, 'A Worldly Law in a Legal World' in Andrea Bianchi and Moshe Hirsch (eds), *International Law's Invisible Frames: Social Cognition and Knowledge Production in International Legal Processes* (OUP 2021) 110–23. The argument made here is different because it targets the epistemology that enables that partition to function: the grammar of thingness by which law stabilizes itself and what it addresses as necessary beings. Instead of merely tracing the dualism between legal discourse and worldly actuality, the present chapter has unpacked the discursive operations – exclusion of perception, foreclosure of the speaking observer, annulment of representation, collapse of agency into self-causation, installation of ancestrality, effacement of labour – through which that dualism is naturalized and made efficacious. In other words, the earlier analysis showed that the bridge between law and world is built by law; the argument here shows that the very ground on which the bridge stands is made thingly by law's own hands.
155 Bruno Latour, *La fabrique du droit: Une ethnographie du Conseil d'État* (La Découverte 2004) 110.

Chapter 5

The fascist grammar of thingness

By shedding light on some figures of legal thingification, the previous chapter has shown that law systematically and constantly thingifies what it encounters, thereby gaining its efficacy from what has been called here a precritical epistemology. By thingifying itself, the State, the people, sex, race, nature, and, law consistently awards itself and these entities the status of necessary beings-in-the-world that present themselves as independent of perception, observation, language, discourse, and representation. It is remarkable that this precritical epistemology manifests itself across all domains of legal discourse and practice. In each instance, law effaces the discursive labour that produces these entities while simultaneously installing them as beings-in-themselves that exclude the speaking observer and foreclose representational debates.

This finding, while already significant for understanding how law secures its efficacy, is yet to be unpacked further. This chapter makes the claim that law's embrace of thingness does not merely constitute a philosophical return to precritical modes of thought but also actively deploys an authoritarian type of epistemology, one that is reminiscent of fascist thought. The chapter more particularly argues that when legal discourse systematically transforms contingent, historical, social constructions into thingly entities and awards them a necessary material existence irrespective of how they are perceived, experienced, named, thought, represented, or interpreted, it deploys the same prescriptive grammar that characterizes fascist thought, a grammar designed to foreclose representational debates, critique, and contestation.

This chapter unfolds its argument as follows. The first section begins by justifying the choice of the concept of fascist grammar as a hyperbolic descriptor to capture the authoritarian epistemology at work in thingness, distinguishing this concept from alternative metaphors like terrorism and totalitarianism (1). The following section once again mobilizes the insights of Roland Barthes and sheds light on the genealogy of the fascist grammar of thingness invoked here, tracing it back to Barthes's famous claim about the fascism of language (2). The third section further theorizes the concept of fascist grammar by examining how thinkers like Louis Althusser, Gilles

DOI: 10.4324/9781003753940-6

Deleuze and Félix Guattari, Theodor Adorno and Max Horkheimer, Herbert Marcuse, and Jacques Rancière have, each in their own way, identified analogous forms of discursive compulsion that relieve the burden of world-making at the cost of the speaking observer (3). The fourth section draws on Bruno Latour's idea of the "fear of the mob" to illuminate how thingness functions as a defensive manoeuvre that closes the space of mediation and contestation by treating facts as already settled and exempt from scrutiny (4). The fifth section ventures a historical comparison with 1930s–1940s authoritarian discourse, drawing on the work of Jean-Pierre Faye, Johann Chapoutot, Victor Klemperer, and Umberto Eco, in order to demonstrate how fascist discourse has commonly been deploying remarkably similar techniques of thingification (5). In the sixth section, this chapter returns to postcolonial thought's findings about the role of thingification in colonialism and about the extent to which colonialism and fascism go hand in hand (6). Finally, the seventh section returns to the legal thingification processes examined in Chapter 4, demonstrating how law, by compelling recognition of contingent arrangements as necessary beings, deploys a fascist grammar as it is understood here (7).

1. Fascism, terrorism, and totalitarianism: The search for a hyperbolic descriptor

Before shedding light on the authoritarian character of the epistemology at work in thingness, a few observations are warranted to explain the descriptive category adopted in this chapter, and especially the choice for the idea of fascist grammar. Three observations are warranted in that respect.

First, the chapter's recourse to the idea of fascist grammar to demonstrate the authoritarian perils of thingness and thingification is a rigorously delimited hyperbolic descriptor that is only meant to shed light on the discursive closure enabled by thingness. Even if Section 5 below will briefly broach a few parallels with some distinctive past discursive practices, the use of such hyperbolic descriptor does not aim at equating the legal practices described in the previous chapter with the totality of past and contemporary fascist governmental regimes but solely at demonstrating the extent to which such practices emulate the semantic tactics historically observed in authoritarian rhetoric. Fascist grammar, as it is used in this chapter, designates the point at which accumulated thingifying moves may consolidate into a discursive apparatus of compulsory recognition hostile to contestability.

Second, it must be emphasized that although fascism is mobilized throughout this chapter as a deliberately hyperbolic descriptor to illuminate the authoritarian epistemology at work in thingness, other descriptors could plausibly be used to sustain the claim made here. Strikingly, Barthes – who is the spearhead of the critical use of the figure of fascism in relation to language and who will be discussed in the next section – also mobilizes the metaphor of "terrorism" to mark the annihilation of discourse.[1] It must be acknowledged that the terrorist metaphor aptly captures the refusal of argumentative mediation and the spectacularization of silence that thingness enacts when it disqualifies contradiction. Yet the fascist analogy, I suggest, better maps the full authoritarian grammar of thingness. A fascist grammar does not merely suspend discourse. It simultaneously institutes an order of forms that pre-assigns places, capacities, and meanings, prescribing compliance with a world presented as already composed. Fascism, in this analytic sense, names more specifically a lasting representational regime in which sign is absorbed by the self-evidence of the thing. If the terrorist category figures the very punctual violence of discourse's abolition, the fascist register figures the more continuous governance of self-evidence through which thingness normalizes the cancellation of representation.

A further terminological remark concerns the possible use of "totalitarianism" to capture what thingness does. In fact, one might plausibly resort to this descriptive category, which is often associated with the fetishizing closure at work in political discourse (as is illustrated by Adorno's analyses of the authoritarian logic that converts concepts into rigid idols[2] and by Enrique Dussel's critiques of the fetishization of power that occludes alterity and mediation).[3] In this sense, totalitarianism can name a regime that aspires to total closure through centralization, saturation, and a fetish of unity. Nevertheless, I prefer the figure of fascism to designate the authoritarian epistemology of thingness. First, in its classical usage, totalitarianism foregrounds central planning, ubiquitous surveillance, and juridico-political omnipotence. Using such reference would run the risk of overdetermining the discussion toward institutional completeness. As was exposed in the previous chapters, thingness, by contrast, primarily works at an infra-institutional level: It entails a being-in-itself that excludes perception, a being-without-a-witness that cancels the speaking observer, and a self-signifying being that expels representation *hors langue* but without constituting an institutional apparatus. Second, totalitarianism often implies a total domination in all domains, whereas thingness operates through a type of everyday self-evidence that presents the world as already composed, self-caused, and ancestral, without simultaneously requiring or realizing full subjugation.[4] In short, if totalitarianism echoes the fetish of unity and the aspiration to total closure, fascism more precisely tracks the infra-institutional epistemic protocols through which thingness converts representational debates into assent and fixes a world that is meant to precede, exceed, and outlast any speaking observer.

2. From Barthes' fascism of language to the fascist grammar of thingness

Describing the epistemology at work in thingness by reference to fascism is not without precedent. It echoes a line of thinking famously inaugurated by Roland Barthes. In fact, Barthes, in his inaugural lecture at the *Collège de*

France, famously insists that "language is neither reactionary nor progressive; it is quite simply fascist; for fascism does not prevent speech, it compels speech".[5] This oft-discussed formulation[6] seeks to indicate that the most coercive force of language lies not in what it bans but in what it obliges speakers to articulate in order to speak at all. Later in his course on "the Neutral",[7] Barthes substantiates that affirmation. He adds that the laws of language secure the speaking subject in that they provide the very possibility of sayability and intersubjective recognition. Yet, he says, they exact a price. That price is the imposition of a "mode of being", that is, a typified subjectivity, dictated by grammatical categories, pronominal systems, syntactic positions, and obligatory rubrics. To speak French, for instance, is to be compelled by its syntax to appear as a certain subject. To address another is to be forced into an affective-distance relation encoded by a distinction between fixed and predetermined personal pronouns. Barthes underscores that what matters are the obligatory functions and categories of language, especially the matrix of selections and positions that prefigure the speaker's stance, relation, and identity.[8] Hence his crucial reversal: In a language, what is important is not what it prevents you from saying but what it obliges you to say. From that perspective, the word fascism names the structural compulsion that pins the subject into predetermined forms of articulation and thus of thought.

The analogy with what thingness does is not unwarranted. As was discussed in Chapter 1, thingness here names the quality of being a thing, i.e. of having a necessary material existence irrespective of how it is perceived, experienced, named, thought, or represented. Calling it fascist stresses that this grammar does not merely frame debate but forecloses it by compelling a prior acceptance of a necessary being. It cancels the speaking observer as a constitutive agent and determines in advance the positions that can be occupied and the predicates that can be assigned. Likewise, thingness, which was earlier described as an epistemology of the contemplation that spares us the labour of representation,[9] compares to Barthes' understanding of language as it also exacts a price. That price is the foreclosure of representational debates and the loss of the speaking observer's of their status as a speaking observer.

3. A fascist grammar in all but name: Althusser, Deleuze and Guattari, Adorno and Horkheimer, Marcuse, and Rancière

As the ambition here is to further theorize the idea that thingness puts in place a fascist grammar, the present chapter cannot solely build on the parallel with Barthes's famous claim about the fascist dimension of language. Indeed, the idea that language compels, constrains, and typifies the subject, pinning speakers into predetermined forms of articulation and modes of being, is not unique to Roland Barthes. While the latter's formulation has attracted sustained commentary and discussion, its core diagnostic has antecedents as well as affiliates across twentieth-century critical theory. Many thinkers, without adopting the figure of fascism to pinpoint what language does, nonetheless describe a analogous compulsion: A grammar, code, or apparatus that precedes the subject, organizes what is sayable, and declares a world already given, already sorted, and not open to contestation at the level of its constitution and representation.

An obvious analogue is Louis Althusser's concept of interpellation which was already mentioned.[10] For Althusser, ideology is not a set of detachable illusions but a material apparatus that "hails" individuals as subjects, recruiting them into the social order by inducing recognition in the address.[11] Althusser's famous paradigmatic scene ("Hey, you there!") is where subjects become subjects by answering the hail, by turning toward the call and assuming the position it assigns. In that sense, the institutions that enact ideology (the "ideological state apparatuses" such as the school, the family, the media, the church) do not simply transmit content. They organize the positions from which content can be enunciated and received. The point is not that speech is prevented, but that speech is possible only as the speech of a subject-position already sanctioned by ideology. For Althusser, interpellation is, in other words, a grammar of compulsion. It provides the subject-form that will speak before any particular utterance is made. The analogy with Barthes is exact at this level. Both Barthes' and Althusser's accounts locate coercion prior to content, in the very possibility of speech, and both construe discourse as a technology of subject-formation whose censorship operates by obligation rather than interdiction. This simultaneously resonates directly with how thingness generates interpellation as one of its main discursive and epistemological effects. The self-signifying thing and its necessary being-in-the-world, once encountered by the former speaking observer, assign the latter a specific place and role, that of a subject of a specific order. The (former) speaking observer is accordingly interpellated by the thing which, through its interpellation, indicates to them its being as a thing and elevates them into a subject of the order of the thing concerned. Being a subject here means being subject to the thing and thus ascribed a specific place and role, not as speaking observer, but as a subordinate.[12]

Gilles Deleuze and Félix Guattari offer a cognate diagnosis through the notions of territorialization, coding, and the "bricking-up" of thought. Their analysis, developed across *Anti-Œdipus* but more extensively in *A Thousand Plateaus*, concerns assemblages of desire, signs, and institutions that tend to fix flows, impose codes, carve enclaves, and install rigid segmentations where open series of transformations might otherwise persist. Territorialization stabilizes relations, assigns identities, and encloses passages. It is a logic of capture that produces safe redundancies and predictable circuits. To "brick up" is to close apertures, convert pathways into walls, and institutionalize minimal differences that nonetheless preempt new ones. Deleuze and Guattari read this logic as characteristic not only of the modern State but also of fascism's micropolitics: The hypertrophy of coding, the saturation of space by rigid segmentarities, and the policing of desire by micro-fascisms embedded in everyday practices and utterances. This is deeply resonant with the epistemology of thingness. To treat the world as a set of ready-made objects, partitioned and coded in advance, is to territorialize thinking, that is, to brick up the scene of appearance so that representation becomes mere adequation to already constituted things. The convenience that such territorialization affords (recognizability, legibility, the comfort of the same) operates by curtailing the de- and reterritorializations that would multiply modes of appearing and speaking.[13] This parallels the differentiation effect of thingness as understood here, i.e. its enabling of a thinking in terms of difference and distinctiveness, allowing the organization of the world into distinct practices, States, actors, peoples, environments, histories, cultures, traditions, races, sexed identities, identities, foreignness, otherness, states of economic development, discriminations, dominations, oppressions, liberations, injustices, inequalities, aggressions, violences, etc.

Elsewhere, Gilles Deleuze has interestingly developed a slightly alternative take on such compulsion but which preserves this chapter's metaphor's force for describing what thingness does. Indeed, in another intervention, he explicitly uses the term fascism to refer to a self-serving process that is destructive of itself and of others,[14] adding that it is a process that celebrates death and always ends up destroying others and itself.[15] This altered understanding of fascism continues to carry a relevant echo for the hyperbolic characterization of thingness that is provided here. In fact, thingness can be approached as a self-fulfilling epistemic state that forecloses all possibilities for the thing, reducing becoming to an 'is' outside language and without any representational alternative. Said differently, viewed through Deleuze's lens of fascism as a self-destructive process, one can further appreciate how thingification – i.e. the drive for thingness – can also be construed as a devastating enterprise that leaves everything in ruins once thingness is produced.

The Frankfurt School, from another angle, sheds light on similar discursive compulsions through critiques of what they call reification, instrumental reason, and the culture industry.[16] For instance, in *Dialectic of Enlightenment*, Adorno and Horkheimer analyse how the Enlightenment's project of liberation transmutes into domination through the universalization of instrumental rationality. Accordingly, means displace ends, concepts are reduced to tools, thinking becomes procedure, and the culture industry standardizes consciousness into passive receptivity. They more particularly argue that cultural commodities are not innocuous entertainment but machines of conformity, producing subjects who consume, identify, and obey.[17] The compulsion here is not the explicit ban, but the formatting of experience such that only certain recognitions are possible and only certain desires legible. Concepts, stripped of negativity, cease to mediate difference and instead ratify sameness. Thingification (in their terms: Reification) generalizes the commodity form to thought itself, for relations appear as things, processes as substantialized facts, and critique as eccentricity or error.[18] Hence the kinship to the idea of a fascist grammar of thingness: The apparatus does not silence but scripts an idiom of assent, a vocabulary of equivalence and exchange that makes dissent unintelligible or unserious. This simultaneously echoes how thingness has been understood as a very sophisticated form of abstraction.[19]

Herbert Marcuse similarly offers some insights that closely approach the spectre of discursive fascism at work in thingness. In *One-Dimensional Man*, Marcuse diagnoses an overwhelming concreteness in which the substantive governs the sentence in an authoritarian manner, turning the sentence into an affirmation one must accept. The declared and codified meaning, he argues, cannot be demonstrated, modified, or denied. Closed language does not demonstrate or explain but communicates decision, diktat, order. Such language exercises control by reducing the linguistic forms of reflection, abstraction, development, and contradiction, often by substituting images for concepts. It negates or absorbs transcendent vocabularies. It does not seek the true and the false so much as establish and impose them. In so doing, Marcuse identifies the authoritarian character of an administrative language in which propositions are not to be argued but to be accepted, where the copula becomes a site of command rather than mediation. The price of communicative efficacy is the dismantling of negativity and the foreclosure of conceptual movement.[20] What Marcuse describes provides an almost literal parallel to the prescriptive dimension of thingness where the thing prescribes to the whole world that it cannot not exist, ordering an absolute obedience to the existence that is so established, the "is" simultaneously being a "must be".[21]

Last but not least, the claim that thingness rests on a fascist grammar finds a revealing echo in Jacques Rancière's well-known distinction between *police* and *politics*. Read through the lens of Jacques Rancière's conception of "police", thingness can be construed as naming a mode of distribution that fixes the world as a necessary being-in-the-world and thereby installs a police of discourse, perception, and representation. More particularly, as a being-in-itself, a being-without-a-witness, and a self-signifying being, thingness prescribes what can be seen, said, and done, and thus enacts what Rancière calls the police, i.e. a partition of the sensible that allocates places, roles, capacities, and incapacities, organizing who counts as a speaking observer and what may appear as speakable, visible, and thinkable.[22] In its self-caused and ancestral register, thingness claims anteriority and necessity for the distribution it imposes, rendering the existing order of places and functions not just factual but obligatory, a presence that continues after the speaking observer has left the scene, thereby enabling the exclusion of certain voices and experiences.[23] Because the thing is self-signifying and outside representation, language is, in turn, disqualified as a site of dissensus. The sign vanishes and only the fixed, self-signifying thing remains, cancelling the very operations – naming, arguing, contradicting – through which political subjectivation interrupts the police order. From the perspective of Rancière's famous dichotomy, thingness thus functions as a police of epistemology. It regulates who can appear as a subject and what can appear as an object, stabilizing a partition of the sensible that forecloses dissensus by converting the contingent distribution of roles and places into a self-effacing necessity, i.e. into a world already given that has no part for what does not fit its allocation.[24] And in doing so, it enables the State and all those who resort to thingness to clear the thingified community of all the excess identities.[25]

It is submitted here that the few critical interventions mentioned here as well as in the previous section all converge in showing how specific discursive forms relieve the burden of world-making at the cost of the speaking observer. Under such conditions, representational disputes are not resolved but declared illegitimate. The result is an epistemological authoritarianism whose tacit maxim is "the world is as it is; there is nothing to discuss; move on!". Whether this takes the form of Barthes's fascism of language, Althusser's interpellation, Deleuze and Guattari's bricking-up of thought, Adorno and Horkheimer's routinization of reason, Marcuse's authoritarian sentence, or Rancière's police, the mechanism is the same. Speech is bound to obligatory forms that secure recognition and allocate roles as well as capacities by sacrificing the speaking observer and representation.

The intellectual kinship between the claim that thingness bespeaks a fascist grammar and the abovementioned accounts of how discursive forms relieve the burden of world-making at the cost of the speaking observer provides support for developing this chapter's claim further. That said, while the authors mentioned in the present and previous sections already provide the necessary stepping stones for substantiating the argument, it remains worthwhile to mobilize the insights of yet one further author. This is the object of the next section.

4. Latour's fear of the mob

Bruno Latour famously invokes the idea of the "fear of the mob" in *Pandora's Hope* to name a recurring anxiety that haunts modern epistemology. If the world is constructed, then what prevents "the mob" (whether a numerical majority, a dominant class, or a populist coalition) from imposing whatever version of the world it prefers? Latour's point is diagnostic rather than celebratory. He argues that bypassing Kantian constructivism, i.e. denying the mediations by which phenomena become stabilized, often stems from precisely this fear. If the presupposition of a permanent construction of the world opens the definition of the world to contestation, then one way to shut down the risk of such redefinition is to insist on things as already-given, self-evident, and immune to debate.[26]

Latour's framing reinterprets a well-known Kantian difficulty that has already been discussed in a previous chapter.[27] As is well-known, Kant insists that we have no access to the thing-in-itself and that what we know appears under conditions of sensibility and understanding. That very acknowledgement of mediation carries a political risk. If the world is built, it might be rebuilt. If it is stabilized, it might be destabilized. Latour's "fear of the mob" thus names the reaction that tries to close this vulnerability by denying the political and practical work of object-construction and by treating the world as made of entities that are outside perception, observation, language, discourse, and representation. From this angle, thingness can be read as a defensive manoeuvre. It cultivates the presupposition that there really is a being-in-itself that requires no further inquiry, interpretation, or public adjudication and which is insulated from (re-)capture or (re-)construction by either a mass or an elite. The payoff of this insulation is epistemic peace. No need to negotiate appearances, methods, or meanings, for the world can go on meaning what it has always meant.

It is important to note that Latour's broader argument suggests that such defence against Kantian constructivism is unstable, if not counterproductive. First, the denial of construction does not actually prevent capture but merely obscures it. Declaring the world to be composed of fixed things often licences their imposition by those with the authority to define what counts as a thing. In practice, thingness can itself become the instrument of elite or majoritarian imposition, for realities are simply locked in and shielded from critique. Second, suppressing processes of construction deprives collectives of the very mechanisms – contestation, testing, iteration – by which the world is forged. Far from protecting dominant representations from the crowd, it weakens the conditions under which representations can be made durable.

This is where the analogy to authoritarian epistemology gains traction. Latour's account shows that closing the space of mediation and contestation, by treating the world as already settled and exempt from scrutiny, pathologizes disagreement as error, alternative articulations and representations being, at best, classified as noise. Such closure concentrates authority in whoever can define what counts as a thing and how it is to be recognized. The result is an epistemic monologism in which a plurality of methods, interpretations, and revisions is displaced. It is in this sense that all closing epistemologies can be deemed authoritarian epistemologies. By foreclosing the mechanisms through which claims can be (publicly) made, tested, and remade, they replace shared processes with unilateral settlement and transform knowledge from a collective practice into a regime of prescription.

5. Daring a comparison: The thingifying grammar of 1930s–1940s authoritarian discourse

The previous sections have shown that the idea of a fascist grammar finds support in the work of Barthes, Deleuze and Guattari, the authors of the Frankfurt School, Rancière, and Latour, and that one should have no qualms about mobilizing this discursive category to describe how thingness compels the speaking observer into an epistemology of the contemplation whereby certain beings are necessary, self-signifying, self-caused, and ancestral. This chapter now ventures to trace the historical resonances between such fascist grammar and the discourses of authoritarian regimes at work in the 1930s–1940s. It is submitted here that this historical comparison, despite all its conceptual and methodological limitations,[28] helps reinforce the emphasis on the degree of compulsion that accompanies thingness and its annihilation of contestation and critique. Indeed, if one defines thingness, as it is done here, as the attribute of a necessary being-in-the-world, then Nazi discourse in the 1930s–1940s offers a striking display of discursive techniques that produce a similar necessity by cancelling perception, witness, representation, the speaking observer, and the present.

Before carrying out this comparative exercise further, an important observation is warranted. It should be stressed that the stakes of the analogy made in this chapter is not to provide thingness with any kind of formal pedigree or genealogy. The point is not to imply any linear and direct continuity between fascist uses of thingification and contemporary legal or political discourses. The point is simply to create disruptive resonance and arouse vigilance.

Here too some scholarly works are mobilized to help clarify and substantiate the historical comparison attempted here. For instance, Jean-Pierre Faye's account of totalitarian discourse is helpful as it clarifies how such categories are stabilized by narrative closure: Labels commonly used by Nazis to designate otherness cease to be positions in an open story and become fixed entities that return the same meaning regardless of context, thereby producing the effect of an entity that signifies by virtue of itself and that requires no mediation by a speaking subject. This is thingness as self-signifying being and as ancestral being, since the discourse speaks from before the speaking observer, as if the nation had always already declared itself.[29] Faye shows that the closure of narrative circuits makes critique structurally redundant: Once every event returns to the same thing – enemy, plot, contamination – the present is sidelined and the temporal horizon becomes that of an immemorial destiny.

In the same vein, Johann Chapoutot compellingly demonstrates how this discursive production of necessity is institutionalized through law and administration. For him, Nazi discourse posits race, nature, and *Volk* as anterior to any human decision, treating them as data rather than norms, so that the legal text behaves as if race existed outside language and independently of judge, administrator, or victim.[30] In files, decrees, and forms, persons are thingified into bearers of racial substance.[31] The effect is a regime of self-causation.[32] Administrative inscription gives categories the force of self-evidence: A line on a form converts identity into a thing that precedes the person, uninstalling the speaking observer and instituting a being-without-a-witness in the very act of bureaucratic finding.[33] At the same time, abstraction and universals are denounced as harmful to the German body politic, inquiry is displaced by the injunction that "there is no why", nature is cast as the prior script that determines essence, position, and vocation, and the enemy is degraded below the threshold of personhood toward objecthood, all such moves normalizing the already-given as necessity and aligning law, knowledge, and action with an organicist order taken to speak for itself.[34]

As similarly documented by Klemperer, key categories of Nazi discourse (e.g. *Volk*, race, blood, nature, enemy, Jew, *Führer*, order) are not presented as contestable constructions but installed as beings-in-themselves that have always already been there and cannot be otherwise, an installation that Klemperer documents in the saturation of everyday speech.[35] Through nominalization and compounding – *Entjudung*, *Endlösung*, *Gleichschaltung* – processes and decisions are transformed into things that present themselves as self-evident and ancestral. Likewise, biologizing metaphors simulate self-causation and self-signification by naturalizing normativity – parasite, *bacillus*, degeneration – so that to contest the category is to contest nature itself, which exemplifies the exclusion of representation and the cancellation of agency entailed by thingness.[36] This is exactly the being-without-a-witness that effaces the speaking observer as co-constitutive of meaning.[37]

Mention must also be made here of Umberto Eco's analysis of "Ur-Fascism" in *How to Spot a Fascist*. Although he does not necessarily focus on the actual 1930s and 1940s experiences, his work illuminates how the authoritarian compulsion of thingness operates as a cancellation of perception, language, and dissensus by declaring the world already composed. Eco observes that, for fascism, there can be no advancement of learning, for the truth has already been announced once and for all.[38] This epistemological closure mirrors the being-in-itself and being-without-a-witness that define thingness: The thing presents itself as a necessary being-in-the-world whose meaning is fixed in advance, making the speaking observer irrelevant to what can be thought, said, experienced, and learned. Likewise, Eco's claim that, for fascism, dissent is betrayal[39] echoes the self-signifying being and the exclusion of representation: When the thing signifies by virtue of itself and becomes *hors langue,* the sign vanishes and contradiction is disqualified as illegitimate, so that representational disputes are not resolved but foreclosed as treason to an already-given-order. Finally, Eco's account of the people as a monolithic entity whose common will is expressed through a leader who claims to be its interpreter restates the self-caused and ancestral register of thingness: A distribution of places and roles that presents itself as anterior and necessary, a presence that continues after the speaking observer has left the scene, thereby naturalizing the exclusion of any voice that does not fit the allocation.[40] In short, Eco's take on the grammar of fascism consolidates the same epistemological authoritarianism at work in thingification: Speech is bound to obligatory forms that secure recognition by sacrificing agency and representation, and the scene of appearance is shut down in favour of a world that declares itself already complete.

At this stage, one may object that Nazism, as is accounted for by the authors mentioned in this section, often emphasizes organicism rather than thingness, life rather than inert matter.[41] It is argued here, however, that Nazi organicism can be construed as a privileged modality of thingness, since it confers on the organism precisely the attributes of necessity, self-causation, ancestrality, and self-signification that define thingness. The *Volk* as organism is self-caused (its law springs from its blood), ancestral (it precedes any individual witness), self-signifying (it "speaks" immediately in the signs of health and sickness), and being-in-itself (it endures outside recognition).[42] Eric Michaud's study of Nazi iconography can also be mentioned here because it shows how monumental bodies and typified figures – peasant, soldier, mother – thingify the organic into sculpted presence. These images present life as form, a thing-like surface of necessity exempt from contingency and history, thereby producing the same representationlessness as thingness.[43]

A final remark is in order. It brings us back to a pre-Kantian and precritical epistemology that has been earlier associated with thingness.[44] The many abovementioned thingification processes at work in fascist discourse similarly produce a world that claims to precede and cancel the speaking observer. Such epistemological compulsion is thus also fundamentally pre-Kantian because it replaces the reflective judgement and the autonomy of the speaking observer with the coercive givenness of what is, turning the correlation between object and speaking observer into irrelevance. Interestingly and somewhat ironically, as Johann Chapoutot demonstrates, Nazi intellectuals attempted to recuperate Kant, albeit precisely in order to underwrite their own processes of thingification. In theoretical works supporting Nazi ideology, Kant is extensively referenced because he belongs to the German tradition but his concepts and his epistemology have been emptied of their constructivist substance.[45] Chapoutot particularly details how Otto Dietrich executes a *coup de force*. This author makes Kant say that the world of experience and representation culminates in the postulate of a collective practical reason (the moral law of the people), thereby translating the transcendental standpoint into a *Volksgebot* and converting critique into obedience.[46] The result, Chapoutot argues, is a "monstre notionnel", a Nazification of Kant.[47] In this recoding, Kant ceases to be an Enlightenment thinker and is remade as a German thinker whose authority is invoked to ratify the primacy of the concrete and identitarian – precisely the self-signifying, self-caused thing that, in fascist discourse, demands assent outside language and beyond the speaking observer.[48] For philosophers outside these circles, such recuperation has never proved convincing because it replaces Kant's autonomy of the speaking observer with the heteronomy of the thing. The latter constitutes the most anti-Kantian move of all, one that annihilates perception, cancels the speaking observer, and forecloses representation, thereby converting critique into tutelage.

6. Thingness, colonialism, and fascism

If thingness is the expression of a fascist epistemology, colonialism manifests the same grammar of necessity, commonly converting persons into administrable objects. As has been compellingly shown in postcolonial thought as well as decolonial theory, the indigenous, the enslaved, and later the colonized are repeatedly reduced to beings-without-a-witness, beings *hors langue*, beings outside representation, whose lives are thingified.

For instance, as has been amply studied in decolonial theory,[49] the thingification of the non-European is already very conspicuous in the legal documents, charters, and legal codes that have constituted the legal architecture of European colonialism from the late 15th century onwards. From the outset, papal and royal instruments framed worlds and peoples as assignable things within a distributive order that preempted representation and installed necessity. As early as 1492, the privileges granted to Columbus crystallized a distributive epistemology by granting titles, monopolies, and rights of extraction over lands and peoples as a bundle, conferring on the admiral the authority to govern, tax, and exploit in terms that fold human and natural resources into a single field of prerogatives, thereby scripting a world of offices and objects in which the indigenous is an element of fiscal and administrative calculation. Likewise, in the 1493 papal bull *Inter Caetera,* non-European lands were designated for donation and partition according to a spatial logic that treated territories and their inhabitants as transferable goods under the sign of evangelization and dominion. The text authorized Christian princes to claim discovered regions and to subdue their inhabitants. The papal bull *Dudum Siquidem*, in the same year, extended this grammar by sweeping into the grant even those lands not yet discovered, converting the indeterminate into a pre-appropriated object and folding possible futures into a prior title, thereby reducing indigenous polities to a remainder of a donation that preceded and cancelled their own forms of appearance. The 1494 Treaty of Tordesillas similarly translated this ecclesiastical apportionment into a bilateral cartography that divided the globe by meridian and measure, treating territory as a divisible res and peoples as included in such division, a geometry of allocation that presupposed a world already made legible as object and susceptible to exchange between crowns. The later 1621 Charter of the Dutch West India Company intensified the conflation between commerce, seizure, imperial violence, and thingification by licensing conquest, fortification, trade monopolies, and the seizure of ships and goods across Atlantic and African theatres, treating coasts, rivers, and human bodies as components of a logistical chain. The Charter authorized the Company to make contracts, appointing governors, and administering justice in territories reduced to corporate jurisdiction and extractive purpose. At the same time, in the plantation's codes, thingification became even more explicit and procedural. The 1661 Barbados Act "for the better ordering and governing of Negroes" classified enslaved Africans as governable property by establishing regimes of control, punishment, and dismemberment calibrated to protect the master's estate, with provisions that equated resistance with damage to goods and instituted surveillance as a technique for preserving value, converting the person into a commodity whose movements and speech were regulated for the security of ownership. The 1740 South Carolina Slave Code then consolidated this regime by fixing status as inheritable chattel, restricting assembly, prohibiting literacy and movement, and prescribing corporal punishment to preserve the proprietary order, legally translating African persons into transmissible assets and legally legible risks to be managed, priced, and immobilized. The 1730 Asiento formalized the traffic in bodies as the crown's fiscal instrument by granting the right to import quantified numbers of Africans into Spanish dominions, fixing volumes, tariffs, and delivery points as if scheduling cargo, a juridical apparatus that enumerated human life as units under licence ("piezas"), thereby giving the clearest expression to the conversion of persons into objects of trade and revenue. Across these instruments, a single operation repeats, namely the world's material division and the other's reduction to an assignable object, where indigenous polities were addressed as annexable, Africans were codified as inheritable chattel, and nature was mapped as divisible resource. In all those instances, the legal form operated as a thing-maker that foreclosed representation and installed imperial governance as the administration of things rather than a relation among speaking subjects.[50]

A similar point has also been made by postcolonial thinkers, especially in relation to the European colonization of Africa. Among others, Frantz Fanon, drawing on psychoanalysis, offers a precise account of the colonial conversion of the Black subject into a thing, a process he figures as a collapse of lived historicity and relational meaning under the weight of racial signification. In *Black Skin, White Masks*, Fanon names the moment of racial interpellation ("Look, a Black person!") as an objectifying hail that sutures epidermis to an imposed being-in-itself, producing what he calls the "epidermalization of inferiority", a fixation that reorganizes perception and bodily schema before the subject can speak or appear for themself. In the scene of racial interpellation he describes, Africans are fixed by a look that overcodes, fixes, and crystalizes their being, thereby excluding them from the discursive economy of signification and reciprocity. This fixation is not merely a misrecognition but a thingification. Indeed, the colonizer's gaze thingifies by installing the Black as an object, converting the field of encounter into a one-way optics where reciprocity is foreclosed and the possibility of mutual address is neutralized. The thingness that is so attributed to the Africans by the European colonizer is a self-effacing epistemology that presents itself as anterior to any witness, a presence without presence that, as Fanon argues, imposes upon the colonized the status of res relegated to a fixed place defined by exterior European predicates. For Fanon, this is a world-making operation. The colonial world is a Manichaean order that distributes value and visibility such that Black existence is apprehended as a function of white perception and policing. The result is a phenomenological foreclosure – what Fanon describes as the "crushing objecthood" – in which the colonized experiences a disarticulation of body and world, a reduction to the status of a usable thing within a racialized economy of signs.[51]

Édouard Glissant, elaborating a poetics of relation, similarly shows how the colonizers' demand for legibility and clarity functions as a technology of thingification. Opacity, which would safeguard the possibility of being outside the colonizer's grid, is rejected, and the colonized is reconfigured as a thing that must be fully knowable according to the colonizer's categories, thus evacuated into a schema of predicates, metrics, and programmes that install an a-perception and a representationlessness.[52] For him, the colonized territory can thus be read as a laboratory of thingification in which the reduction of persons to objects is both doctrinal and practical, operating through law, police, medicine, and pedagogy.[53]

From the perspective of the thinkers mentioned in this section, thingification thus appears as a cornerstone of the colonial scene which systematically produces a world of things. Their insights make Albert Memmi's assertion that *colonialism is a form of fascism* even more compelling. His claim names the identical operation by which individuals are forced into thingness, outside language, outside representation, while effacing their discursive production, a devastating enterprise that leaves everything in ruins once necessity is installed. This is nothing other than the mark of fascism.[54]

7. The fascist grammar of the legal discourse

Now that the idea of a fascist grammar has been unpacked and historicized, it is possible to return to the thingification processes enabled by law that were examined in Chapter 4. Seen through the hyperbolic descriptor developed in this chapter, the picture for lawyers – and for anyone who invokes or deploys law and legal arguments – is stark, if not sinister. In fact, a large share of law's efficacy owes to its recourse to a fascist grammar, in the specific sense established here. There is, in other words, a great deal of fascism in law's thingification of what it encounters because it installs a discursive and epistemological machinery that turns contingent, historical, and contested practices into necessary beings-in-themselves, that effaces representation and the speaking observer, that collapses agency into self-causation, and that anchors itself in ancestrality. Law, even when it is commonly systematized and theorized around modern and Kantian principles, can accordingly be said to operate through an authoritarian epistemology. In other words, law, despite its liberal veneer, serves as a theatre for authoritarian epistemological practices that compel recognition. Fascist grammar, as is understood here, one of the grammars through which law operates.

It is acknowledged that such claim requires careful calibration and qualification. The point is of course not that law is fascist "full stop", a claim that would be both conceptually empty and normatively counterproductive. First, fascism has been mobilized here as a hyperbolic descriptor to capture the authoritarian epistemology at work in thingness, not to draw direct and comparisons with totalizing fascist experiences. The analogy operates at the level of discursive and epistemological technology rather than institutional arrangements or governmental programmes. Second, the association between fascism and law is limited to specific discursive and epistemological traits around which legal discourse articulates itself, particularly the compulsion to recognize certain beings as necessary, self-signifying, and ancestral. Third, law encompasses multiple registers and discursive practices that cannot be reduced to thingification, including procedural safeguards, rights protections, and deliberative mechanisms that operate through different epistemological logics. Most importantly, the ambition here is not to repudiate and invalidate law wholesale. Especially these days, law may indeed be what one must cling to when authoritarianism returns in its more familiar institutional forms. The point is rather that highlighting the fascist grammar along which law operates serves as a diagnostic tool to make lawyers and anyone invoking law aware of how law does what it does to the world and to people. Thingness undoubtedly participates in the efficacy of law, as demonstrated in the previous chapter, by providing stable categories, reducing transaction costs, and enabling coordination across diverse contexts. Yet, one of the lessons of this chapter is that the efficacy of law should not be pursued to an extent that revives the sinister practices of epistemological closure and the foreclosure of dissensus that characterized historical fascist regimes.

Recognizing the fascist grammar of law represents the first step toward restoring those capacities that are stifled by legal thingification processes, i.e. those very capacities by which speaking observers can participate in the making of the worlds they inhabit rather than being compelled to acknowledge a world already composed, capacities that are indispensable for critique, including for the critique of law. Restoring such capacities while resisting thingness is what will be attempted in the next chapter. It is important to stress that the following experiment ought not to make us reinvent legal thought and practice beyond all materiality, a move that might exact too high a cost in terms of discursive efficacy and might relegate law to a museum of dead discourses.[55] Nor does such experiment call us to reinvent critique itself beyond any materiality or to abandon the critical tools that have proven effective in exposing relations of domination and exclusion. Instead, what the next chapter endeavours to achieve is a move that, while resisting the precritical and authoritarian features of the thingness around which law is articulated, strategizes the recourse to materiality.

Notes

1 Roland Barthes, *Le Neutre: Cours au Collège de France (1977–1978)* (Éditions du Seuil 2002) 209 ('Le terrorisme n'aime pas le discours. Il ne pratique pas le discours. Il ne discourt pas d'ailleurs et c'est ce qui accroit sans doute auprès de la masse des gens l'impression de folie et d'horreur').
2 Theodor W Adorno and Max Horkheimer, *Dialectic of Enlightenment* (Stanford University Press 2002) 'The Concept of Enlightenment' 1–34; Theodor W Adorno, *Negative Dialectics* (Seabury Press 1973) pt I, chs 1–3.
3 Enrique Dussel, *20 Theses on Politics* (Duke University Press 2008) theses 1–4; Enrique Dussel, *Ethics of Liberation: In the Age of Globalization and Exclusion* (Duke University Press 2013) pt I, chs 1–3.
4 Theodor W Adorno, *The Jargon of Authenticity* (Northwestern University Press 1973) chs 1–2.
5 Roland Barthes, *Leçon* (Seuil 1978) 7–9.
6 On this famous claim of Barthes, see Jean-Jacques Lecercle, *De l'interpellation: Sujet, langue, idéologie* (Editions Amsterdam 2019) 90. See also Laurent de Sutter, *Superfaible: Penser au XXIe siècle* (Climats 2023) 238–39. See also e.g. H Noghrehchi, 'Language is Fascist' (2017) 186(2) *Littérature* 34–43.
7 Roland Barthes, *Le Neutre: Cours au Collège de France (1977–1978)* (Éditions du Seuil 2002).
8 Roland Barthes, *Le Neutre: Cours au Collège de France (1977–1978)* (Éditions du Seuil 2002) 119–20.
9 See ch 1, s 2.1 above.
10 See ch 1, s 2.6 above.
11 On the idea that the social world is composed of acts of interpellation, see Didier Eribon, *Principes d'une pensée critique* (Fayard 2016) 94–95.
12 Louis Althusser, *Initiation à la philosophie pour les non-philosophes* (Presses Universitaires de France 2014) 228; Louis Althusser, 'Ideology and Ideological State Apparatuses' in Louis Althusser, *Lenin and Philosophy and Other Essays* (Monthly Review Press 1971) 127–88, esp 170–77.
13 Gilles Deleuze and Félix Guattari, *L'Anti-Œdipe* (Editions de Minuit 1972) 306–07; Gilles Deleuze and Félix Guattari, *Mille plateaux: Capitalisme et schizophrénie 2* (Editions de Minuit 1980) 382–404.
14 Gilles Deleuze, *Sur les lignes de vie: Cours, mai–juin 1980* (Editions de Minuit 2025) 42–43.
15 Ibid 50–51.
16 On the critique of reification by the Frankfurt School, see Seyla Benhabib, *Critique, Norm, and Utopia: A Study of the Foundations of Critical Theory* (Columbia University Press 1987).
17 Max Horkheimer and Theodor W Adorno, *Dialectic of Enlightenment: Philosophical Fragments* (Stanford University Press 2002) 94–136.
18 Max Horkheimer and Theodor W Adorno, *Dialectic of Enlightenment* (Stanford University Press 2002) 'The Culture Industry: Enlightenment as Mass Deception'

94–136; 'The Concept of Enlightenment' 1–34; Theodor W Adorno, 'On the Fetish-Character in Music and the Regression of Listening' in Andrew Arato and Eike Gebhardt (eds), *The Essential Frankfurt School Reader* (Continuum 1982) 270–99.

19 See ch 1, s 2.9 above.

20 Herbert Marcuse, *One-Dimensional Man: Studies in the Ideology of Advanced Industrial Society* (Beacon Press 1964) 95–134 and 135–72.

21 See ch 1, s 2.8 above.

22 Jacques Rancière, *La mésentente: Politique et philosophie* (La Fabrique 1995) 48. See also Jacques Rancière, *Le partage du sensible: Esthétique et politique* (La Fabrique 2000) 14.

23 Jacques Rancière, *La mésentente: Politique et philosophie* (La Fabrique 1995) 51.

24 The claim that such mechanisms, supported by law, dispossess the political of its initiative is further developed in the chapter 'Démocratie et consensus' in Jacques Rancière, *La mésentente: Politique et philosophie* (La Fabrique 1995) 129–61.

25 Jacques Rancière, *La mésentente: Politique et philosophie* (La Fabrique 1995) 165.

26 This is the claim of Bruno Latour, *L'Espoir de Pandore* (Didier Gille tr, La Découverte 2007) 14.

27 See ch 1, s 3.1 above.

28 On the unavoidable limits and pitfalls of any exercise of comparison, see Günter Frankenberg, 'Critical Comparisons: Re-thinking Comparative Law' (1985) 26 *Harvard International Law Journal* 411; Pierre Legrand, 'The Same and the Different' in Pierre Legrand and Roderick Munday (eds), *Comparative Legal Studies: Traditions and Transitions* (CUP 2003) 240–311; Jean d'Aspremont, 'Comparativism and Colonizing Thinking in International Law' (2020) 57 *Canadian Yearbook of International Law* 89–112.

29 Jean-Pierre Faye, *Langages totalitaires* (Hermann 1972).

30 Johann Chapoutot, *La loi du sang: Penser et agir en nazi* (Gallimard 2014) 29–66 and 127–70.

31 Ibid 151–64.

32 Ibid 167–70.

33 Ibid 151–64.

34 Johann Chapoutot, *La révolution culturelle nazie* (Gallimard 2017) 11–13, 18–19, 119 and 145.

35 Victor Klemperer, *The Language of the Third Reich* (Continuum 2000) 46–53 and 97–104.

36 Ibid 46–53.

37 Ibid 14–22, 46–53.

38 Umberto Eco, *How to Spot a Fascist* (Richard Dixon and Alastair McEwen trs, Harvill Secker 2020) 17.

39 Ibid 19–20.

40 Ibid 24–25.

41 On the relationship between thingness and organicism, see ch 1, s 4.2 above.

42 Johann Chapoutot, *La révolution culturelle nazie* (Gallimard 2017) 95–126.

43 Eric Michaud, *Un art de l'éternité* (Gallimard 1996) 71–110.

44 See ch 2, s 3 above.

45 Johann Chapoutot, *La révolution culturelle nazie* (Gallimard 2017) 118–21.

46 Ibid 130–31.

47 Ibid 133–134.

48 Ibid 140.

49 See eg Malcolm Ferdinand, *Une écologie décoloniale: Penser l'écologie depuis le monde caribéen* (Seuil 2019) 88; Aníbal Quijano, 'Coloniality of Power, Eurocentrism, and Latin America' (2000) 1 *Nepantla: Views from South* 533.
50 Sylvie Laurent, *Capital and Race: The History of a Modern Hydra* (Polity Press 2026).
51 Frantz Fanon, *Peau noire, masques blancs* (Éditions du Seuil 1952) 90–97, 106–13, 116–21 and 179–86; Frantz Fanon, *Les Damnés de la terre* (François Maspero 1961) 31–41 and 57–63.
52 Édouard Glissant, *Poétique de la relation* (Gallimard 1990) 21–31 and 189–97.
53 See also Édouard Glissant, *Discours antillais* (Gallimard 1981) 145–60. On the colonial archive and the annulment of creolized speech, see Achille Mbembe, *Critique de la raison nègre* (La Découverte 2013) 41–55.
54 Albert Memmi, *Portrait du colonisé, précédé de Portrait du colonisateur* (Buchet/Chastel 1957) 163–70.
55 I have used this metaphor elsewhere. See Jean d'Aspremont, 'International Law as a Crisis Discourse: The Peril of Wordlessness' in Makane Mbengue and Jean d'Aspremont (eds), *Crisis Narratives in International Law* (Brill 2021) 69–84.

Chapter 6

Countermateriality

It has been argued in previous chapters that the thingness that law attributes to what it encounters undoubtedly participates in its own efficacy.[1] Yet, at the same time, it has been shown that law's thingification processes have come at the price of reviving the sinister epistemological practices, namely the foreclosure of dissensus characteristic of fascist modes of thinking.[2] In this chapter, it is contended that, more often than not, legal thingification ought to be resisted, if not totally unmade. This is certainly the case when law thingifies itself, the State, the people, sex, race, nature, and culture, thereby displaying its fascist attributes.

This chapter makes the case for a specific mode of resistance to legal thingification that is called *countermateriality*.[3] This chapter starts with an important terminological remark on the notion of materiality which provides the terminological and conceptual skeleton of this mode of resistance (1). It then moves on to show that a complete dematerialization of legal thought and practice can be detrimental to critique and that some minimal materiality is inevitable for critical action (2). A third section briefly introduces a precursory use of materiality as a tool of critique that has been developed under the banner of *Thing Theory* and which has blaized the trail for the type of resistance attempted through the idea of countermateriality (3). It is in a fourth section that the notion of countermateriality is fully unpacked (4). Lastly, this chapter elaborates on what the mobilization of countermateriality, as it has been theorized here, concretely entails in legal thought and practice (5).

1. Preliminary remarks: From thingness to materiality

Before anything else, a terminological remark is in order. Through the idea of countermateriality, this chapter resorts to the notion of materiality, which has not been used to define thingness and thingification in previous chapters. Such omission was deliberate, for materiality has been reserved to introduce a type of epistemology that breaks away from that of thingness. Materiality, as understood here, does not presume a necessary, mind-independent being that is *hors langue* and outside representation. It names only the worldly

DOI: 10.4324/9781003753940-7

arrangements, texts, bodies, media, infrastructures, and resistances through which practices take hold and consequences are felt.[4] In other words, for the sake of this book, the idea of thing does not have a monopoly on materiality. One can speak materially without installing the ancestrality, self-cause, and *hors-langue* pretensions that define thingness.

Three specific features of materiality must be foregrounded to further elucidate its difference from thingness. First, materiality can be relational, emergent, and mediated rather than foundational or self-signifying. Objects are not granted a sovereign outside to language, perception, discourse, or experience. Matter appears through use, mobility, and habit, not through ancestral self-presence.[5] Second, materiality can be assembled rather. This is reminiscent of actor-network approaches in Science and Technology Studies that treat matter as composites of instruments, inscriptions, labour, energy, and institutions. The material is real because it is maintained, measured, and contested, not because it precedes representation.[6] Third, materiality can be processual and performative rather than static. In that regard, feminist and postcolonial accounts have shown how bodies, relations, and environments are produced while denying that such production secures necessity.[7] This aligns with the insight that materiality can be historically sedimented and iterated or stratified and morphogenetic,[8] without collapsing into a self-caused thing.

2. The material register of critique

Having clarified its terminology, this chapter now makes the point that resistance to thingness must keep enough materiality to preserve demonstration, accountability, and intervention, through texts, traces, and measures while systematically suspending any slide back into thingness and its precritical epistemology. In other words, to provincialize thingness is not to subtract matter, but to reorganize material presence so that perception, representation, and the speaking observer return to the scene. The point is that minimal materiality is therefore not an optional addendum to critique but the register in which consequences and resistances become legible enough to interrupt the *hors langue* without reinstalling matter as ancestral or self-signifying as thingness does.

The very first reason why one could not envisage a critique of thingness that does away with materiality is simply that, throughout this book, the very categories of thingness and thingification have always been materially staged by this book itself. They have not only been textualized to be apprehended. More fundamentally, it is their materialization through legal texts, scholarship, literature, archives, and traces that has permitted us to shed light on their manufacture and functioning.[9]

Second, the strategic necessity of minimal materiality has been usefully epitomized in recent decades of contemporary climate politics where the hasty relinquishment of material presence has allowed climate change denial to thrive. In that regard, Bruno Latour has usefully demonstrated that scientists, commonly eager to acknowledge their constructivist epistemology and the permanently tentative character of any of their findings, conceded too hastily that their findings are constructions, allowing climate sceptics to cleverly turn Kantian epistemology on its head, restricting debate to facts and asserting that the material facts are not there.[10] In such striking reversal, scientists came to appear as the activists while sceptics occupied the role of sober savants.[11] Latour's lesson is precise: The point is not to deny construction, but to warn that shedding materiality, and thus mistaking constructivism for dematerialization, exposes inquiry to performative nihilism. The cautionary lesson from Latour is that critique must safeguard material presence without elevating it into an epistemological closure.

Third, one finds additional support for the necessity to disjoin materiality from thingness in Althusserian materialism. For Althusser, ideology is not merely textual or discursive but has a material existence[12] insofar as it is enacted in practices and embodied in institutions (through training and habituation, repetition and ritualization, evaluation and sanction, taking concrete form in school curricula, media routines, political ceremonials, workplace architectures, bureaucratic procedures, and digital interfaces).[13] As a result, studying the production of necessity requires analysing the apparatuses and practices through which subjects are formed and social relations reproduced. Even if this book does not approach thingness and thingification through a strict ideology-critique prism, Althusser's materialism teaches us that the awareness of the representationless system of representation provided by thingness and the denunciation of its material inscriptions on the world by no means sufficient to resist are it.[14] Resisting entails engaging with the very material *dispositifs* of law that concretize and routinize the exclusions of perception, representation, and the speaking observer.

Fourth, the need for minimal materialization in the critique of thingness finds confirmation in the way in which, as shown by Marxist thought, the proletariat commonly thingifies itself in order to play its role and contest the bourgeois order. In its struggle, the proletariat is said to have commonly crystallized itself into an agent of history by adopting determinate forms of organization, visibility, and strategic articulation (party, union, strike, slogan, platform) whose material presence enables confrontation as well as solidarity.[15] Such thingification is not a metaphysical relapse but a tactical and dialectical move through which a class-for-itself emerges from a class-in-itself, converting dispersed vulnerabilities into coordinated action. The proletariat's self-materialization shows that critique of thingness and thingification cannot remain a purely discursive practice but must pass through forms, texts, practices, and embodiments that render antagonism operative while remaining revisable and contestable.

Fifth, multiple critical traditions, despite being predicated on a constructivist epistemology, have unsurprisingly upheld a great deal of materialism and shown that, in order to appreciate what a discourse does and how it does what it does, one must grasp its material implications, i.e. how it produces bodies, colours, subjectivities, identities, and worlds without confusing such material production with epistemological necessity.[16] Feminist critical thought, which has already been amply mentioned in this book, is particularly illustrative in that respect. Judith Butler, for instance, has compellingly challenged the assumption that sex is a prediscursive given and shown how the heterosexual imperative materializes bodies through performative reiteration.[17] Sex, on this account, is not an inert substrate upon which gender is imposed but a cultural norm that governs the materialization of bodies, forming the speaking "I" through the process of assuming a sex, enabling certain identifications and foreclosing others.[18] Matter is thereby rethought not as inert surface but as a process of materialization that stabilizes over time to produce the effects of boundary, fixity, and surface called matter.[19] Against caricatures of constructivism as linguistic idealism, Butler thus concedes the materiality of sex while showing that such concession is always a concession to some specific formation of materiality. For her, language and materiality are fully embedded in one another without collapsing into one another, for every reference to materiality occurs through signifying practices that are themselves materially instantiated.[20]

Last but not least, within legal theory specifically, similar insights on the need for some minimal materiality can be gathered from Margaret Davies, who has articulated the most sustained account of how to retain materiality without epistemological closure in relation to law. In calling for renewed attention to matter and objects in legal theory, she shows convincingly why some legal thingification processes remain attractive while also clarifying how a critical materialism can avoid epistemological closure. She specifically argues for a new materialism in the study of law, i.e. an approach that takes seriously the physicality of objects, infrastructures, and environments with which law interacts, and that recognizes the plural epistemologies that law convenes rather than presuming a single metaphysical order.[21] Her insistence on the physical presence of objects (the roads, files, bodies, machines, rivers, and architectures that co-constitute legal practice) speaks to the intuition that legal efficacy often depends on engaging what appears as possessing thingness. Yet, it is important to stress that Davies's materialism does not collapse into the self-effacing epistemology that thingness puts in place. By linking pluralism to practice, she resists the ancestral and self-caused thingness and instead frames objects as embedded in networks of relations, meanings, and practices. In this way, she offers lawyers a route to keep the focus on matter and objects without ceding the exclusion of perception and representation, maintaining instead an open grammar of contestation around the very materialities law must handle. By analysing how objects are staged, circulated, and stabilized juridically, Davies equips legal theory with a sensitivity to the production of object-worlds and to the ways in which law's reliance on apparent physicality can both enable intervention and conceal politics. Thus, her account, like many other critical traditions, underwrites a view in which keeping a certain degree of materiality may be justified when it facilitates urgent action or clarify responsibility, provided that one simultaneously denecessitates the epistemological pretensions of materiality and re-opens the discursive scene where objects are negotiated.

3. The intellectual companionship of Thing Theory

Possibly the best model for the resort to a type of materiality that evades the pitfall of the precritical epistemology of thingness is provided by Thing Theory, a famous conceptual framework that provides a useful precedent for the attitude of resistance envisaged here under the banner of countermateriality. The project of Thing Theory, as famously developed by Bill Brown, stages a confrontation between the sensible, formed, and perceived object and a surplus that eludes objecthood, i.e. an opacity or recalcitrance indexed as thingness.[22] From the outset, Brown distinguishes thingness from objecthood by drawing on philosophy's long-standing efforts to separate the in-itself from the for-us and by foregrounding the modern arts' fascination with the inscrutable, the unassimilable, the strange remainder that fits nowhere on the grid of intelligibility. It is this remainder that gives thingness its critical force, for it marks a presence that resists reduction to function, concept, or utility and that solicits, interrupts, or even assaults perception.[23] One might say that Thing Theory seeks to recover the drama that occurs when objects cease to be merely objects – when they stop working, break down, or suddenly appear as alien – and thereby disclose the epistemological excess of things over the categories that domesticate them. Brown's claim is that literature and the visual and plastic arts have been meticulously preserving this drama, awaiting its excavation, because their modes of staging and material play can dramatize what is rarely the task of theory: How things impress themselves upon consciousness to upset epistemic security. In this sense, Thing Theory describes both a constellation of critical concerns and a method of attentiveness attuned to the moments when an object, stripped of its familiar profile, offers itself as a thing.[24]

Brown's account unfolds against the background of contemporary intellectual movements that privilege language and sign as well as against the transformations that have dematerialized material culture. The so-called "turn to discourse", the structuralist and poststructuralist focus on signification, and various theories of subjectivity seem to marginalize the being of objects as secondary or beside the point.[25] At the same time, the digitization of the world and the progressive dematerialization of cultural artefacts cultivate a sense that objects might be disappearing or losing their semantic plenitude.[26] Brown, in reaction, nurtures a quest for some new engagement with the object, an effort to forestall disappearance or to cling to a world where things remain repositories of meaning. This quest parallels the emergence, in critical theory, of a renewed fascination with the material stuff of life, i.e. a return of things that seeks resources in phenomenology and in arts to re-situate material presence after long seasons of textualization. On this occasion, Brown emphasizes minimalism's interest in the inscrutability of the thing, an aesthetics that resists interpretation to expose how certain presences evade our grids. Duchamp's Fountain remains paradigmatic in that respect. By selecting and relocating a urinal, he inscribes – not simply represents – the arbitrariness of the art object, the boundaries and authority of the art system, and the capacity of things to interrupt the conventions that confer intelligibility.[27] From this perspective, Duchamp's Fountain constitutes a meta-object that addresses the conditions of objecthood, performing a materialist explication that makes the object's thingness critical by placing it just outside the normal circuits of recognition.[28]

For the sake of the resistance attempted in this chapter, it must be added that thingness, for Brown, is not merely a property but a relational event defined partly by the absence of human witness: It is a state made critical by the absence of looking, akin to the Kantian thing-in-itself, outside the spatiotemporal grid of experience that furnishes the for-us.[29] Yet the condition is not pure unknowability. It is the irreducibility of the object to any object form, the remainder that persists when the apparatus of perception fails or falters. For him, things are critical when there is no one to see them, when their state remains outside the phenomenological capture of the subject. But in practice, the interest lies in how objects grasp you, how they elicit attention, interrupt concentration, and assault the consciousness.[30] This is why the arts, for Brown, are so fascinating. They advance a speculative realism, not by endorsing metaphysical claims about access to the in-itself, but by ignoring the discrepancy between the phenomenal and the material to lay bare the materiality effect.[31]

For legal scholars, immersion in Thing Theory can surely help visibilize the invisible, and especially law's process of thingification. In particular, it can help legal scholars grasp those objects that routinely pass as transparent instruments (files, forms, contracts, borders, property parcels, bodily samples, courtroom architectures, procedural devices) while allowing them to better appreciate the materiality effect through which law hides its operations. It can also make them more alert to the vitality of concrete things, how they disturb coherence and unsettle claims to necessity, thus preparing legal reasoning to acknowledge breakdowns, resist fetishization, and recover the contested production of necessity.

Yet, it is submitted here that not all the tools provided by Thing Theory are relevant for resisting legal thingification as described in this book. And this is where the type of resistance envisaged here, and more fully described in the next section, distances itself from Thing Theory. A few of these differences between Thing Theory and the mode of resistance put forward here must be mentioned here. First, while Thing Theory succeeds in dramatizing the irreducible remainder beyond object form, the type of resistance promoted here is premised on upholding materiality without endorsing the epistemological closure of thingness. The critical issue for legal scholars is not merely that objects hide a surplus of thingness. It is rather that law produces an ancestral, self-caused status for itself, its objects, its environments, and its identities, converting them into immovable stones and installing zones of uncriticability. Thing Theory's emphasis on opacity and inscrutability provides a salutary counter to precritical epistemology, but what one needs to insist on is a different tactic, namely saturating and rematerializing the juridical scene to show how necessity is manufactured and how the "must-be" is staged. If Thing Theory privileges the moment of arrest, i.e. when the thing assaults perception, what must be privileged here is the iterative work of intervention, thereby provincializing claims to ancestrality by exposing thingification processes. What is more, Thing Theory's inheritance from aesthetics, i.e. its confidence that art can disclose thingness better than philosophy, offers invaluable methods for the critique of legal thingification but can risk relocating resistance into well-delineated encounters that are episodic and exemplary rather than iterative. The resistance that is needed here, by contrast, is dialectical, for it proposes the thingification of thingification, the reflexive materialization of the process that produces thingness. It is by giving the production of thingness its own seams, supports, and failures that the resistance envisaged here abolishes the epistemological necessity. The result is a practice for dismantling closures that Thing Theory helps us recognize but does not necessarily instruct us to unmake. Finally, Thing Theory's allegiance to speculative realism within the arts may encourage what is, from a legal standpoint, an insufficiently discriminating embrace of the "beyond-representation". Law's regimes of representation are not merely discursive screens but are also the material means by which harms are recognized, claims registered, and domination contested. Resistance to legal thingification refuse to valorize being totally outside representation as such. Instead, it must re-insert representation as an instrument for dismantling the *hors langue* claims that immunize legal thingification processes and the thingness they create from critique.

The foregoing should suffice to show that it would not help to seek to simply and mechanically translate Thing Theory into a mode of resistance against legal thingification. Such resistance, albeit taking its cue from some of the moves promoted by Thing Theory, must be thought anew, almost from scratch. This is the object of the next section that more systematically and more thoroughly introduces what is meant by countermateriality.

4. The notion of countermateriality

Countermateriality names the mode of resistance advanced here against thingification that, as argued in the previous sections, strategically upholds some minimal materiality but allows thingness, in all its epistemological dimensions, to be kept at bay. Countermateriality is not a monolithic doctrine or method but a composite attitude that advances a set of moves that unsettle thingness from multiple angles. It begins with a clear stance that thingness is historically made rather than given (what is called *foundational constructivism*), then continues by dissolving the word/thing split (what is called *non-dual mediation*), overtextualizing the process of attribution of thingness (*thingification-of-thingification*), saturating what is endowed with thingness with dense and material specificities until unity fissures (*overmateriality*), moving what has been thingified across vantage points (*transperspectivism*), and ends by recalibrating the figurative language that sustains thingification (*countermetaphorism*). Taken together, these moves reinsert perception and representation into what had, until then, presented itself as necessary and self-caused, thereby reintroducing the possibility of construction, debate and contestation.

The way these various moves function can be sketched out as follows. Foundational constructivism sets the horizon and prevents metaphysical relapse into a precritical epistemology. Non-dual mediation blocks representational dualism and establishes the co-constitutive terrain for countermateriality. Thingification-of-thingification targets claims to mute exteriority early, clarifying how thingness is always staged. Overmateriality performs saturation that fractures unity at the level of description and experience, turning thingness into an obscene scene of excessive performances. Transperspectivism maintains the fracture by demonstrating non-coincidence across perspectives, exposing how unity is an achievement of coordination rather than a thing. Countermetaphorism cleans the figurative regime that re-stabilizes things, disciplining language so that critique can move without reinstalling thingness.

It is important to stress that, in the view of the author of these lines, one does not need to embrace each and every one of the abovementioned moves to espouse countermateriality. Neither do these moves need to be applied in a rigid sequence. Rather, performing some of these moves will suffice to resist precritical epistemologies and interrupt processes of thingification.

4.1 Foundational constructivism

Countermateriality remains constructivist and does not relapse into a precritical epistemology.[32] Rather, it mobilizes a minimal, situated materiality – archives, texts, traces, infrastructures, bodies, devices – as an evidentiary and interruptive resource for critique, superposed upon the very processes of thingification it seeks to unsettle. In such epistemology, materiality functions as a disciplined register of consequences and resistances within practices, not as an underlying substrate preceding representation. This approach is reminiscent of critical theories that show how objects and institutions acquire object-status through historical assemblage and rule-bound enunciation, where things are effects of practices that remain revisable and contestable.[33] It also echoes those approaches that treat form, practice, and mediation as constitutive, while retaining enough grip to record harm and accountability.[34] This constructivist premise simultaneously resonates with genealogical methods that elucidate how forms, objects, and institutions are historically assembled and maintained within regimes of enunciation.[35] Such a move also finds an echo in the delinking strategy found in decolonial theory where the first move is always to unveil the modern and colonial theo- and geopolitics of knowledge and understanding at work in our engagement with the world.[36] Foundational constructivism accordingly names the refusal to anchor critique in substances or essences, and insists that what appears as sovereign thingness has been formed, codified, and stabilized.

4.2 Non-dual mediation

Countermateriality breaks decisively with the distinction between word and thing, between thing and representation, moving toward the proposition that neither a fixed word nor a fixed thing precedes mediation. Discourse, inscription, gesture, and material supports co-constitute what appears as stability. They do so iteratively and without final closure. This is not a claim about textual omnipotence but about the co-presence of language and material traces within practices of reference and world-making. To illustrate such a move, one can refer to Derrida's work on iterability, trace, and *différance* as it captures this co-constitutive movement, particularly when he shows how writing saturates speech and how presence is marked by the very spacing that renders meaning repeatable and revisable.[37] Foucault offers a similar intuition as he remarks that the French title of his famous book *Les mots et les choses* was a trap, precisely to indicate that discourse is autonomous, exterior to both words and things.[38] From such a perspective, non-dual mediation affirms a terrain in which a border, an identity, or an artefact is neither purely linguistic nor purely material but an articulation across registers, times, and vantage points, such that any appeal to *hors langue* is always the product of mediations.

4.3 Thingification-of-thingification (ultracontextualism)

Countermateriality, as was said, does not do away with all materiality. Materiality is preserved by thingifying the process of thingification itself in a way that interrupts it. Instead of accepting the thing as a given outside representation, one materializes the discursive action of thingification and turns thingness over its head. Once the thingification itself is thingified, the necessity is abolished. One sees the apparatuses, rituals, and infrastructures that enact the exclusion of perception and representation, and in seeing them as material, one recovers the capacity to contest and reconfigure them. In that sense, the thingification-of-thingification is a form of *ultracontextualism*. In fact, the formation of thingness is contextualized to such an extreme that all its material and components come to appear as a composition that can only be an artefact of discourse and can no longer be taken as a necessary being.

It must be acknowledged that such a move is not novel in critical thinking. It particularly resonates with feminist critical theory, which commonly articulates how material vulnerabilities and solidarities are forged at the intersection of discourse and world without attributing to matter a self-signifying being that cancels critique.[39] Such lessons from feminist critical thought are crucial here. Indeed, they teach us that critique requires a diagnostic move that shifts from constructivism to the identification of how constructs have been endowed with a material aura. Resistance thus begins by rendering visible the discursive labour by which bodies, identities, and natures are made to appear necessary and independent of language, representation, and the observing subject.

4.4 Overmateriality

This further move within countermateriality is where the materiality of countermateriality is most discernible. In such a move, countermateriality entails the saturation of the thingified law, state, people, sex, race, nature, or culture with so much materiality that the thingness so attributed begins to fissure itself. In fact, overmateriality multiplies the registers, densities, and textures of material presence (historical sedimentations, infrastructural entanglements, bodily vulnerabilities, ecological interdependences, economic circuits, etc.) until the claim of self-signifying necessity becomes untenable. One materializes the object so extensively, with its networks, residues, affordances, and frictions, that it is no longer possible to take its thingness seriously. So understood, saturation works like a magnification that reveals seams, joints, and sutures. The alleged immovable stone appears as laminated layers produced by discursive and institutional practices. An overmaterialized border, for example, becomes a complex set of fences, sensors, roads, contracts, budgets, algorithms, and labour arrangements. An overmaterialized identity becomes a confluence of documents, databases, rituals, clothing, medical procedures, and kinship economies. In such saturation, the claim that the border or the identity is ancestrally self-caused dissolves into the specificity of assembly and maintenance. The very excess of materiality reintroduces representation by forcing attention to how materialities are staged, designed, patched, and enforced. In this sense, overmateriality becomes the antidote to the representationlessness of thingness. It shows how representation, far from being absent, is folded into the practices that present the thing as beyond representation.[40]

This specific move can be read as reminiscent of Derrida's *surinterprétation* (overinterpretation), the labour of reading that multiplies meanings beyond any stable closure. From such a perspective, overmateriality may be understood as a material correlative to *surinterprétation*, multiplying material readings of composition, history, and operation until the alleged *hors langue* collapses.[41] Where overinterpretation refuses to let the text rest in a definitive sense, overmateriality refuses to let the object rest in a definitive thingness. Both strategies are meant to destabilize the pretension to presence by insisting on traces and iterability that mark dependence on mediations claimed to be transcended.

4.5 Transperspectivism

Transperspectivism names the movement across technical, experiential, scalar, and institutional viewpoints so the same object is revealed as a composite articulation rather than a stable essential and necessary being, thereby preventing unity from re-coalescing, making the object's conditions of appearance distributed, contestable, and non-coincident. To put it differently, the constant traversal across micro, meso, and macro perspectives ensures that the thing endowed with thingness cannot remain the same across vantage points. What appears unified from one perspective becomes heterogeneous or differently articulated at another. Permanently shifting perspectives is thus a critical operation that reveals the non-coincidence of objecthood. The point is to demonstrate that unity is a function of the chosen horizon. The object transforms with each traversal, exposing the fragility of thingness and the difficulty of sustaining it across time and space. Transperspectivism thereby provides countermateriality with a tool to deflate thingness. It records how necessary being is distributed, not self-caused, and how what counts as the "same" thing is an achievement of alignment across vantage points rather than an ancestral identity.[42]

4.6 Countermetaphorism

A final move within countermateriality consists of recasting the figurative scaffolding that sustains thingness by positing that the language in which thingness is verbalized is irreducibly metaphoric.[43] The aim is thus to recalibrate the metaphor through which thingness is expressed to displace all organic tropes. This entails, for instance, doing away with metaphors of voice, life, and essence ("The treaty is a living instrument", "The body of law", "The spirit of the law") which silently confer necessity and self-significance on objects. Countermetaphorism thus substitutes figures that foreground exposure, representation, signification, coupling, and situatedness. It disciplines its own language by avoiding metaphors that thingify and bring about epistemological closures. Countermetaphorism is accordingly a discursive practice that refuses the metaphors by which thingness enables imperative acknowledgement and that simultaneously cultivates figures capable of keeping representation in view. In that sense, this ultimate move echoes Walter Mignolo's delinking by refusing the rhetorical capture through which coloniality/modernity naturalizes its own epistemic norms.[44] Where delinking affirms modes of knowing disqualified as premodern, local, or non-scientific, countermetaphorism interrupts metaphoric regimes that organicize and self-authorize dominant objects (law, the State, institutions, the people, nature, culture) as living, self-speaking entities. By stripping these metaphors of their epistemological privilege and reopening the conditions of legibility, countermetaphorism performs an epistemic disobedience. It detaches critique from the grammar of necessity, affirms pluriversal principles of knowledge, and re-situates sense in relations that thingness had rendered mute.

5. Countermateriality at work

The preceding section has envisaged countermateriality as a composite attitude composed of several moves (foundational constructivism, non-dual mediation, thingification-of-thingification, overmateriality, transperspectivism, and countermetaphorism), each of which unsettles thingness from a distinct angle while preserving the minimal materiality without which critique would lose its grip on the world. What remains to be shown is what countermateriality concretely entails when it is applied to the specific figures of legal thingification examined in Chapter 4. The present section undertakes this task. Its ambition is to demonstrate that the six moves composing countermateriality are not merely theoretical postures but very concrete interventions capable of interrupting the precritical epistemology that law installs when it thingifies the State, the people, sex, race, nature, culture, and itself.

This section begins by applying countermateriality to the thingification of the State (5.1), the people (5.2), sex (5.3), race (5.4), nature (5.5), and culture (5.6) – that is, to the objects that law encounters, constitutes, and governs. In each instance, the discussion shows how one or several moves of countermateriality can interrupt the production of thingness while safeguarding the material scaffolding through which law protects, adjudicates, and intervenes. This section then turns to the application of countermateriality to the thingification of law itself (5.7). Here too the stakes are high, for law's self-thingification, as has been shown throughout this book, is the condition of its own discursive efficacy, and yet it is also the site where the precritical epistemology is equally deeply entrenched.

5.1. The State

The thingification of the State, as shown in Chapter 4, operates by installing the State as a being-in-itself whose necessary materiality appears to precede perception and survive the withdrawal of any speaking observer. The Montevideo criteria, the declaratory theory of recognition, the veneration of territorial integrity, and the dense bureaucratic apparatus of files, registries, and chains of command all conspire to present the State as a self-caused, ancestral entity that simply is. Countermateriality intervenes in this scene not by denying that the State has material consequences – it manifestly does, and those consequences include both the capacity to manage populations and the capacity to annihilate them – but by refusing to let the State's materiality congeal into an epistemological closure.

Overmateriality is possibly the most immediately operative move here. When the State is saturated with the full density of its material composition – the labour contracts of its civil servants, the concrete and barbed wire of its borders, the algorithms of its surveillance systems, the budgetary lines that fund its prisons and its schools, the diplomatic cables that negotiate its recognition, the census forms that enumerate its population, the weapons systems that ensure its security – the impression of a self-caused and seamless entity dissolves. The State appears not as a thing but as a laminated assemblage whose layers can be peeled apart, inspected, and contested. An overmaterialized State is a State whose seams are visible: The border is not an ancestral membrane but a composite of fences, sensors, bilateral agreements, private security contracts, and racialized policing practices. The territorial integrity that international law venerates is not an impenetrable male body, as feminist critiques have compellingly shown, but a patchwork of infrastructural maintenance, diplomatic negotiation, and military expenditure whose continuation requires daily labour. Once this labour is made visible, the self-effacing character of the State's thingness is interrupted. The speaking observer returns to the scene, and with that return, the question of how the State is assembled – and for whom – becomes articulable.

Transperspectivism reinforces this interruption. When the State is traversed from the perspective of the refugee detained at its border, the Indigenous community whose territory it claims, the international monitor assessing its compliance with human rights obligations, and the fiscal auditor tracing its budgetary flows, the unity of the State-thing fractures into non-coincident articulations. What appears as a mighty whole from the vantage point of the General Assembly is a site of dispossession from the vantage point of the displaced. What appears as territorial integrity from the vantage point of the Security Council is an apparatus of confinement from the vantage point of those locked in camps. The constant traversal of perspectives prevents the State from recoalescing into a self-signifying being and reveals that its unity is an achievement of discursive coordination rather than a thing.

Yet, and this is where the double operation of countermateriality is most visible, the suspension of the State's thingness does not entail the dissolution of the State as a site of legal accountability. On the contrary, it is precisely by refusing to treat the State as a self-caused, ancestral thing that one can hold it responsible for what it does. A thingified State is a State that appears to act by necessity, whose violence is naturalized as the expression of an epistemological given. A countermaterialized State is a State whose actions are returned to the register of choice, assembly, and maintenance, and therefore to the register of accountability. When the International Court of Justice adjudicates a claim of genocide, it must be able to attribute conduct to a State; but such attribution is more rigorous, not less, when it proceeds through the material traces of command structures, budgetary allocations, and institutional routines rather than through the invocation of a self-signifying sovereign entity. The materiality is preserved while the thingness is suspended.

5.2. The people

The thingification of the people, as Chapter 4 has shown, operates through the circular temporality of constitutional founding (the "We the People" that both speaks and installs the subject who speaks) and through the archival apparatus of censuses, registries, and electoral rolls that produce the object they enumerate while hiding their productive force. The right to self-determination further installs "peoples" as bearers of a right whose addressees are States, producing a narrow class of collectivities eligible to inhabit the category. Countermateriality intervenes here by exposing the curatorial labour that produces the people as a thingly entity while preserving the material and institutional scaffolding through which collective self-governance and anti-colonial struggle remain possible.

The thingification-of-thingification is the most pertinent move in this context. Instead of accepting the people as a self-caused, ancestral being that authorizes the constitutional text, one materializes the very process by which the people are constituted: The drafting committees, the exclusions from the franchise, the negotiations over census categories, the diplomatic determinations of which colonial units qualify as "peoples" under Resolution 1541, the administrative standardization of identity documents. Once these processes are themselves rendered material – given their own seams, supports, and failures – the necessity that surrounds the people is abolished. One sees, concretely, that the people are a composition, i.e. a product of inclusions and exclusions, of naming and silencing, of archival practices and bureaucratic routines. The imperative of acknowledgement – the "must be" that attaches to the "is" of the people – is thereby returned to the register of contestation.

Countermetaphorism further disciplines the figurative language through which the people's thingness is sustained. The organic tropes that pervade constitutional discourse (the body politic, the will of the people, the living constitution) silently confer self-signifying necessity on a collective subject that is always constructed. Substituting figures that foreground composition, articulation, and situatedness – the people as an ongoing negotiation, a provisional alignment, a contested assembly – displaces the ancestrality without dissolving the capacity for collective action. The point is not that the people do not exist or that self-determination is a fiction. The point is that the people exist as a material achievement of discursive and institutional practices, and that recognizing it as such is the condition for subjecting its composition to debate. When decolonization movements invoke the right to self-determination, they mobilize a material claim, namely a claim grounded in histories of dispossession, in the concrete suffering of colonized populations, in the infrastructural violence of imperial administration. Countermateriality preserves this material claim while refusing to let the category "peoples" congeal into a self-effacing administrative kind whose boundaries are policed by the very discourses that produced them.

5.3 Sex

The thingification of sex, as examined in Chapter 4, operates through the binary grammar of international instruments (principally the CEDAW) that presuppose "women" as a unitary, already-known category and consolidate sex as a self-signifying referent through definitional choices, reporting practices, and managerial techniques. Countermateriality intervenes here by drawing on the rich resources of feminist critical theory (Butler's materialization thesis, Crenshaw's intersectionality, Federici's and Fraser's accounts of social reproduction) to suspend the thingness of sex while preserving the material category through which discrimination is identified, harms are named, and protections are enforced.

Overmateriality is again a decisive move. When the category "women" is saturated with the full density of its material composition – the intersecting axes of race, class, sexuality, disability, migration status, and colonial history that co-constitute gendered experience – the impression of a unitary, self-signifying subject dissolves. An overmaterialized account of sex does not deny that discrimination against women is real and consequential. On the contrary, it insists that the reality of such discrimination is more complex, more layered, and more materially dense than the binary grammar the CEDAW can capture. It is important to stress that the saturation does not subtract matter but adds so much matter that the thingness of the category fissures. What appeared as a self-caused, ancestral binary reveals itself as a laminated assemblage of medico-legal protocols, kinship regulations, labour market structures, welfare architectures, and bioclinical interventions whose continuation requires daily maintenance. The speaking observer, i.e. the embodied subject whose life exceeds the template, returns to the scene, and with that return, the question of whose experience counts and whose is rendered peripheral becomes articulable.

Non-dual mediation further interrupts the word/thing split that sustains sex's thingness. The assumption that sex is a pre-discursive biological datum upon which gender is merely imposed is precisely the representational dualism that countermateriality refuses. Following Butler, one affirms that language and materiality are fully embedded in one another. Every reference to the materiality of sex occurs through signifying practices that are themselves materially instantiated. This does not mean that sex is merely linguistic. It means that the materiality of sex is always a materiality-in-mediation, produced through the iterative citation of regulatory norms, and therefore revisable. The legal consequence is significant. If sex is not a self-signifying thing but a mediated materiality, then the instruments that protect against sex-based discrimination can be redesigned to accommodate the full spectrum of embodied experience without losing their material grip. The CEDAW Committee's interpretive expansions (especially General Recommendations No. 28, 33, and 35) already gesture in this direction, but countermateriality insists that such expansions must be accompanied by a systematic refusal to let the binary grammar reconstitute itself as a self-effacing background. The protection must remain but the thingness must not.

The stakes here are concrete. When law fails to protect against gender-based violence, forced marriage, or reproductive coercion, the failure is not merely conceptual. It is material. Bodies are harmed, lives are truncated, possibilities are foreclosed. Countermateriality invites us to preserve the evidentiary and institutional density through which harms are registered and redressed. At the same time, it does not ask law to abandon the category 'women' or to dissolve the protections that the CEDAW provides. Rather, it invites us to treat such category as a provisional, revisable, and internally heterogeneous articulation rather than as a self-caused, ancestral thing.

5.4 Race

The thingification of race, as Chapter 4 has shown, operates through the legal grammar of the ICERD and CERD's treaty-body practices, which presuppose race, colour, or ethnic origin as stable attributes that can be identified, disaggregated, and administered. The apparatus of census, registry, administrative typology, and indicator dissolves into invisibility, leaving race to signify by itself as if it did not need the work of representation. The resort to countermateriality to suspend such legal thingification is most relevant but needs to be carefully calibrated because the thingification of race by law is entangled with histories of colonial violence, enslavement, and genocide whose material traces demand recognition and redress.

Against this background, the thingification-of-thingification proves particularly indispensable. One must materialize the very process by which race is produced as a legal category: The imperial taxonomies of the sixteenth century, the colonial census practices that sorted populations into administrable kinds, the bioclinical protocols that policed the boundary between races, the diplomatic negotiations that determined which categories would appear in the ICERD's definitional clause, the bureaucratic routines through which States supply disaggregated data to the CERD. Once these processes are themselves rendered visible as material compositions (with their own histories, interests, exclusions, and failures) the ancestral, self-caused character of race is interrupted. Race appears not as a self-signifying envelope but as a product of classificatory labour whose continuation requires institutional maintenance. The imperative of acknowledgement, that is the silent command to treat race as a necessary being-in-the-world, is thereby returned to a discursive space where contestation is enabled.

It must be acknowledged that the operation of countermateriality is nowhere more delicate than when mobilized to unsettle the legal thingification of race. Indeed, the material traces of racial violence (the archives of the slave trade, the mass graves of colonial massacres, the statistical evidence of systemic discrimination, the bodily scars of police brutality) are precisely the evidentiary resources through which accountability is pursued and reparation is claimed. To dissolve all materiality in the name of constructivism would be to perform what Latour warned against: A dematerialization that hands the terrain to those who deny the reality of racial harm. Countermateriality therefore insists on a double gesture. It suspends the thingness of race – the pretension that race is a self-caused, ancestral, biological thing – while saturating the legal scene with the material density of racial harm – the economic circuits of extraction, the infrastructural violence of segregation, the bodily vulnerabilities produced by racialized policing, the intergenerational transmission of dispossession. An overmaterialized account of race does not deny that racial discrimination is felt and experienced. It insists that the actuality of racial discrimination is more materially dense, more historically sedimented, and more institutionally entangled than the administrative category "race" can capture. The saturation fractures the thingness of the category while amplifying the material category through which harm is made legible and accountability is pursued.

Transperspectivism further ensures that the legal category of race cannot recoalesce into a self-signifying unity. When racial discrimination is traversed from the perspective of the descendant of enslaved persons, the Indigenous community subjected to extractive industry, the migrant racialized at the border, and the populations excluded from civic participation, the non-coincidence of racial experience becomes palpable. The category "race" transforms with each traversal, revealing that its unity is a function of the chosen horizon rather than an ancestral thingness. This does not weaken the legal claim against discrimination. It strengthens it by making visible the multiple, intersecting, and non-analogous modes through which racialization operates. As Butler cautions, power works fundamentally differently with respect to racism, homophobia, and misogyny, and countermateriality honours this non-equivalence by refusing to let the legal enumeration of protected grounds flatten the specificity of racial harm into a listable, interchangeable object.

5.5 Nature

The thingification of nature, as Chapter 4 has demonstrated, operates through the legal grammar of environmental and climate instruments that translate nature into measurable, scalable, and administrable substrates: Ambient air quality standards, biodiversity coverage percentages, carbon accounting units, temperature goals. The apparatus of metrication dissolves into invisibility, leaving nature to appear as a self-signifying, self-caused being whose limits and thresholds speak for themselves. Countermateriality intervenes here by suspending the thingness of nature while preserving the material category through which ecological destruction is identified, planetary boundaries are articulated, and accountability for environmental harm is pursued.

Overmateriality is the most immediately operative move when it comes to the legal thingification of nature. When the environment is saturated with the full density of its material composition – the entangled ecological interdependences, the labour of Indigenous communities who maintain biodiversity, the economic circuits of extraction and pollution, the infrastructural networks of energy production and waste disposal, the bodily vulnerabilities of communities exposed to toxic contamination – the impression of a self-signifying, scalable substrate dissolves. An overmaterialized account of nature does not deny that climate change is actual or that biodiversity loss is catastrophic. On the contrary, it insists that ecological destruction is more materially dense, more relationally entangled, and more contested than the Paris Agreement's temperature goal can capture. The saturation reintroduces the speaking observer (e.g. the situated community, the affected body, the Indigenous knowledge system) into a scene from which metrication had expelled them.

Countermetaphorism further disciplines the figurative language through which nature's thingness is sustained. The hydraulic metaphors of "natural capital", "ecosystem services", and "carbon sinks" silently confer self-signifying necessity on what are in fact negotiated, contested, and politically produced categories. Substituting figures that foreground relation, vulnerability, and interdependence (e.g. nature as kin, as commons) displaces the ancestrality without dissolving the capacity for legal intervention. The rights-of-nature experiments also examined in Chapter 4 (e.g. Ecuador's constitutional recognition, the Atrato River's legal personality, the Whanganui River's status as ancestor) already gesture toward such countermetaphorical practice by reinstalling witness, guardianship, and relational epistemology at the heart of legality. Countermateriality reads these experiments not as definitive solutions but as partial interruptions of thingification whose capacity to de-thingify depends on whether they maintain revisability and refuse the self-effacing erasure that thingness demands.

5.6 Culture

The thingification of culture, as Chapter 4 has shown, operates through the legal grammar of heritage instruments (e.g. the 1972 Convention Concerning the Protection of the World Cultural and Natural Heritage, the 2003 Convention for the Safeguarding of the Intangible Cultural Heritage, the 2005 Convention on the Protection and Promotion of the Diversity of Cultural Expressions) that install culture as a self-signifying corpus endowed with outstanding universal value, ancestral transmission, and a self-effacing curatorial apparatus. Once inscribed on a list, a cultural practice or site acquires a stabilized identity whose value appears intrinsic, even as it is produced by expert missions, committee politics, and diplomatic negotiation. Countermateriality intervenes here by exposing the discursive labour that produces cultural thingness while preserving the material category through which cultural destruction is identified and cultural diversity is defended.

The thingification-of-thingification is the most pertinent move here. One materializes the very process by which outstanding universal value (OUV) is produced: The nomination dossiers, the expert evaluations, the committee deliberations, the geopolitical negotiations over inscription, the tourism economies that redirect living practices toward staged performances, the intellectual property regimes that commodify cultural expressions. Once these processes are themselves rendered visible as material compositions, the self-signifying universality is interrupted. OUV appears not as an intrinsic quality but as a product of institutional labour whose criteria, hierarchies, and exclusions can be contested. The ancestral being that heritage discourse installs is returned to representational practices, where the question of whose past counts and whose is erased becomes articulable and debatable.

Transperspectivism reinforces this interruption by traversing the same cultural object from the perspective of the community that practises it, the tourist who consumes it, the State that reports on it, the expert who evaluates it, and the diaspora community that claims it from afar. The non-coincidence of these perspectives reveals that the unity of the cultural object is an achievement of alignment rather than an ancestral thing. What appears as a seamless tradition from the vantage point of the UNESCO listing is a site of internal contestation, hybridization, and ongoing reinterpretation. The constant traversal prevents culture from recoalescing into a self-effacing thing and insists that the speaking observer (e.g. the practitioner, the critic, the dissenter) remains constitutive of cultural meaning.

Yet here too the operation of countermateriality must be carefully calibrated. When cultural heritage is destroyed in the course of armed conflict, the destruction is not merely symbolic. It is material, for irreplaceable traces of human creativity and historical sedimentation are annihilated. The legal instruments that protect cultural property in armed conflict (the 1954 Hague Convention, the Rome Statute's criminalization of attacks on cultural objects) require a material category through which destruction is identified, documented, and adjudicated. In that sense, countermateriality requires that the evidentiary and institutional density through which cultural destruction is made cognizable as a wrong is preserved while holding the category of cultural heritage open and treating it as a provisional, revisable, and internally heterogeneous articulation rather than as a self-signifying, ancestral thing.

5.7 Law

The application of countermateriality to the thingification of law itself is the most perilous operation examined in this section, which is why it is examined last. As Chapter 4 has argued, law always begins by thingifying itself. It frames its own rules, doctrines, sources, practices, and institutions as endowed with thingly materiality, thereby harvesting the discursive and epistemological effects of thingness (independence from perception, the cancellation of the speaking observer, representationlessness, originary causation, ancestrality, etc.). The metaphor of the "sources of law", the image of the "body of law", the rulist picture of law as a system of well-defined building blocks, and the hermeneutic configuration of the legal text as a corpus containing meaning, all conspire to present law as a necessary being-in-the-world that simply is. Countermateriality can help us unsettle such self-thingification without destroying the discursive architecture through which law enables accountability for wrongs, makes suffering legible, and intervenes against the most grievous forms of violence.

This is no minor challenge. If law's self-thingification is entirely dissolved, law risks losing the grip that makes it consequential in the world. A law that presents itself as nothing more than a contingent discursive practice – floating, revisable, without purchase – is a law that cannot prohibit genocide, cannot criminalize torture, cannot bar the destruction of ecosystems, cannot compel States to account for the confinement of human beings in camps, etc. This was said many times in the previous chapters. The discursive efficacy of law depends, in part, on its capacity to present its prohibitions and obligations as bearing the stamp of necessity. Countermateriality does not deny this. It insists, however, that the necessity of law's most pressing rules can be sustained without the full epistemological closure of thingness. For instance, the rule that prohibits genocide does not need to be presented as a self-caused, ancestral, self-signifying being-in-itself in order to be binding and consequential. It needs to be presented as a historically produced, institutionally maintained, and materially world-changing achievement whose force derives not from its pretension to exist outside representation but from the density of the material traces that ground it (e.g. the archives of previous atrocities, the testimonies of survivors, the institutional memory of tribunals, the iterative practice of States that have committed themselves to its observance, etc.). In other words, countermateriality proposes that law's force be grounded in material density rather than in epistemological closure.

Foundational constructivism proves a very germane posture in that regard. It names the refusal to anchor law's discursive efficacy in substances, and especially in the "nature of law", the "spirit of the law", or the "body of law". It stresses that what appears as thingness has been formed, codified, and stabilized through historical processes that remain revisable. This does not mean that law is arbitrary or that its prohibitions are without foundation. It means that law's foundations are historical, institutional, and material rather than ancestral and self-caused. To recognize this labour is not to weaken legal rules but to re-situate their discursive efficacy in the practices that sustain them rather than in a pretension to self-signifying necessity.

The thingification-of-thingification is equally decisive. When the process by which law thingifies itself is itself materialized, that is, when one renders visible the drafting committees, the codification projects, the restatement processes, the archival practices, the citational routines, the conventional hermeneutic practices through which law acquires its thingly appearance, the self-causation is interrupted. The "sources of law" appear not as primordial fountains from which legal norms spring but as institutional sites of production whose outputs are shaped by the interests, exclusions, and compromises of those who operate them. The "body of law" similarly appears not as a self-signifying organism but as a textual assemblage whose coherence is shaped by scholars, judges, and practitioners whose labour is ordinarily effaced. Likewise, the hermeneutic scene (in which meaning is configured as a thing-in-the-thing, a deposit to be extracted from the textual body) appears not as a mechanism of discovery but as a factory of thingness that manufactures both text and meaning as things and then validates its own operations by proclaiming that it has merely uncovered what was always already there. Once this productive labour is made visible, the speaking observer returns to the interpretive scene, and with that return, the question of who interprets and creates meaning, from what position, and with what consequences becomes articulable.

Countermetaphorism further helps debunk the figurative language through which law's self-thingification is sustained. It has been shown that the hydraulic metaphor of the "sources of law", the organic metaphor of the "body of law", the archaeological metaphor of "finding" the law silently confer self-signifying necessity on what are in fact institutional productions. Substituting figures that foreground composition, maintenance, and situatedness displaces such ancestrality without dissolving the capacity for normative intervention. A law that presents itself as a maintained infrastructure rather than as a self-caused organism is a law that can still prohibit torture, still criminalize aggression, still compel the protection of civilians, but it is also a law that acknowledges its own conditions of production and thereby opens itself to the critique and revision that thingness forecloses.

The foregoing should suffice to elucidate what countermateriality concretely means when it is brought to bear on the thingification of law by law. From the perspective of countermateriality, law must not choose between thingness and discursive efficacy. Countermateriality produces a law whose discursive efficacy is grounded in material density and institutional practice rather than in epistemological closure. The argument is that law's discursive efficacy in the face of mass atrocities, genocide, starvation, discrimination, the confinement of human beings in camps, the destruction of the planet, and fascist politics is better served by a countermaterial epistemology than by a precritical one. A law that presents itself as a self-caused and ancestral thing is a law that immunizes itself from critique. A law that acknowledges its own conditions of production is a law that can be held accountable for what it produces. Obviously, such a law is more vulnerable to critique but this vulnerability is precisely its strength. Indeed, countermateriality preserves the material scaffolding through which law prohibits genocide, criminalizes torture, protects civilians, bars discrimination, reins in the destruction of ecosystems, while systematically suspending the precritical epistemology through which law forecloses the speaking observer and converts the contingent into the necessary. The result is a law that retains its grip on the world, i.e. its capacity to intervene, to protect, to prohibit, to adjudicate, while remaining open to the perception, representation, and contestation that thingness had expelled. After all, only once the critique of law, and of the conditions of its production, has been seriously carried out can we credibly begin to mobilize law in the service of people and of the world, in a way that keeps fascist grammar at bay.

Notes

1 See ch 4, s 8.
2 See ch 5.
3 Cf Martti Koskenniemi's notion of counter-disciplinarity, which is an attitude of resistance against the usual division of labour between international law and international relations and against the moves whereby one field declares certain questions not properly legal or not properly political/scientific. See Martti Koskenniemi, "Law, Teleology and International Relations: An Essay in Counter-Disciplinarity' (2012) 26(1) *International Relations* 3.
4 See Bruno Latour, *Face à Gaïa: Huit conférences sur le nouveau régime climatique* (La Découverte 2015) 37–52; Bruno Latour, 'Why Has Critique Run out of Steam? From Matters of Fact to Matters of Concern' (2004) 30 *Critical Inquiry* 225, 232–47.

5 On the idea that key figures of postmodernism constitute thing theorists, see Matthew Mullins, 'Postmodernism and Thing Theory' (Arcade, 2017) https://shc.stanford.edu/arcade/interventions/postmodernism-and-thing-theory?locale=en accessed 9 March 2026. See gen Matthew Mullins, *Postmodernism in Pieces: Materializing the Social in U.S. Fiction* (OUP 2019); Maurice Merleau-Ponty, *Phénoménologie de la perception* (Gallimard 1945) 203–60.
6 Bruno Latour, *Reassembling the Social: An Introduction to Actor-Network-Theory* (OUP 2005) chs 1–2, 1–62; Susan Leigh Star, 'The Sociology of the Invisible: The Primacy of Work in the Writings of Anselm Strauss' in Wiebe E Bijker, Thomas P Hughes and Trevor Pinch (eds), *The Social Construction of Technological Systems: New Directions in the Sociology and History of Technology* (MIT Press 1987) 257–82.
7 See eg Judith Butler, *Notes Toward a Performative Theory of Assembly* (Harvard University Press 2015) 1–30; Gayatri Chakravorty Spivak, *A Critique of Postcolonial Reason: Toward a History of the Vanishing Present* (Harvard University Press 1999) 1–68.
8 Gilles Deleuze, *Différence et répétition* (Presses Universitaires de France 1968) 206–40; Gilbert Simondon, *L'individuation à la lumière des notions de forme et d'information* (Millon 2005) 23–72.
9 See the remarks of Susan Marks about reification as a reified category. See Susan Marks, 'Introduction' in Susan Marks (ed), *International Law on the Left: Re-examining Marxist Legacies* (CUP 2008) 1, 6.
10 Bruno Latour, *Face à Gaïa: Huit conférences sur le nouveau régime climatique* (La Découverte 2015) 39–40.
11 Ibid 40.
12 See also Louis Althusser, *Pour Marx* (La Découverte 1996) 227–49.
13 Louis Althusser, *Positions (1964–1975)* (Éditions sociales 1976) 67–125.
14 See also Louis Althusser, *Pour Marx* (La Découverte 1996) 236.
15 See the remarks of Gilles Deleuze and Félix Guattari, *L'Anti-Œdipe* (Éditions de Minuit 1972) 307.
16 See how materiality and embodiment are rendered politically salient without ontological closure in Gayatri Chakravorty Spivak's work on subalternity and representation (Gayatri Chakravorty Spivak, *A Critique of Postcolonial Reason: Toward a History of the Vanishing Present* (Harvard University Press 1999) 1–68). On the idea that the body becomes the seat of the true reality, see Stuart Hall, *Race, ethnicité, nation: Le triangle fatal* (Éditions Amsterdam 2019) 58. Michel Foucault can also be read as treating discursive practices as materially consequential objects of critique, securing a grip upon them through their "object-level" features, and affirming that critique requires a disciplined material register – texts, architectures, procedures, files, norms. See Michel Foucault, *Entretiens radiophoniques 1961–1983* (Flammarion/Vrin/INA 2024) 486 and 516. On the idea that feminists and race theorists have maintained an emphasis on the material conditions because materially experienced oppression is at the basis of their critique, see Margaret Davies, *Law Unlimited: Materialism, Pluralism, and Legal Theory* (Routledge 2017) 51. On the inescapability of materialist thinking, see Jacques Derrida, *Spectres de Marx* (Seuil 2024) 198–99.
17 Judith Butler, *Bodies That Matter: On the Discursive Limits of "Sex"* (Routledge 2011) xii–xiii.
18 Ibid xiii–xiv.
19 Ibid xviii–xix.
20 Ibid xix–xx, 37–39.

21 Margaret Davies, *Law Unlimited: Materialism, Pluralism, and Legal Theory* (Routledge 2017) 1–54.
22 Bill Brown, *Other Things* (University of Chicago Press 2015) 5. See also Sarah Wasserman, 'Thing Theory 2017: A Forum' (Arcade, 2017) https://shc.stanford.edu/arcade/interventions/thing-theory-2017-forum accessed 9 March 2026.
23 See also Bill Brown, 'Things – In Theory' (Arcade, 2017) https://shc.stanford.edu/arcade/interventions/things-theory accessed 9 March 2026.
24 Bill Brown, *Other Things* (University of Chicago Press 2015) 9–11.
25 Ibid 12–13.
26 Ibid 12. See also Sarah Wasserman, 'Thing Theory 2017: A Forum' (Arcade, 2017) https://shc.stanford.edu/arcade/interventions/thing-theory-2017-forum accessed 9 March 2026.
27 Bill Brown, 'Thing Theory' (2001) 28 *Critical Inquiry* 1, 13.
28 Bill Brown, *Other Things* (University of Chicago Press 2015) 9–13.
29 Ibid 18.
30 Bill Brown, 'Thing Theory' (2001) 28 *Critical Inquiry* 1, 3, 16, 24.
31 Bill Brown, *Other Things* (University of Chicago Press 2015) 24–41. See also Bill Brown, 'Things – In Theory' (Arcade, 2017) https://shc.stanford.edu/arcade/interventions/things-theory accessed 9 March 2026.
32 On the idea that we are bound to be heirs of Kantian constructivism and correlationism, see Quentin Meillassoux, *Après la finitude: Essai sur la nécessité de la contingence* (Seuil 2006) 52. See contra the attempt of Manuel DeLanda to design an ontology that enables existence that is conception independent, see Manuel DeLanda, *A New Philosophy of Society: Assemblage Theory and Social Complexity* (Bloomsbury 2019) 2.
33 Bruno Latour, *Reassembling the Social: An Introduction to Actor-Network-Theory* (OUP 2005) chs 1–2, 1–62. See also Bruno Latour, *L'Espoir de Pandore* (Didier Gille tr, La Découverte 2007).
34 Judith Butler, *Notes Toward a Performative Theory of Assembly* (Harvard University Press 2015) 1–30; Judith Butler, *Bodies That Matter: On the Discursive Limits of "Sex"* (Routledge 2011) xix–xxiv.
35 Michel Foucault, *L'archéologie du savoir* (Gallimard 1969) 63–76, 171–76.
36 Walter Mignolo, 'Delinking: The Rhetoric of Modernity, the Logic of Coloniality, and the Grammar of Decoloniality' (2007) 21 *Cultural Studies* 449–514, 463 and 485.
37 Jacques Derrida, *De la grammatologie* (Éditions de Minuit 1967) 77–114; Jacques Derrida, *Marges de la philosophie* (Éditions de Minuit 1972) 365–93.
38 Michel Foucault, *Entretiens radiophoniques 1961–1983* (Flammarion/Vrin/INA 2024) 485–86.
39 Judith Butler, *Notes Toward a Performative Theory of Assembly* (Harvard University Press 2015) 1–30; Gayatri Chakravorty Spivak, *A Critique of Postcolonial Reason: Toward a History of the Vanishing Present* (Harvard University Press 1999) 1–68.
40 On the technique of saturation and the strategy of making material supports visible against regimes of transparency, see Bruno Latour's insistence on reassembling the social through its material mediators (Bruno Latour, *Reassembling the Social: An Introduction to Actor-Network-Theory* (OUP 2005) 63–90). On the idea that representationlessness is a mode of representation, see ch 1, s 1.3.
41 Jacques Derrida, *Marges de la philosophie* (Éditions de Minuit 1972) 183–96.
42 Cf Bruno Latour, *Reassembling the Social: An Introduction to Actor-Network-Theory* (OUP 2005) 21–46.

43 On the idea that language is always metaphoric, see Hayden White, *Tropics of Discourse: Essays in Cultural Criticism* (Johns Hopkins University Press 1978) 252; see also Steven L Winter, *A Clearing in the Forest: Law, Life, and Mind* (University of Chicago Press 2001) 65.

44 Walter Mignolo, 'Delinking: The Rhetoric of Modernity, the Logic of Coloniality, and the Grammar of Decoloniality' (2007) 21 *Cultural Studies* 449–514, 463 and 485.

Epilogue

A dinner at Fayard[1]

The French publishing house Fayard had outdone itself. Crystal chandeliers hung from the vaulted ceiling of the private dining room on the Rue des Saints-Pères in Paris, casting prismatic light across white linen tablecloths and an arrangement of peonies so extravagant it bordered on the geological. The occasion: The Prix Thiers, awarded this year to Donald T. for his collection of memos, *The Real American History of Greenland*, freshly translated into French and published, improbably, by Fayard. The guests had assembled in the anteroom, circling one another with the wariness of philosophers who suspect they have been invited to the same dinner party by mistake.

Bruno L. stood near the window, examining a potted fern with the intensity of someone who had spent decades insisting that such objects deserved a parliament. He wore a rumpled linen jacket and an expression of profound ambivalence. Judith B. had arrived in a black turtleneck, already engaged in what appeared to be an internal debate about whether to stay. Jean D. was leafing through the evening's programme with visible incredulity, wondering why he was there at all, while the others' glances made it clear they had no idea who he was. Bill B. lingered near the bookshelf, running his fingers along the spines as though expecting one of them to resist. Kimberlé C. had positioned herself near the door, observing the room with the practised eye of someone who had spent a career watching legal categories harden into instruments of exclusion. She exchanged a glance with Frantz F., who stood apart from the others, arms crossed, his gaze fixed on a portrait of Napoleon that hung above the mantelpiece. And then there was Donald T., who had arrived fifteen minutes early, commandeered the largest armchair, and was now holding forth to no one in particular about the "tremendous" quality of the canapés.

"Beautiful shrimp", Donald T. announced, gesturing with a toast point. "The best shrimp. People don't know this, but the French invented shrimp. True story. I read it somewhere. Probably in my book".

The maître d'hôtel appeared and ushered the guests toward the dining table. Bruno L. found himself seated between Judith B. and Donald

T., a configuration that struck him as either a cruel joke or a sociological experiment.

"Monsieur Bruno L.", the maître d'hôtel murmured, "the seating was arranged by the committee".

"Of course it was", Bruno L. replied. "The committee. That marvellous fiction we invoke to explain why things are as they are".

Donald T. leaned over. "You're the science guy, right? The one who says facts aren't real?"

Bruno L. winced. "That is a spectacular misreading of my work".

"I like it", Donald T. said, nodding vigorously. "Facts aren't real. I've been saying that for years. Nobody listened. Now I've got a prize".

Judith B., seated on Bruno L.'s other side, raised an eyebrow. "The prize, I should note, is for a book about Greenland".

"Tremendous book", Donald T. said. "Very thick. Lots of words. Some of them French now".

"And yet", Judith B. continued, "Greenland remains, as a matter of international law, a territory of Denmark".

Donald T. waved a hand. "Details. Greenland is a thing. A big, beautiful thing. Ice, minerals, strategic location. You can't argue with a thing".

Across the table, Frantz F. set down his glass with a sharp click. "And there it is. The thing. The irresistible facticity of the colonial gaze. Greenland is a thing because you have decided it is a thing. Its people, its history, its self-determination – all of this vanishes the moment you project thingness upon it".

"I don't know what you just said", Donald T. replied, "but it sounded very negative".

Jean D. cleared his throat, a small, betrayed gesture that revealed just how stressed he was. "Perhaps we might approach this more systematically. The argument, as I understand it, is that thingness refers to a quality of being that presents itself as independent of perception, representation, and the speaking observer. The thing simply *is*. It owes its existence to itself and not to any act of representation".

"Exactly", Donald T. said. "Greenland is. I saw it on a map. Big and white. Very real".

"But that is precisely the problem", Jean D. continued. "The map is not the territory. The map is a representational practice. And yet thingness effaces that practice. It makes the map disappear so that only the territory remains – a territory that appears to have been there all along, awaiting no observer, requiring no representation".

Bill B. leaned forward, his eyes bright with the particular enthusiasm of someone who had spent decades thinking about objects. "This is the crux of Thing Theory, of course. The thing is what exceeds the object. The object is domesticated, functional, legible. But the thing – the thing is what resists. It is the remainder, the opacity, the moment when the object stops working and suddenly *appears* as something strange".

"My book works", Donald T. interjected. "Very well. Bestseller".

"I was speaking metaphorically", Bill B. said.

"I don't do metaphors", Donald T. replied. "Too complicated. I like things. Simple things. Greenland. Walls. Deals".

Kimberlé C., who had been listening with growing impatience, set down her fork. "The simplicity is the point, isn't it? Thingness operates by collapsing complexity into unity. It takes a territory with Indigenous populations, with histories of colonization, with competing claims and layered sovereignties, and it stamps it: *Thing*. One word. One object. One deal".

"Stamping is good", Donald T. said. "I stamp things all the time. Executive orders. Very effective".

"And yet", Kimberlé C. continued, "the stamp is never benign. It is always an act of selection. It decides what counts as visible, what counts as sayable, what counts as thinkable. The thing is not discovered; it is produced. And the production always serves someone".

Frantz F. pushed back his chair slightly, as though to gain distance from the table. "What strikes me most forcefully is the ancestrality of the thing. The claim that it has always been there, prior to any encounter, prior to any history. This is the colonial move par excellence. The coloniser arrives and declares: This land was empty. These people were not people. This culture was not culture. And because the thing is ancestral, because it precedes the present, there is nothing to discuss. The thing simply *was*".

"Greenland was", Donald T. said, nodding. "Before Denmark. Before anybody. Just ice. Waiting".

"Waiting for whom?" Frantz F. asked, his voice sharp.

"For someone to see its potential. To make a deal".

"And the Inuit? The Kalaallit? The people who have lived there for thousands of years?"

Donald T. shrugged. "They can stay. I'm not unreasonable. But the thing is the thing. You can't argue with geography".

Judith B. removed her glasses and polished them slowly. "This is what the book of Jean D. calls the *being-without-a-witness*. The thing is held to exist in a scene from which the speaking observer has been expelled. It requires no perception, no representation, no language. It simply *is*, in a universe where the world unfolds without any human presence".

"I like that", Donald T. said. "No witnesses. Very clean".

"It is the grammar of fascism", Judith B. replied quietly.

The table fell silent.

Bruno L. broke the silence by reaching for the wine. "I confess I find myself in an awkward position. I have spent my career arguing against the Kantian settlement – against the idea that we are forever trapped behind a veil of representation, unable to access the thing-in-itself. And yet here we are, confronting a mode of thought that claims direct access to the thing, that bypasses representation entirely, and the result is" – he gestured vaguely toward Donald T. – "this".

"You're welcome", Donald T. said.

"I did not mean it as a compliment".

"Everything's a compliment if you're winning".

Jean D. intervened. "The question, surely, is not whether we can access the thing, but what happens when we claim to have done so. Thingness, as theorized in my book, is not merely an epistemological posture. It is a *discursive action*. It produces effects. It interpellates subjects. It forecloses debate".

"Interpellates", Donald T. repeated, frowning. "Is that French?"

"It is Althusserian", Judith B. said.

"Sounds French".

Kimberlé C. leaned in. "The interpellation is the key. The thing does not simply exist; it *hails* us. It assigns us a place, a role, a position within its order. And that position is not one of sovereignty or agency. It is one of subjection. We become subjects *of* the thing – not speaking observers, but subordinates who must acknowledge its necessity".

"People acknowledge me all the time", Donald T. said. "Very gratifying".

"That is precisely the mechanism", Kimberlé C. replied. "The thing demands acknowledgement. And in acknowledging it, we confirm its necessity. We become complicit in its production".

Bill B. had been sketching something on his napkin – a diagram of overlapping circles that appeared to represent nothing in particular.

"What fascinates me", he said, looking up, "is the claim that thingness is *representationless*. The thing signifies by virtue of itself. It requires no language, no naming, no symbolic mediation. And yet – and this is the paradox – the very claim to representationlessness is itself a representational practice. It is a way of *staging* the thing as outside representation".

"Staging is good", Donald T. said. "I do rallies. Very big. Lots of flags".

"The flags are representations", Bill B. observed.

"The flags are things", Donald T. countered. "Red, white, blue. You can touch them. Very real".

Frantz F. shook his head. "And here we see the violence of thingness. The flag is not merely a thing. It is a sign, a symbol, a condensation of histories – of conquest, of slavery, of exclusion. But thingness strips all of that away. It presents the flag as a brute materiality, a self-evident presence that requires no representation. And in doing so, it silences every voice that might contest its meaning".

"I don't silence people", Donald T. said. "I just talk louder".

The main course arrived: A delicate arrangement of duck confit that seemed, under the circumstances, almost satirically French. The sommelier poured a Burgundy that Bruno L. examined with the attention he usually reserved for laboratory inscriptions.

"What troubles me", Bruno L. said, swirling his glass, "is the depoliticisation. Thingness, as described here, removes the thing from the sphere of politics. It is simply *there*, and there is nothing to discuss. But politics – genuine politics – requires precisely the opposite. It requires that we treat the given as contestable, that we refuse the closure of necessity".

"I close deals", Donald T. said. "That's politics".

"That is transaction", Bruno L. replied. "Politics is what happens when the transaction fails. When the thing refuses to stay put. When the excluded return to contest the distribution of the sensible".

Judith B. nodded. "Rancière's point exactly. The police order – and I use 'police' here in his technical sense – is the arrangement that distributes places, roles, and capacities. It determines what counts as visible, sayable, thinkable. Thingness is the police order par excellence. It forecloses dissensus by presenting the world as already settled, already *there*".

"The world is there", Donald T. said. "I didn't make it up. It's real. Very real. The realest".

"And yet", Judith B. continued, "the 'real' is precisely what is at stake. The permanent exhibition of the real – the injunction to concreteness, to facts, to things – is the ordinary form of police in contemporary societies. It saturates perception with what already is, and in doing so, it neutralises the capacity to imagine what might be otherwise".

Jean D. set down his knife and fork with deliberate precision. "I wonder if we might turn to the question of resistance. My book proposes something called *countermateriality* – a mode of engagement that retains enough materiality to preserve demonstration and accountability, while systematically suspending any slide back into thingness".

"Countermateriality", Donald T. repeated. "Sounds like a scam".

"It is the opposite of a scam", Jean D. said. "It is a disciplined practice of material resistance. It refuses to treat the thing as a self-caused, ancestral being, while retaining the material supports – texts, traces, inscriptions, infrastructures – that allow critique to gain traction".

Bill B. looked intrigued. "This resonates with Thing Theory, though it moves in a different direction. Thing Theory seeks to recover the opacity of the thing, the moment when it exceeds our categories. Countermateriality, as I understand it, seeks to *saturate* the thing with so much materiality that its unity fissures".

"Overmateriality", Jean D. said. "Yes. The idea is to multiply the registers, densities, and textures of material presence until the claim of self-signifying necessity becomes untenable. One materialises the object so extensively – with its networks, residues, affordances, and frictions – that it is no longer possible to take its thingness seriously".

Donald T. frowned. "You're saying if you look at something too closely, it falls apart?"

"In a sense, yes".

"That's why I don't read briefings. Too many details. Ruins the thing".

Kimberlé C. laughed – a sharp, unexpected sound. "And there, in a single sentence, is the entire epistemology of thingness. The refusal of detail. The insistence on unity. The fear that complexity might undo the stamp".

Frantz F. had been silent for some time, his gaze distant. When he spoke, his voice carried the weight of decades. "What I find most compelling in this analysis is the notion of *thingification-of-thingification*. The idea that one might turn the process of thingification back upon itself. That one might materialise the discursive action that produces thingness, and in doing so, abolish its necessity".

"You lost me", Donald T. said.

"I suspect that is often the case", Frantz F. replied. "But consider: when you declare Greenland a thing, you are performing an act. You are selecting, framing, excluding. You are deciding what counts as relevant and what does not. Thingification-of-thingification means making that act visible. It means showing the seams, the joints, the sutures. It means revealing that the thing is not a given but a production".

"I produce things", Donald T. said. "Buildings. Shows. Books. Very productive".

"And yet", Frantz F. continued, "the production is always hidden. The building appears as if it had always been there. The show appears as if it were simply entertainment. Your book appears as if it were simply history. Thingness effaces its own making. It presents the product as a necessity rather than a choice".

Judith B. leaned forward. "This is why Jean D.'s book insists that thingness is *self-effacing*. It hides the specific type of epistemology it puts in place. It makes the existence of its beneficiary – the thing – beyond doubt, while concealing the exclusions that made such certainty possible".

"I don't hide anything", Donald T. said. "I'm very transparent. The most transparent".

"Transparency", Bruno L. observed, "is itself a mode of concealment. It suggests that there is nothing to represent, nothing to contest. The thing is simply *there*, available to anyone who cares to look. But availability is not neutrality. The frame determines what is seen".

The dessert arrived: A tarte Tatin that glistened under the chandeliers like a philosophical proposition awaiting refutation. Donald T. examined it with suspicion.

"Is this apple?"

"It is", the waiter confirmed.

"Good. I like apples. Very American".

Kimberlé C. seized the moment. "And here we return to the central claim of Jean D.'s book: that thingness, when deployed in certain ways, exhibits what the author calls a *fascist grammar*. Not fascism in the narrow historical sense, but a mode of thinking that forecloses dissensus, that installs zones of uncriticability, that demands acknowledgement without permitting contestation".

"I'm not a fascist", Donald T. said. "I'm a businessman".

"The categories are not mutually exclusive", Kimberlé C. replied. "The fascist grammar is not about ideology in the conventional sense. It is about the structure of thought. It is about the way certain claims are made immune to critique by being presented as things – as necessary, self-evident, ancestral beings that require no justification".

Frantz F. nodded slowly. "This is what I have always understood about colonialism. It is not merely a political arrangement. It is an epistemology. It is a way of knowing the world that turns the colonised into things – into objects to be managed, exploited, erased. And the most insidious aspect of this epistemology is that it presents itself as no epistemology at all. It presents itself as simply *seeing what is*".

"I see what's there", Donald T. said. "Greenland. Big. White. Mine".

"Not yours", Jean D. said quietly.

"Not yet", Donald T. replied, smiling.

Bruno L. pushed his dessert plate aside and leaned back in his chair. "I confess I am moved by this conversation, though I remain uncertain about my own position within it. I have spent my career arguing against the bifurcation of nature and culture, against the idea that there is a realm of brute facts untouched by human practice. And yet I have also worried – perhaps too loudly – about the 'fear of the mob.' The fear that if we acknowledge the constructed character of our knowledge, we will lose all grounds of authority, all capacity to distinguish better from worse".

"The mob is fine", Donald T. said. "I love the mob. Very enthusiastic".

"I did not mean it as an endorsement", Bruno L. said. "My point is that constructivism has been weaponised. It has been turned against the very sciences that might help us address the crises of our time. Climate deniers have learned to say: 'You claim that facts are constructed? Very well, then your facts about climate change are merely constructions.' And suddenly the scientists appear as activists, while the deniers occupy the position of sober sceptics".

Judith B. nodded. "This is why Jean D.'s book insists on *minimal materiality*. The point is not to abandon materiality altogether – that would be performative nihilism. The point is to retain enough material traction to preserve demonstration and accountability, while refusing to let materiality congeal into thingness".

"Materiality is good", Donald T. said. "I like materials. Gold. Marble. Very classy".

"Those are commodities", Bill B. observed.

"Same thing".

"They are not the same thing", Bill B. said. "A commodity is an abstraction. It is a form that structures social relations while appearing to be concrete, natural, and objective. Marx understood this. The commodity fetish is precisely the confusion of the abstract with the material".

Donald T. shrugged. "Marx lost. I won".

Kimberlé C. had been making notes on her napkin – a habit, she explained, from years of legal practice. "What strikes me most forcefully is the application of this analysis to law. Jean D.'s book argues that law is a primary site of thingification. It takes complex social relations and stamps them: property, rights, corporations, jurisdictions. And once stamped, these categories acquire a prescriptive force that shapes conduct, allocates resources, and forecloses alternatives".

"Law is good", Donald T. said. "I have lawyers. Many lawyers. The best lawyers".

"And yet", Kimberlé C. continued, "the law's thingification is always selective. It decides what counts as a person, what counts as property, what counts as a crime. And these decisions are not benign. They reflect and reinforce existing distributions of power. Intersectionality, as I have theorised it, is precisely an attempt to make visible the ways in which legal categories interact to produce specific forms of exclusion – forms that are invisible when each category is considered in isolation".

Jean D. leaned in. "This is where assemblage thinking becomes crucial. The law is not a monolithic thing. It is a composite of drafting conventions, translation practices, filing standards, jurisprudential styles, registrar routines, and enforcement logistics. Countermateriality means saturating the legal object with these specificities until its unity fissures".

"Fissures are bad", Donald T. said. "I like things solid. No cracks".

"The cracks are where the critique gets in", Frantz F. said quietly.

The coffee arrived. Donald T. examined his cup with the suspicion of someone who had been served something insufficiently large. "Small cup", he observed.

"It is an espresso", the waiter said.

"In America, we have big cups. Very big. You can see them from space".

Bruno L. smiled despite himself. "And there, perhaps, is the final lesson. Thingness is always a question of scale. The thing appears unified, self-evident, necessary – but only from a certain distance. Move closer, and the unity dissolves. Move further away, and it disappears into a larger assemblage. The trick is to find the scale at which critique becomes possible".

Judith B. rose from her chair, gathering her things. "The conclusion of Jean D.'s book, as I understand it, is that thingness must be resisted – not by abandoning materiality, but by reorganising material presence so that perception, representation, and the speaking observer return to the scene. Countermateriality is the practice of this return".

"I never left the scene", Donald T. said. "I'm always on the scene. Very present. The most present".

Frantz F. stood as well, his expression unreadable. "The question is not whether you are present. The question is whether your presence forecloses the presence of others. Whether your thingness, your insistence on being a thing, on treating the world as composed of things, silences the voices that might contest your claims".

"I don't silence anyone", Donald T. said. "I just win".

"Winning", Kimberlé C. observed, "is itself a thingification. It stamps the outcome as necessary, as inevitable, as the way things simply are. But outcomes are not things. They are productions. And productions can be undone".

The guests filed out into the Paris evening. The Rue des Saints-Pères was quiet, the cobblestones slick with recent rain. Bruno L. paused at the doorway, looking back at the dining room where Donald T. remained, examining the remnants of the tarte Tatin.

"Do you think he understood any of it?" Jean D. asked.

"Understanding is not the point", Bruno L. replied. "The point is that we understood. That we saw the mechanism. That we named the process by which thingness is produced and the ways in which it might be resisted".

Bill B. adjusted his scarf. "Thing Theory was always about the moment when the object stops working – when it suddenly appears as strange, as opaque, as resistant to our categories. Perhaps this evening was such a moment".

"Or perhaps", Judith B. said, "it was simply a dinner. A material event. An assemblage of bodies, words, food, and wine. Nothing more, nothing less".

Frantz F. had already begun walking toward the Seine. He did not look back. But his voice carried in the night air: "The thing is never simply a thing. It is always a wound. And wounds, if we attend to them, can teach us how to heal".

Kimberlé C. fell into step beside him. "The healing begins with the refusal. The refusal to accept the stamp. The refusal to acknowledge the thing as necessary. The refusal to let the world congeal into immovable stones".

Behind them, through the window of Fayard, Donald T. could be seen shaking hands with the maître d'hôtel, posing for a photograph, holding up his prize. The flash illuminated the room for an instant – a brief, bright assertion of presence.

And then the light faded, and the night reclaimed the scene, and the speaking observers walked on into a world that remained, as it had always been, open to contestation.

The thing is never the last word. The last word is always the return of the speaking observer, the reopening of the scene, the insistence that what appears as necessity is only ever a production. Productions, however solid they may seem, can always be unmade.

Note

1 This epilogue is a work of fiction. The views expressed by the characters are invented and do not represent statements actually made by any person one could recognize behind such characters. The author accepts no responsibility for any thingification that may occur in the reading for it is the responsibility of the reader alone. The format of this epilogue is largely inspired by Pierre Schlag, 'My Dinner at Langdell's' (2004) 52 *Buffalo Law Review* 851.

Bibliography

Adorno TW, *The Jargon of Authenticity* (Northwestern University Press 1973)
Adorno TW, *Negative Dialectics* (Seabury Press 1973)
Adorno TW, 'On the Fetish-Character in Music and the Regression of Listening' in Andrew Arato and Eike Gebhardt (eds), *The Essential Frankfurt School Reader* (Continuum 1982)
Agamben G, *L'irréalisable* (Seuil 2025)
Allott P, 'Language, Method and the Nature of International Law' (1971) 45 *British Yearbook of International Law* 79
Althusser L, *Être marxiste en philosophie* (Presses Universitaires de France 2015)
Althusser L, 'Idéologie et appareils idéologiques d'État' in *Positions* (Éditions Sociales 1976)
Althusser L, 'Ideology and Ideological State Apparatuses' in Louis Althusser, *Lenin and Philosophy and Other Essays* (Monthly Review Press 1971)
Althusser L, *Initiation à la philosophie pour les non-philosophes* (Presses Universitaires de France 2014)
Althusser L, *Positions (1964–1975)* (Éditions sociales 1976)
Althusser L, *Pour Marx* (La Découverte 1996) (first published 1965)
Anderson B, *Imagined Communities* (Verso 2006)
Anghie A, *Imperialism, Sovereignty and the Making of International Law* (CUP 2005)
Aquinas T, *De Ente et Essentia* (Armand Maurer tr, Pontifical Institute of Mediaeval Studies 1968)
Aquinas T, *Summa Theologiae* (Fathers of the English Dominican Province tr, CUP 2006)
Arendt H, *The Human Condition* (2nd edn, University of Chicago Press 2018)
Aristotle, *Categories and De Interpretatione* (John Lloyd Ackrill tr, OUP 1963)
Aristotle, *Metaphysics* (WD Ross tr, Jonathan Barnes rev, in Jonathan Barnes (ed), *The Complete Works of Aristotle: The Revised Oxford Translation*, vol 2 (Princeton University Press 1984)
Armstrong D, Farrell T and Lambert H, 'The Nature of International Law' in David Armstrong, Theo Farrell and Hélène Lambert, *International Law and International Relations* (2nd edn, CUP 2012)
Atrey S, *Intersectional Discrimination* (OUP 2019)
Augustine of Hippo, *Confessions* (Henry Chadwick tr, OUP 2008)

Augustine of Hippo, *De Doctrina Christiana* (Roger PH Green tr, OUP 1995)
Aust A, *Modern Treaty Law and Practice* (CUP 2007)
Austin JL, *How to Do Things with Words* (OUP 1962)
Balibar E, *Passions du concept: Epistémologie, théologie et politique. Écrits II* (La Découverte 2020)
Balibar E and Wallerstein I, *Race, nation, classe: Des identités ambiguës* (La Découverte 2018)
Barthes R, *L'aventure sémiologique* (Seuil 1985)
Barthes R, *Le bruissement de la langue: Essais critiques IV* (Seuil 1984)
Barthes R, *Critique et vérité* (Seuil 1999)
Barthes R, *Le degré zéro de l'écriture* (Editions du Seuil 1972)
Barthes R, 'Le discours de l'histoire' (1967) 6(4) *Social Science Information* 63
Barthes R, *Leçon* (Seuil 1978)
Barthes R, *Mythologies* (Éditions du Seuil 1957)
Barthes R, *Le Neutre: Cours au Collège de France, 1977–1978* (Éditions du Seuil 2002)
Baudrillard J, *Le crime parfait* (Galilée 1995)
Baudrillard J, *Le système des objets* (Gallimard 1968)
Bayart J-F, *L'énergie de l'État: Pour une sociologie historique et comparée du politique* (La Découverte 2022)
Beneyto JM and Kennedy D, *New Approaches to International Law: The European and the American Experiences* (Springer 2013)
Benhabib S, *Critique, Norm, and Utopia: A Study of the Foundations of Critical Theory* (Columbia University Press 1986)
Bentham J, *Bentham's Theory of Fictions* (CK Ogden ed, Routledge 2007)
Berger P and Luckmann T, *The Social Construction of Reality: A Treatise in the Sociology of Knowledge* (Penguin Books 1967)
Bergson H, *Essai sur les données immédiates de la conscience* (Flammarion 2013)
Bergson H, *Introduction à la métaphysique* (Presses Universitaires de France 2011)
Berkeley G, *A Treatise Concerning the Principles of Human Knowledge* (Jonathan Dancy ed, OUP 1998)
Berman HJ, *Law and Revolution: The Formation of the Western Legal Tradition* (Harvard UP 1983)
Berros MV and Yaksic NE (eds), *Perspectivas latinoamericanas sobre derechos de la naturaleza* (Tirant lo Blanch 2020)
Berry T, *The Great Work* (Bell Tower 1999)
Bethlehem D, 'The End of Geography: The Changing Nature of the International System and the Challenge to International Law' (2014) 25 *European Journal of International Law* 9
Bettio F and Bottazzi A, 'The Istanbul Convention and Gender-Based Violence: Challenges of Implementation' (2021) 28(2) *Social Politics* 453
Bewes T, *Reification or The Anxiety of Late Capitalism* (Verso 2002)
Bhabha HK, *Nation and Narration* (Routledge 1990)
Bianchi A, 'The Game of Interpretation in International Law: The Players, the Cards, and Why the Game is Worth the Candle' in Andrea Bianchi, Daniel Peat and Matthew Windsor (eds), *Interpretation in International Law* (OUP 2015)

Bishop I, 'Everyday Hegemony: Reification, the Supermarket, and the Nuclear Family' (2004) 7 *Open Philosophy* 1
Blake J, *International Cultural Heritage Law* (OUP 2015)
Bond J, 'International Intersectionality: A Theoretical and Pragmatic Exploration of Women's International Human Rights Violations' (2003) 52 *Emory International Law Review* 71
Borgen CJ, 'The Language of Law and the Practice of Politics: Great Powers and the Rhetoric of Self-Determination in the Cases of Kosovo and South Ossetia' (2009) 10 *Chicago Journal of International Law* 1
Bourdieu P, *Ce que parler veut dire: L'économie des échanges linguistiques* (Fayard 1982)
Bourdieu P, 'The Force of Law: Toward a Sociology of the Juridical Field' (1987) 38 *Hastings Law Journal* 814
Brandom R, *Making It Explicit: Reasoning, Representing, and Discursive Commitment* (Harvard University Press 1994)
Brown B, *Other Things* (University of Chicago Press 2015)
Brown B, 'Thing Theory' (2001) 28 *Critical Inquiry* 1
Brown B, 'Things—In Theory' (*Arcade*, 2017) https://shc.stanford.edu/arcade/interventions/things-theory accessed 9 March 2026
Burri M, *Public Service Broadcasting 3.0* (Routledge 2015)
Butler J, *Bodies That Matter: On the Discursive Limits of "Sex"* (Routledge 2011)
Butler J, *Gender Trouble: Feminism and the Subversion of Identity* (2nd edn, Routledge 1990)
Butler J, *Notes Toward a Performative Theory of Assembly* (Harvard University Press 2015)
Canguilhem G, *Idéologie et rationalité dans l'histoire des sciences de la vie* (Vrin 1977)
Cass DZ, 'Navigating the Newstream: Recent Critical Scholarship in International Law' (1996) 65 *Nordic Journal of International Law* 341
Cassese A, *Self-Determination of Peoples* (CUP 1995)
Certeau M de, *Histoire et psychanalyse entre science et fiction* (Gallimard 2016)
Certeau M de, *L'écriture de l'histoire* (Gallimard 1975)
Césaire A, *Discourse on Colonialism* (Joan Pinkham tr, Monthly Review Press 2000)
Chakrabarty D, 'The Climate of History: Four Theses' (2009) 35(2) *Critical Inquiry* 197
Chanson V, 'La réification comme concept "épistémologique" chez Adorno' in Vincent Chanson, Alexis Cukier and Frédéric Monferrand (eds), *La Réification: Histoire et actualité d'un concept critique* (La Dispute 2014)
Chanson V, Cukier A and Monferrand F (eds), *La Réification: Histoire et actualité d'un concept critique* (La Dispute 2014)
Chapoutot J, *La loi du sang: Penser et agir en nazi* (Gallimard 2014)
Chapoutot J, *La révolution culturelle nazie* (Gallimard 2017)
Charbonnier V, 'La réification chez Lukács' in Vincent Chanson, Alexis Cukier and Frédéric Monferrand (eds), *La Réification: Histoire et actualité d'un concept critique* (La Dispute 2014)
Charlesworth H and Chinkin C, *The Boundaries of International Law: A Feminist Analysis* (Manchester UP 2000)

Charlesworth H, Chinkin C and Wright S, 'Feminist Approaches to International Law' (1991) 85 *American Journal of International Law* 613
Châtelet F, *Une histoire de la raison* (Seuil 1992)
Chatterjee P, *Nationalist Thought and the Colonial World* (University of Minnesota Press 1986)
Chatterjee P, *The Nation and Its Fragments* (Princeton UP 1993)
Chimni BS, 'New Approaches to International Law: The Critical Scholarship of David Kennedy and Martti Koskenniemi' in *International Law and World Order: A Critique of Contemporary Approaches* (CUP 2017)
Chomsky N and Foucault M, *The Chomsky-Foucault Debate on Human Nature* (The New Press 2006)
Colin P and Quiroz L, *Pensées décoloniales: Une introduction aux théories critiques d'Amérique Latine* (Zones 2023)
Conaghan J, *Law and Gender* (OUP 2013)
Coronil F, *The Magical State* (University of Chicago Press 1997)
Cover R, 'Nomos and Narrative' (1983) 97 *Harvard Law Review* 4
Crawford J, *The Creation of States in International Law* (2nd edn, OUP 2006)
Crenshaw KW, 'Demarginalizing the Intersection of Race and Sex' (1989) *University of Chicago Legal Forum* 139
Crenshaw KW, 'Mapping the Margins: Intersectionality, Identity Politics, and Violence against Women of Color' (1991) 43(6) *Stanford Law Review* 1241
Crenshaw KW, 'Race, Reform, and Retrenchment: Transformation and Legitimation in Antidiscrimination Law' (1988) 101 *Harvard Law Review* 1331
Crutzen PJ and Stoermer EF, 'The "Anthropocene"' (2000) 41 *Global Change Newsletter* 17
Culler J, *Literary Theory: A Very Short Introduction* (OUP 1997)
Cullinan C, *Wild Law: A Manifesto for Earth Justice* (Siber Ink 2002)
d'Aspremont J, *After Meaning: The Sovereignty of Forms in International Law* (Edward Elgar 2021)
d'Aspremont J, 'A Worldly Law in a Legal World' in Andrea Bianchi and Moshe Hirsch (eds), *International Law's Invisible Frames: Social Cognition and Knowledge Production in International Legal Processes* (OUP 2021)
d'Aspremont J, 'Bindingness' in Jean d'Aspremont and Sahib Singh (eds), *Concepts for International Law: Contributions to Disciplinary Thought* (Edward Elgar 2019)
d'Aspremont J, 'The Chivalric Pursuit of Coherence in International Law' (2024) 37 *Leiden Journal of International Law* 191
d'Aspremont J, 'Comparativism and Colonizing Thinking in International Law' (2020) 57 *Canadian Yearbook of International Law* 89
d'Aspremont J, 'Consenting to International Law in Five Moves' in Samantha Besson (ed), *Consent in International Law* (CUP 2023)
d'Aspremont J, 'Critical Histories of International Law and the Repression of Disciplinary Imagination' (2019) 7 *London Review of International Law* 89
d'Aspremont J, *The Critical Attitude and the History of International Law* (Brill 2019)
d'Aspremont J, 'Current Theorizations About the Treaty' in Duncan B Hollis (ed), *The Oxford Guide to Treaties* (2nd edn, OUP 2020)

d'Aspremont J, *The Discourse on Customary International Law* (OUP 2021)
d'Aspremont J, 'The Doctrine of Fundamental Rights of States and Anthropomorphic Thinking in International Law' (2015) 4(3) *Cambridge Journal of International and Comparative Law* 503
d'Aspremont J, *The Epistemology of the Secret: International Law as Revelation* (CUP 2025)
d'Aspremont J, *The Experiences of International Organizations: A Phenomenological Approach to International Institutional Law* (Edward Elgar 2023)
d'Aspremont J, 'International Law and the Rage against Scienticism' (2022) 33 *European Journal of International Law* 679
d'Aspremont J, 'International Law as a Crisis Discourse: The Peril of Wordlessness' in Makane Mbengue and Jean d'Aspremont (eds), *Crisis Narratives in International Law* (Brill 2021)
d'Aspremont J, *International Law as a Belief System* (CUP 2017)
d'Aspremont J, 'The International Law of Statehood and Recognition: A Post-Colonial Invention' in Thierry Garcia (ed), *La reconnaissance du statut d'État à des entités contestées: approches de droit international, régional et interne* (Pedone 2018)
d'Aspremont J, 'Is an International Organization a Thing?' 23 *International Organizations Law Review* (2026)
d'Aspremont J, 'The Law of Statehood as a Constellation of Hybrids' in Jure Vidmar, Sarah McGibbon and Lea Raible (eds), *Research Handbook on Secession* (Edward Elgar 2022)
d'Aspremont J, 'The Love for International Organizations' (2023) 20 *International Organizations Law Review* 111
d'Aspremont J, 'Time Travel in the Law of International Responsibility' in Samantha Besson (ed), *Theories of International Responsibility Law* (CUP 2022)
d'Aspremont J, 'Turntablism in the History of International Law' (2020) 22 *Journal of the History of International Law* 472
d'Aspremont J, 'Two Attitudes towards Textuality in International Law: The Battle for Dualism' (2022) 42 *Oxford Journal of Legal Studies* 963
Davies M, *Law Unlimited: Materialism, Pluralism, and Legal Theory* (Routledge 2017)
DeLanda M, *A New Philosophy of Society: Assemblage Theory and Social Complexity* (Bloomsbury 2019)
Deleuze G, *Différence et répétition* (Presses Universitaires de France 1968)
Deleuze G, *Proust et les signes* (PUF 1964)
Deleuze G, *Sur l'appareil d'État et la machine de guerre: Cours de novembre 1979–mars 1980* (Éditions de Minuit 2025)
Deleuze G, *Sur les lignes de vie: Cours, mai–juin 1980* (Éditions de Minuit 2025)
Deleuze G and Guattari F, *L'Anti-Œdipe* (Éditions de Minuit 1972)
Deleuze G and Guattari F, *Mille plateaux* (Éditions de Minuit 1980)
de Man P, *The Resistance to Theory* (University of Minnesota Press 1986)
Derrida J, *De la grammatologie* (Éditions de Minuit 1967)
Derrida J, 'Declarations of Independence' (1986) 7(1) *New Political Science* 7
Derrida J, *L'écriture et la différence* (Éditions du Seuil 1967)
Derrida J, *Mal d'Archive: Une impression freudienne* (Éditions Galilée 1995)
Derrida J, *Marges de la philosophie* (Éditions de Minuit 1972)

Derrida J, *Papier Machine: Le ruban de machine à écrire et autres réponses* (Éditions Galilée 2001)
Derrida J, *Parages* (Galilée 1986)
Derrida J, *Positions* (Éditions de Minuit 1972)
Derrida J, *Spectres de Marx* (Seuil 2024)
Descola P, *Par-delà nature et culture* (Gallimard 2005)
Descartes R, *Meditations on First Philosophy* (John Cottingham tr, CUP 2017)
Descartes R, *Principles of Philosophy* (Valentine Rodger Miller and Reese P Miller trs, Kluwer Academic Publishers 1991)
Descombes V, *Le Même et l'Autre: Quarante-cinq ans de philosophie française (1933–1978)* (Éditions de Minuit 1979)
Dimick M, 'Race and Reification' (2023) 31 *Historical Materialism* 69
Du Bois WEB, *The Souls of Black Folk* (AC McClurg 1903)
Dugard J and Raic D, 'The Role of Recognition in the Law and Practice of Secession' in Marcelo Kohen (ed), *Secession: International Law Perspectives* (CUP 2006)
Dumézil G, *Histoires romaines* (Gallimard 1973)
Dumézil G, *L'Idéologie des trois fonctions dans les épopées des peuples indo-européens* (Gallimard 1968)
Dumézil G, *Types épiques indo-européens: Un héros, un sorcier, un roi* (Gallimard 1971)
Dussel E, *Ethics of Liberation: In the Age of Globalization and Exclusion* (Eduardo Mendieta, Camilo Pérez Bustillo and Yolanda Angulo trs, Duke University Press 2013)
Dussel E, *The Invention of the Americas: Eclipse of the Other and the Myth of Modernity* (Michael D Barber tr, Continuum 1995)
Dussel E, *Philosophie de la Libération* (PUF 2023)
Dussel E, *20 Theses on Politics* (Duke University Press 2008)
Dworkin R, *Law's Empire* (Harvard UP 1986)
Eco U, *How to Spot a Fascist* (Richard Dixon and Alastair McEwen trs, Harvill Secker 2020)
Eribon D, *Principes d'une pensée critique* (Fayard 2016)
Fanon F, *Black Skin, White Masks* (Charles Lam Markmann tr, Grove Press 1967)
Fanon F, *Les Damnés de la terre* (Maspero 1961)
Fanon F, *Peau noire, masques blancs* (Éditions du Seuil 1952)
Fanon F, *The Wretched of the Earth* (Richard Philcox tr, Grove Press 2004)
Farnsworth EA, *Farnsworth on Contracts* (4th edn, Wolters Kluwer 2019)
Fausto-Sterling A, *Sexing the Body: Gender Politics and the Construction of Sexuality* (Basic Books 2000)
Faye J-P, *Langages totalitaires* (Hermann 1972)
Federici S, *Caliban and the Witch: Women, the Body and Primitive Accumulation* (Autonomedia 2004)
Federici S, *Le capitalisme patriarcal* (La Fabrique 2019)
Ferdinand M, *Une écologie décoloniale: Penser l'écologie depuis le monde caribéen* (Seuil 2019)
Fields KE and Fields BJ, *Racecraft: The Soul of Inequality in American Life* (Verso 2022)
Fish S, 'Fish v Fiss' (1984) 36 *Stanford Law Review* 1325
Fish S, *Is There a Text in This Class?* (Harvard University Press 1980)

Fish S, 'With the Compliments of the Author: Reflections on Austin and Derrida' (1982) 8 *Critical Inquiry* 693
Fiss OM, 'Objectivity and Interpretation' (1982) 34 *Stanford Law Review* 739
Fitzpatrick P, *The Mythology of Modern Law* (Routledge 1992)
Foucart S, 'Donald Trump et Elon Musk plongent la science américaine dans un indescriptible chaos' *Le Monde* (24 February 2025)
Foucault M, *L'archéologie du savoir* (Gallimard 1969)
Foucault M, *The Archaeology of Knowledge* (Routledge 2002)
Foucault M, *Dits et écrits, vol I (1954–1975)* (Gallimard 2001)
Foucault M, *Dits et écrits, vol II* (Gallimard 2001)
Foucault M, *Entretiens radiophoniques 1961–1983* (Flammarion/Vrin/INA 2024)
Foucault M, *« Il faut défendre la société »: Cours au Collège de France, 1976* (Gallimard 1997)
Foucault M, *Le Discours philosophique* (Gallimard/Seuil 2023)
Foucault M, *Leçons sur la volonté de savoir: Cours au Collège de France 1970–1971* (Seuil/Gallimard 2011)
Foucault M, *Les mots et les choses* (Gallimard 1966)
Foucault M, *Naissance de la biopolitique: Cours au Collège de France (1978–1979)* (Gallimard/Seuil 2004)
Foucault M, *Naissance de la clinique* (PUF 1963)
Foucault M, *L'ordre du discours* (Gallimard 1971)
Foucault M, *Phénoménologie et Psychologie 1953–1954* (Gallimard/Seuil 2021)
Foucault M, *Sécurité, territoire, population: Cours au Collège de France, 1977–1978* (Gallimard 2004)
Foufas N, *La critique de la réification chez Lukács* (L'Harmattan 2020)
Francioni F, 'World Heritage Convention' in Francesco Francioni and Martin Scheinin (eds), *Cultural Heritage, Cultural Rights, Cultural Diversity* (OUP 2008)
Frankenberg G, 'Critical Comparisons: Re-thinking Comparative Law' (1985) 26 *Harvard International Law Journal* 411
Fraser N, *Fortunes of Feminism: From State-Managed Capitalism to Neoliberal Crisis* (Verso 2013)
Frier P-L and Donnier J-B, *Droit du patrimoine culturel* (Dalloz 2015)
Gabel P, 'Reification in Legal Reasoning' (1980) 3 *Research in Law and Sociology* 25
Gadamer H-G, *Truth and Method* (Joel Weinsheimer and Donald G Marshall trs, Bloomsbury Academic 2013)
Garcia T, *Forme et objet: Un traité des choses* (PUF 2011)
Geertz C, *The Interpretation of Cultures* (Basic Books 1973)
Gerstenblith P, *Art, Cultural Heritage, and the Law* (Carolina Academic Press 2019)
Giddens A, *The Consequences of Modernity* (Polity 1990)
Glissant É, *Discours antillais* (Gallimard 1981)
Glissant É, *Poétique de la relation* (Gallimard 1990)
Goldberg DT, *Are We All Postracial Yet?* (Polity 2015)
Goldberg DT, *The Racial State* (Blackwell 2002)
Graeber D, 'Fetishism as Social Creativity: Or, Fetishes Are Gods in the Process of Construction' (2005) 5(4) *Anthropological Theory* 407
Grzybowski J and Koskenniemi M, 'International Law and Statehood: A Performative View' in Robert Schuett and Peter MR Stirk (eds), *The Concept of the State*

in International Relations: Philosophy, Sovereignty and Cosmopolitanism (Edinburgh UP 2015)

Hacking I, *Historical Ontology* (Harvard UP 2002)

Hacking I, *The Social Construction of What?* (Harvard UP 1999)

Hafstein VT, *Making Intangible Heritage* (Indiana UP 2018)

Hall S, 'Cultural Identity and Diaspora' in Jonathan Rutherford (ed), *Identity: Community, Culture, Difference* (Lawrence & Wishart 1990)

Hall S, 'New Ethnicities' in David Morley and Kuan-Hsing Chen (eds), *Stuart Hall: Critical Dialogues in Cultural Studies* (Routledge 1996)

Hall S, 'The Question of Cultural Identity' in Stuart Hall, David Held and Tony McGrew (eds), *Modernity and Its Futures* (Polity Press/Open University 1992)

Hall S, 'Race, Articulation and Societies Structured in Dominance' in *Sociological Theories: Race and Colonialism* (UNESCO 1980)

Hall S, *Race, ethnicité, nation: Le triangle fatal* (Éditions Amsterdam 2019)

Hall S, 'The Spectacle of the "Other"' in Stuart Hall (ed), *Representation: Cultural Representations and Signifying Practices* (Sage/Open University 1997)

Hall S, 'The Work of Representation' in Stuart Hall (ed), *Representation: Cultural Representations and Signifying Practices* (Sage/Open University 1997)

Harris CH, 'Whiteness as Property' (1993) 106 *Harvard Law Review* 1707

Hart HLA, *The Concept of Law* (2nd edn, OUP 1994)

Heidegger M, *Being and Time* (Joan Stambaugh tr, Dennis J Schmidt rev, State University of New York Press 2010)

Heidegger M, *Introduction to Metaphysics* (Gregory Fried and Richard Polt trs, Yale University Press 2014)

Heidegger M, *Qu'est-ce qu'une chose?* (Jean Reboul and Jacques Taminiaux trs, Gallimard 1971)

Hobbes T, *Leviathan* (Richard Tuck ed, CUP 1996)

Hobsbawm E, 'Mass-Producing Traditions: Europe, 1870–1914' in Eric Hobsbawm and Terence Ranger (eds), *The Invention of Tradition* (CUP 1983)

Hobsbawm E and Ranger T (eds), *The Invention of Tradition* (CUP 1983)

Hollis D, 'Why State Consent Still Matters: Non-State Actors, Treaties, and the Changing Sources of International Law' (2005) 23 *Berkeley Journal of International Law* 1

Honneth A, *Reification: A New Look at an Old Idea* (OUP 2008)

Horkheimer M and Adorno TW, *Dialectic of Enlightenment: Philosophical Fragments* (Stanford University Press 2002)

Husserl E, *Ideas Pertaining to a Pure Phenomenology and to a Phenomenological Philosophy: First Book* (Fred Kersten tr, Kluwer Academic Publishers 1983)

Hyppolite J, *Logique et existence* (Presses Universitaires de France 1952)

Jappe A, 'Aliénation, réification et fétichisme de la marchandise' in Vincent Chanson, Alexis Cukier and Frédéric Monferrand (eds), *La Réification: Histoire et actualité d'un concept critique* (La Dispute 2014)

Jasanoff S, *The Fifth Branch: Science Advisers as Policymakers* (Harvard UP 1990)

Jasanoff S, 'The Idiom of Co-production' in Sheila Jasanoff (ed), *States of Knowledge: The Co-production of Science and Social Order* (Routledge 2004)

Jasanoff S, 'Ordering Knowledge, Ordering Society' in Sheila Jasanoff (ed), *States of Knowledge: The Co-production of Science and Social Order* (Routledge 2004)

Jasanoff S (ed), *States of Knowledge: The Co-production of Science and Social Order* (Routledge 2004)
Jasanoff S, 'Technologies of Humility' (2007) 450 *Nature* 33
Johns F, 'Critical International Legal Theory' in JL Dunoff and MA Pollack (eds), *International Legal Theory: Foundations and Frontiers* (CUP 2022)
Jovanović MA, *The Nature of International Law* (CUP 2019)
Jullien F, *L'incommensurable* (L'Observatoire 2022)
Kang W, 'Thing' (*Oxford Research Encyclopedias: Literature*, 23 February 2021) https://www.oxfordreference.com/ accessed 9 March 2026
Kant I, *Critique of Pure Reason* (Paul Guyer and Allen W Wood trs, CUP 1998)
Kennedy D, 'Critical Theory, Structuralism and Contemporary Legal Scholarship' (1985–1986) 21 *New England Law Review* 209
Kennedy D, 'Form and Substance in Private Law Adjudication' (1976) 89 *Harvard Law Review* 1685
Kennedy DW, 'A New Stream of International Law Scholarship' (1988) 7 *Wisconsin International Law Journal* 1
Kirshenblatt-Gimblett B, *Destination Culture* (University of California Press 1998)
Klabbers J, *The Concept of Treaty in International Law* (Kluwer 1996)
Klemperer V, *The Language of the Third Reich* (Continuum 2000)
Koskenniemi M, *The Gentle Civilizer of Nations: The Rise and Fall of International Law 1870–1960* (CUP 2001)
Koskenniemi M, 'Law, Teleology and International Relations: An Essay in Counter-Disciplinarity' (2012) 26(1) *International Relations* 3
Koskenniemi M, 'What Should the International Lawyer Learn from Karl Marx?' in Susan Marks (ed), *International Law on the Left: Re-examining Marxist Legacies* (CUP 2008)
Lacey N, 'Feminist Legal Theory and the Rights of Women' in Heikki Pihlajamäki and others (eds), *The Oxford Handbook of European Legal History* (OUP 2018)
Latour B, *An Inquiry into Modes of Existence* (Harvard University Press 2013)
Latour B, *L'Espoir de Pandore* (Didier Gille tr, La Découverte 2007)
Latour B, *La fabrique du droit: Une ethnographie du Conseil d'État* (La Découverte 2004)
Latour B, *Face à Gaïa* (La Découverte 2015)
Latour B, *Nous n'avons jamais été modernes: Essai d'anthropologie symétrique* (La Découverte 1991)
Latour B, *Pandora's Hope: Essays on the Reality of Science Studies* (Harvard University Press 1999)
Latour B, *Politiques de la nature: Comment faire entrer les sciences en démocratie* (La Découverte 1999)
Latour B, *Reassembling the Social: An Introduction to Actor-Network-Theory* (OUP 2005)
Latour B, *Science in Action: How to Follow Scientists and Engineers Through Society* (Harvard University Press 1987)
Latour B, 'Why Has Critique Run out of Steam? From Matters of Fact to Matters of Concern' (2004) 30 *Critical Inquiry* 225
Latour B and Woolgar S, *Laboratory Life: The Construction of Scientific Facts* (2nd edn, Princeton University Press 1986)

Laurent S, *Capital and Race: The History of a Modern Hydra* (Polity Press 2026)
Lauterpacht H, *Recognition in International Law* (CUP 1947)
Laval C, *Jeremy Bentham: Le pouvoir des fictions* (PUF 1994)
Lecercle J-J, *De l'interpellation: Sujet, langue, idéologie* (Éditions Amsterdam 2019)
Legendre P, *L'Amour du Censeur: Essai sur l'ordre dogmatique* (Seuil 2005)
Legendre P, *L'empire de la vérité: Introduction aux espaces dogmatiques industriels* (Fayard 1983)
Legendre P, *Leçons VI: La fabrique de l'homme occidental* (Fayard 1996)
Legendre P, *Sur la question dogmatique en Occident: Aspects théoriques* (Fayard 1999)
Legrand P, 'The Same and the Different' in Pierre Legrand and Roderick Munday (eds), *Comparative Legal Studies: Traditions and Transitions* (CUP 2003)
Letsas G, 'Strasbourg's Interpretive Ethic: Lessons for the International Lawyer' (2010) 21 *European Journal of International Law* 509
Lévi-Strauss C, *Structural Anthropology*, vol II (M Layton tr, University of Chicago Press 1976)
Litowitz D, 'Reification in Law and Legal Theory' (2000) 9 *Southern California Interdisciplinary Law Journal* 401
Lixinski L, *Intangible Cultural Heritage in International Law* (OUP 2013)
Lixinski L, 'Selecting Heritage: The Interplay of Art, Politics and Identity' (2011) 22 *European Journal of International Law* 81
Locke J, *An Essay Concerning Human Understanding* (Peter H Nidditch ed, OUP 1979)
Locke J, *Two Treatises of Government* (Peter Laslett ed, CUP 1988)
Lordon F, *Capitalisme, désir et servitude: Marx et Spinoza* (La Fabrique 2010)
Lordon F, *La société des affects: Pour un structuralisme des passions* (Seuil 2013)
Lucretius, *De Rerum Natura* (William Ellery Leonard tr, rev edn, University of Wisconsin Press 2008)
Lukács G, *Histoire et conscience de classe: Essais de dialectique marxiste* (K Axelos and J Bois trs, Éditions de Minuit 1960) (first published 1923)
Lyotard J-F, *La Condition postmoderne* (Éditions de Minuit 1979)
Lyotard J-F, 'Matière et temps' in *Matière et philosophie* (Éditions du Centre Pompidou 1988)
Lythgoe G, *The Rebirth of Territory in International Law: Space, Governance, and the Legal Imagination* (CUP 2024)
Lythgoe G, 'Reimagining Territory in International Law' (2022) 35 *Leiden Journal of International Law* 247
MacCormick N, *Institutions of Law* (OUP 2005)
Macé A, *La matière* (GF Flammarion 1998)
MacKinnon CA, 'Are Women Human?' in Catharine A MacKinnon, *Are Women Human? And Other International Dialogues* (Harvard UP 2006)
MacKinnon CA, *Toward a Feminist Theory of the State* (Harvard UP 1989)
Mamdani M, *Citizen and Subject: Contemporary Africa and the Legacy of Late Colonialism* (Princeton UP 1996)
Mamdani M, *Define and Rule: Native as Political Identity* (Harvard UP 2012)
Mamdani M, *Neither Settler nor Native: The Making and Unmaking of Permanent Minorities* (Harvard UP 2020)

Marcuse H, *One-Dimensional Man: Studies in the Ideology of Advanced Industrial Society* (Beacon Press 1964)
Marks S, 'Introduction' in Susan Marks (ed), *International Law on the Left: Re-examining Marxist Legacies* (CUP 2008)
Marks S (ed), *International Law on the Left: Re-examining Marxist Legacies* (CUP 2008)
Marmor A, *Social Conventions* (Princeton UP 2009)
Marx K, *Capital: A Critique of Political Economy, Volume I* (Ben Fowkes tr, Penguin Classics 1990)
Mbembe A, *Critique de la raison nègre* (La Découverte 2013)
Mbembe A, *Critique of Black Reason* (Duke UP 2017)
Meillassoux Q, *After Finitude: An Essay on the Necessity of Contingency* (Ray Brassier tr, Continuum 2008)
Meillassoux Q, *Après la finitude: Essai sur la nécessité de la contingence* (Seuil 2006)
Memmi A, *Portrait du colonisé, précédé de Portrait du colonisateur* (Buchet/Chastel 1957)
Merleau-Ponty M, *Phénoménologie de la perception* (Gallimard 1945)
Merry SE, *The Seductions of Quantification* (University of Chicago Press 2016)
Merry SE, Davis KE and Kingsbury B (eds), *The Quiet Power of Indicators* (CUP 2015)
Merryman JH, *The Civil Law Tradition* (3rd edn, Stanford UP 2007)
Merryman JH, 'Two Ways of Thinking About Cultural Property' (1986) 80 *American Journal of International Law* 831
Michaud E, *Un art de l'éternité* (Gallimard 1996)
Miéville C, *Between Equal Rights: A Marxist Theory of International Law* (Pluto Press 2005)
Mignolo W, 'Delinking: The Rhetoric of Modernity, the Logic of Coloniality, and the Grammar of Decoloniality' (2007) 21 *Cultural Studies* 449
Mills CW, *The Racial Contract* (Cornell UP 1997)
Morton T, *Hyperobjects: Philosophy and Ecology after the End of the World* (University of Minnesota Press 2013)
Mullins M, 'Postmodernism and Thing Theory' (*Arcade*, 2017) https://shc.stanford.edu/arcade/interventions/postmodernism-and-thing-theory?locale=en accessed 9 March 2026
Mullins M, *Postmodernism in Pieces: Materializing the Social in U.S. Fiction* (OUP 2019)
Mutua M, *Human Rights: A Political and Cultural Critique* (University of Pennsylvania Press 2002)
Noghrehchi H, 'Language is Fascist' (2017) 186(2) *Littérature* 34
O'Keefe R, *The Protection of Cultural Property in Armed Conflict* (CUP 2006)
Oreskes N and Conway EM, *Merchants of Doubt: How a Handful of Scientists Obscured the Truth on Issues from Tobacco Smoke to Global Warming* (Bloomsbury Press 2010)
Otto D, 'Lost in Translation: Re-scripting the Sexed Subjects of International Human Rights Law' in Anne Orford (ed), *International Law and Its Others* (CUP 2006)
Otto D, 'Queering Gender [Identity] in International Law' (2015) 33(4) *Nordic Journal of Human Rights* 299

Pahuja S, *Decolonising International Law: Development, Economic Growth and the Politics of Universality* (CUP 2011)
Pashukanis EB, *The General Theory of Law and Marxism* (Barbara Einhorn tr, Transaction 2002)
Pinton CI, 'From Ego Conquiro to Ego Cogito: Dussel's Latin American History of Philosophy' (2025) 29 *RUDN Journal of Philosophy* 704
Pistor K, *The Code of Capital* (Princeton UP 2019)
Pitkin HF, 'Rethinking Reification' (1987) 16 *Theory and Society* 263
Plato, *Phaedo* (David Gallop tr, OUP 2009)
Plato, *Republic* (Christopher Rowe tr, Penguin Classics 2012)
Ponge F, 'My Creative Method' in Francis Ponge, *The Voice of Things* (Beth Archer tr and ed, McGraw-Hill 1972)
Popper K, *Conjectures and Refutations: The Growth of Scientific Knowledge* (Routledge Classics 2002)
Pottage A and Mundy M (eds), *Law, Anthropology, and the Constitution of the Social: Making Persons and Things* (CUP 2004)
Prieto de Pedro J, *Patrimonio Cultural: Concepto y Régimen Jurídico* (Civitas 1996)
Prott LV and O'Keefe PJ, *Law and the Cultural Heritage* (vol 1, Professional Books 1984)
Quijano A, 'Coloniality of Power, Eurocentrism, and Latin America' (2000) 1(3) *Nepantla: Views from South* 533
Rancière J, *La Leçon d'Althusser* (La Fabrique 2011)
Rancière J, *La mésentente: Politique et philosophie* (La Fabrique 1995)
Rancière J, *Le partage du sensible: Esthétique et politique* (La Fabrique 2000)
Raustiala K, 'Form and Substance in International Agreements' (2005) 99 *American Journal of International Law* 581
Raz J, *Practical Reason and Norms* (2nd edn, OUP 1999)
Ricoeur P, *De l'interprétation: Essai sur Freud* (Seuil 1965)
Ricoeur P, *La mémoire, l'histoire, l'oubli* (Seuil 2000)
Robinson CJ, *Black Marxism: The Making of the Black Radical Tradition* (UNC Press 1983; revised edn 2000)
Rosen L, *Law as Culture* (Princeton UP 2006)
Rousseau J-J, *The Social Contract* (Victor Gourevitch ed, CUP 1997)
Said EW, *Orientalism* (Pantheon 1978)
Said EW, *The World, the Text, and the Critic* (Harvard University Press 1983)
Sapir E, *Language: An Introduction to the Study of Speech* (Ishi Press International 1921)
Saussure F de, *Course in General Linguistics* (Charles Bally and Albert Sechehaye eds, Open Court 1986)
Sayers S, 'What Is Marxism?' (2021) 11 *International Critical Thought* 377
Schachter O, 'The Twilight Existence of Nonbinding International Agreements' (1977) 71 *American Journal of International Law* 296
Schauer F, 'Amending the Presuppositions of a Constitution' in Sanford Levinson (ed), *Responding to Imperfection: The Theory and Practice of Constitutional Amendment* (Princeton Press 1995)
Schauer F, 'Is the Rule of Recognition a Rule?' (2012) 3(2) *Transnational Legal Theory* 1

Schauer F, *Playing by the Rules* (Clarendon Press 1991)
Schlag P, 'My Dinner at Langdell's' (2004) 52 *Buffalo Law Review* 851
Schofield P, Cléro J-P and Laval C (eds), *Jeremy Bentham, De l'ontologie et autres textes sur les fictions* (Éditions du Seuil 1997)
Schorlemer S von and Stoll P-T, *The UNESCO Convention on the Protection and Promotion of the Diversity of Cultural Expressions* (Springer 2012)
Searle JR, *The Construction of Social Reality* (Free Press 1995)
Sedgwick EK, *Epistemology of the Closet* (University of California Press 2008)
Sellars W, *Empiricism and the Philosophy of Mind* (Harvard University Press 1997) (first published 1956)
Serres M, *Le Contrat naturel* (François Bourin 1990)
Serres M, *Le Mal propre: Polluer pour s'approprier* (Le Pommier 2008)
Serres M, *Les Origines de la géométrie: Tiers livre des fondations* (Flammarion 2011)
Serres M, *Statues: Le second livre des fondations* (Champs 2014)
Shapin S and Schaffer S, *Leviathan and the Air-Pump* (Princeton University Press 1985)
Simondon G, *L'individuation à la lumière des notions de forme et d'information* (Millon 2005)
Simpson AWB, 'The Common Law and Legal Theory' in AWB Simpson (ed), *Oxford Essays in Jurisprudence* (OUP 1973)
Smart C, *Feminism and the Power of Law* (Routledge 1989)
Smith L, *Uses of Heritage* (Routledge 2006)
Södersten A and Patterson D, 'The Nature of International Law' in Dennis Patterson and Anna Södersten (eds), *A Companion to European Union Law and International Law* (John Wiley & Sons 2016)
Søreide T and Gloppen S, 'Gender-Based Violence and the Law: A Critical Review' (2021) 76 *Crime, Law and Social Change* 179
Spivak GC, *A Critique of Postcolonial Reason: Toward a History of the Vanishing Present* (Harvard University Press 1999)
Spivak GC, *In Other Worlds: Essays in Cultural Politics* (Routledge 2006)
Star SL, 'The Sociology of the Invisible: The Primacy of Work in the Writings of Anselm Strauss' in Wiebe E Bijker, Thomas P Hughes and Trevor Pinch (eds), *The Social Construction of Technological Systems: New Directions in the Sociology and History of Technology* (MIT Press 1987)
Stengers I, *Au temps des catastrophes: Résister à la barbarie qui vient* (La Découverte 2009)
Stengers I, *Cosmopolitiques VII: Pour en finir avec la tolérance* (La Découverte/Les Empêcheurs de penser en rond 1997)
Sunstein CR, *Legal Reasoning and Political Conflict* (OUP 1996)
Sutter L de, *Superfaible: Penser au XXIe siècle* (Climats 2023)
Tairako T, 'Reification, Thingification, and Alienation in Marx's Economic Manuscripts' (2025) 55 *Hitotsubashi Journal of Social Studies* 1
Thirlway H, 'The Nature of International Law and the Concept of "Sources"' in Hugh Thirlway, *The Sources of International Law* (2nd edn, OUP 2019)
Thomas DA, *Exceptional Violence* (Duke UP 2013)
Thompson EP, *The Making of the English Working Class* (Penguin Classics 2013)

Timmer A, 'Judging Stereotypes: What the European Court of Human Rights Can Do to Address Sexist Stereotypes' (2015) 33(4) *Nordic Journal of Human Rights* 369
Tushnet M, 'Defending the Indeterminacy Thesis' (1996) 16 *Quinnipiac Law Review* 339
Unger RM, *The Critical Legal Studies Movement* (Harvard UP 1986)
Vaihinger H, *The Philosophy of "As If"* (Routledge 2021) (first published 1911)
Van Den Meerssche D, 'International Organizations and the Performativity of Measuring States: Discipline through Diagnosis' (2018) 15(1) *International Organizations Law Review* 168
Vandenberghe F, 'La notion de réification: Réification sociale et chosification méthodologique' (1992) 103 *L'Homme et la société* 81
van Marle K and Kotzé LJ, 'Earth Jurisprudence and Rights of Nature: The Emergence of a New Legal Paradigm' in Louis J Kotzé and Duncan French (eds), *Sustainable Development, Global Governance and the Law* (Edward Elgar 2018)
Veyne P, *Foucault: Sa pensée, sa personne* (Albin Michel 2008)
Vismann C, *Files: Law and Media Technology* (Stanford UP 2008)
Wade S, *Foucault in California* (Heyday 2019)
Wasserman S, 'Thing Theory 2017: A Forum' (*Arcade*, 2017) https://shc.stanford.edu/arcade/interventions/thing-theory-2017-forum accessed 9 March 2026
Weber M, *Economy and Society* (University of California Press 1978)
White H, *Tropics of Discourse: Essays in Cultural Criticism* (Johns Hopkins University Press 1978)
Whitehead AN, *The Concept of Nature* (Cosim 2007) (first published 1920)
Whitehead AN, *Process and Reality* (corrected edn, The Free Press 1978)
Wieacker F, *A History of Private Law in Europe* (OUP 1995)
Willoughby WW, 'The Legal Nature of International Law' (1908) 2 *American Journal of International Law* 357
Winter SL, *A Clearing in the Forest: Law, Life, and Mind* (University of Chicago Press 2001)
Zarbiyev F, *Le discours interprétatif en droit international contemporain* (Pedone 2015)

Index

For Product Safety Concerns and Information please contact our EU representative GPSR@taylorandfrancis.com Taylor & Francis Verlag GmbH, Kaufingerstraße 24, 80331 München, Germany